Reinventing Public Education

Reinventing

HOW CONTRACTING CAN

Public

TRANSFORM AMERICA'S SCHOOLS

Education

Paul T. Hill
Lawrence C. Pierce
James W. Guthrie

THE UNIVERSITY OF CHICAGO PRESS
Chicago and London

Paul T. Hill is research professor in the Graduate School of
Public Affairs at the University of Washington and Director
of the Joint University of Washington-RAND Program on
Reinventing Public Education. **Lawrence C. Pierce** is a senior
staff member of the Program on Reinventing Public Education
and former dean of the College of Education, Louisiana State
University, Baton Rouge. **James W. Guthrie** is professor of
education and public policy and director of the Center on
Education Policy, Vanderbilt University.

The University of Chicago Press, Chicago 60637
The University of Chicago Press, Ltd., London
© 1997 by RAND Corporation
All rights reserved. Published 1997
Printed in the United States of America
06 05 04 03 02 01 00 99 98 97   1 2 3 4 5

ISBN: 0-226-33651-4 (cloth)
0-226-33652-2 (paper)

Library of Congress Cataloging-in-Publication Data

Hill, Paul Thomas, 1943–
    Reinventing public education : how contracting can transform
America's schools / Paul T. Hill, Lawrence C. Pierce, and James W. Guthrie
        p.   cm. — (A RAND research study)
    Includes bibliographical references and index.
    ISBN 0-226-33651-4 (alk. paper). — ISBN 0-226-33652-2 (pbk. : alk. paper)
    1. Performance contracts in education—United States.
    2. Educational change—United States. 3. Educational accountability—
United States. 4. Privatization in education—United States.
    I. Pierce, Lawrence C. II. Guthrie, James W. III. Title. IV. Series.
LB2806.2.H56   1997
379.1'1—dc21   96-39542
                                                                     CIP

⊗ The paper used in this publication meets the minimum requirements of the American National Standard for Information Sciences—
Permanence of Paper for Printed Library Materials, ANSI Z39.48-1984.

CONTENTS

A fter a decade of efforts to improve American public schools incrementally, the initiative for education reform has shifted to outsiders who propose radical measures. Communities and states are now seriously debating reform options, such as vouchers and charter schools, that would have been considered implausible only a few years ago. Many current reform proposals seriously challenge the defining features of the American public school system that developed after World War II—direct operation of schools by elected school boards, compliance-based accountability, civil service employment for teachers, mandatory assignment of students to schools, and control of funds by central district bureaucracies.

Starting with publication of Chubb and Moe's *Politics, Markets and America's Schools,* various fundamental reform proposals would replace regulatory compliance with student performance standards, make schools' existence and staff members' jobs contingent on performance, give families choices among public schools, and transfer control of public funds from centralized bureaucracies to individual schools. These proposals attempt to redefine public education, to include schooling in any form and by any provider that can meet community standards for student learning and can guarantee nondiscriminatory access. They challenge the dominant way of thinking that equates "public" with "government-run."

Some of these proposals would place education almost entirely into private hands, allowing parents to choose any licensed school and relying on private initiative to develop and run schools. Such proposals are based on the belief that public education has evolved into a government- and professionally run bureaucracy that takes too little account of family concerns. Parents in big cities find public schools particularly unresponsive. City schools have become so constrained by rules and regulations made elsewhere—governing, for example, how students and teachers are selected, which teachers can help which students, how long a child must be kept out of regular classes in order to receive a particular kind of remedial instruction, what a principal must go through in order to remove a disruptive student, and what work teachers may and may not do—that many are unable to respond to the needs of students and parents. As Ted Sizer has noted, parents experiencing the blank bureaucratic face of such schools have reason to question whether they are really public at all: they appear profoundly private, controlled by government on behalf of teachers' unions and interest groups that have managed to capture the agendas of school boards and state legislatures.

Our collaboration on this book was based on our shared belief that something must be done to restore balance between the private and public interests in education. As people who had devoted their careers to education, we shared public education's commitment to equity, but we thought schools needed greater control of their funds, staffs, and instructional methods than existing public schools now have. As political scientists, we knew that any reform proposal must be politically feasible and that total school autonomy is an illusion: no one who takes the public's funds and educates the public's children should totally escape government oversight. We hoped to give policymakers, parents, and community leaders an option, a way of reforming schools that neither relied entirely on government nor rejected any role for it.

Our proposal tries to restore the partnership between schools and families that has been destroyed during a period of regulatory excess. It recognizes the public interest in schooling, and in ensuring that students learn basic skills, prepare for responsible lives as earners and citizens, and understand basic democratic values. To protect these public interests, our proposal requires that every school operate under an explicit agreement with a duly authorized local school board. It makes room for the private interest in schooling by allowing families to choose among schools that take different approaches to education. Most importantly, our proposal creates conditions under which schools can serve both public and private interests effectively.

We propose a new form of governance for public education based on contracting and family choice. Under the plan presented in this book, all public schools would operate under contracts that define each school's mission, its guarantee of public funding, and its grounds for accountability. These contracts would have two parties—the local school board and the individual school. A local school board would be party to many different contracts, one with each school. Contracts with failing schools or schools that did not attract students could be terminated. New contracts could be offered to groups or organizations that have run successful schools or that propose programs deemed likely to succeed.

Our proposal takes contracting literally: school boards would contract out for whole schools and schools would be run by independent organizations that would have complete control over their budgets, programs, hiring, firing, and staff training. In the early 1990s, school boards in Baltimore and Hartford hired Education Alternatives, Inc (EAI) to run some schools—in the case of Hartford, the entire district—but the boards retained control of budgets and staffing. After periods of mutual frustration the contracts were canceled, with the school boards complaining about disappointing results and the school operators claiming they had been prevented from making necessary changes. Our proposal takes account of the lessons learned from earlier failures. To make a difference in school performance, contracting must require that school boards give up trying to control school operations.

Our form of contracting would redefine the public school. Any school supported with public funds and operating under a funding and performance agreement with a duly constituted public education board would be, by definition a public school. Every pubic school would have such an agreement. Contracting extends the charter school concept, which allows small numbers of schools to gain control of money, staff, and programs, to the entire public school system.

Contract schools would differ from one another, offering different instructional methods and extracurricular activities. Some might even operate at different hours of the day or for different numbers of days each year. With such a variety of alternatives available there would be no justification for requiring a family to send a child to a particular school, especially if the parents knew of another school that would better fit the child's needs or the family's ideas about a good education. Families would be free to choose among local public contract schools. Because their freedom to choose would be bounded by the range of schools available in their locality, parents could petition the local school board to establish a new contract for a type of school that was not locally available, or to reproduce a school that had become so popular that it could admit no more students. The local board could authorize new schools, but it could also decide that a particular type of school was not likely to be effective or could not attract a large enough student body to be financially viable.

Contracting would also redefine define a public school board as a local community agent responsible for providing a portfolio of school alternatives that meet the needs of the community's children. School boards would no longer have authority to run schools directly or to create systems of regulation that exhaustively constrain what all schools may do. They would no longer have responsibility for directly hiring, evaluating, paying, or dismissing teachers, administrators, or other employees for individual schools. Their only responsibility would be finding, hiring, paying, and monitoring the performance of the independent contractors that would run schools.

The local board would identify the need for particular schools: for example, a district with a significant population of Spanish-speaking children might decide to run a bilingual elementary school, or a district containing a new high-technology industry might want to provide a school whose curriculum was built to help students understand and prepare for careers in that industry. The local board would then seek operators for the schools, through requests for proposals or by negotiating directly with qualified providers. It would monitor schools to determine that all admit students without respect to race or income, that no child is obliged to attend a bad school, and that students attending failing schools are provided with viable alternatives. As a portfolio manager, the board would not be required to guarantee that everyone liked, or even approved of, a particular school. Because families could choose among schools, no private individual would have standing to interfere with a school's operation on grounds that its focus or program was offensive to him or her. Schools could therefore run consistent and coherent programs, free of the need to be all things to all people.

A local board could replace contractors who failed to honor their promises, or to ensure that schools make substantial quality improvements if performance fell below acceptable levels. A board could also maintain quality by "pruning" its portfolio of schools, meaning the lowest-performing schools could be closed and replaced.

School evaluation would have to be based on state or local student performance standards. The task of applying these standards fairly to all schools, given the inevitable differences in school instructional methods and students' levels of preparation, would be a serious challenge. Contracting makes this challenge unavoidable, but it does not create it: any governance system seriously concerned with school performance—including the existing one—must solve the problem of how to hold different schools to universal standards.

Schools would hire teachers, either on the open market or from a registry of certified teachers, depending on the terms of their contracts. Teachers would be employees of individual schools. This would create a true labor market for instructional and administrative staff. Schools would make decisions about hiring, evaluating, and terminating their own staff members. Teachers and administrators would be free to assess and select their workplaces. Salaries would be set by the market, and schools might compete for good staff by providing incentives to prospective teachers, such as a good benefits package or training programs. Teachers could demand higher pay for difficult situations or heavy responsibilities, and schools could offer bonuses for high performance.

Teachers' unions would act as hiring halls for schools in search of teachers. Unions might even accept full management responsibility for certain schools. If they were awarded school contracts, then teachers' unions would no longer simply be "labor. " They would also become entrepreneurs or providers, as are professionals in other fields like law, medicine, and accounting.

New laws would be necessary in many states to authorize school boards to contract out for whole schools and to pay contractors on per-pupil basis. Many states would also need new collective bargaining laws that allowed individual schools to employ teachers and to hire on the basis of fit with the school's mission and instructional approach.

We hope will readers agree that contracting is an important and practical idea. It encourages innovation and diversity in public education, avoiding the need for a whole community to make a single choice in favor of one method of instruction. It eliminates zero-sum conflicts among families that have different ideas about how children should learn: since public schools can differ and parents can choose, there is no need for parents to contend with one another about the one best model of schooling. It also promotes efficient use of limited public funds, by focusing money and decisions at the school level. Contracting can produce these results without abandoning public education's concern for fairness, equality of opportunity, and progress for the disadvantaged. Though it would create stressful changes in the lives of some administrators and union leaders, it would create new opportunities for parents and teachers alike.

Contracting is not a modest proposal but it need not be treated as an all-or-nothing proposition. It would take time to make a transition. States might experiment with contracting by establishing it first in big city districts where there are few good schools and thousands of students in desperate need of a more effective alternative. Similarly, cities might try it first as an alternative for neighborhoods where the regular public school system has failed for decades to provide good schools.

PH, LP, JG

PART I

THE CASE FOR CONTRACT SCHOOLS

ONE

Preserving Public Education

The Vaughn Next Century Learning Center, located in the heart of Los Angeles, California, now operates autonomously from the local school district and is in control of its entire budget. Under the leadership of Dr. Yvonne Chan, the school, made up of 99 percent Latino and African-American children, has seen dramatic improvement in student performance. Language arts scores have gone up from the 9th to the 39th percentile. Math scores have risen from the 14th to the 57th percentile. Attendance is now 99 percent and average class size has dropped from 31 to 26. Discipline referrals have dropped from 500 to 100 a year. The school serves 69 gifted students where before there were none. Dr. Chan and her staff of teachers have accomplished these results while saving $1 million out of a $4.6 million budget in the school's first year. With these extra funds, the school has reduced class size, restored salary cuts, built new classrooms, installed computers, increased the number of instructional days, and contributed money to seventeen neighboring schools.

Today the Vaughn Next Century Learning Center is the exception in American public education. The purpose of this book is to propose a reform that will make it possible for all schools to have the control of funds and accountability for results that enabled Vaughn to improve so dramatically. This reform will eliminate the practice of controlling schools with politically created mandates and enable teachers and principals to concentrate on making their schools more effective. It will also enhance the range of public school options available to families and provide far higher levels of educational equality than now characterize much of American schooling.

The new arrangement we propose retains the best features of the current system and simultaneously enables schools to be more bold, imaginative, adaptable, and suited to the needs of the children and families. It can also make schools into good places for teachers to work, where teachers are treated as adults who take responsibility for children's learning and are rewarded for results.

The strategy we propose is straightforward. It would replace the current system of detailed political and bureaucratic controls on school operations with a system of school-specific agreements that would define each school's mission, guarantee of public funding, and grounds for accountability. These agreements would be similar to the agreements under which the best magnet and special-program schools now gain freedom to control their own programs and select only those staff members who fit the school's instructional strategy. The difference is that the agreements we propose would be more explicit and reliable than the informal grants of permission that now permit a few schools to innovate and vary from the norm. These agreements would be formal *contracts* between two legally equal parties: the local school board, which would eliminate detailed controls on school expenditures, services, and hiring in order to allow every school to provide a focused and distinctive instructional program; and individual schools, which would enter binding legal commitments to provide specific programs of instruction, use public funds and assets responsibly, work to ensure success for all students, and produce agreed-upon rates of student achievement.

Contracts of the kind sketched here can clarify the relationships between individual schools and public authorities, allowing schools to pursue their instructional missions free from the continual changes in policy and mandates that legislatures, courts, and local school boards inevitably create. Contracting would be a radical change in the way Americans operate public schools, yet it would preserve the public character of public education. Parents, students, and teachers would gain the advantages of choice but preserve their recourse to public officials if the schools do not serve them well. School board members would remain the politically accountable authorities responsible for ensuring that every child in a community had access to a quality education. School boards would no longer operate schools directly, but they would gain new powers and options to support truly innovative schools and to intervene to transform or replace weak and failing schools.

If all public schools were governed by the kinds of contracts we propose, a local school board would be party to many different agreements, one with each school. Each school's agreement would specify the amount of public funds it would receive, the type of instructional program it would provide, and types and levels of student outcomes its managers agree to produce and be accountable for. A local school board's contracts with failing schools or schools that did not attract students could be terminated. Boards could offer new contracts to groups or organizations that have run successful schools or that can assemble highly qualified staffs and show how they will provide a well-grounded instructional program.

The suggestions in this book have been tried and found promising in public service sectors other than K–12 education. A 1995 survey of 82 cities in 34 states showed that contracting for public services from private companies is common. All of these cities use private companies to provide food at public facilities. Sixty percent of the cities contract out rubbish collection, 40 percent contract for security and street maintenance, 35 percent use private companies to operate parking garages and provide tree-trimming services, and approximately 20 percent contract out health and medical services, street sweeping, and food for jails (*The Economist*, August 19–25, 1995, pp. 25–26). Public contracting strategies simply have not heretofore been applied widely to public education or in any systematic manner.

We propose an entire governance system that gives individual schools full control over key resources and staff, under agreements that specify each school's instructional approach and expected student outcomes. Readers may wonder how our hopes for contracting square with the experience of Educational Alternatives, Inc. (EAI), a private firm that first won and then lost school management contracts with school boards in Baltimore and Hartford. The answer is that we are not proposing just any arrangement that goes under the name of contracting. EAI entered agreements under which they neither controlled resources and staff nor were accountable for strictly defined performance.[1] In Baltimore, EAI was forced to accept teachers assigned under union contract provisions and to persuade teachers who were members of a union that hated the very idea of EAI management of schools to learn and implement EAI's instructional methods. EAI also accepted accountability provisions so vague that no one knew who would evaluate the schools, when, or by what standards. The result was that the first evaluations were done by EAI's most aggressive critic, the American Federation of Teachers. Evaluation of EAI-managed schools' performance subsequently became an exercise in polemic and counterpolemic. Subsequent evaluations conducted after termination of

1. For an overview of EAI's experience, see Thomas Toch, "Do Firms Run Schools Well?" *U.S. News and World Report*, January 8, 1996, pp. 46–49.

EAI's Baltimore contract showed rapidly improving student achievement, but to this day no one can confidently say whether EAI students learned more or less than comparable Baltimore students.

The proposed contracting system requires comprehensive changes in the roles, missions, and legal authorities of all actors in public education, particularly school boards, teacher unions, and school staff. School boards now make detailed operational decisions affecting all schools and act as employers of school personnel. Teacher unions now act as sole-source labor contractors, who supply teachers to schools on the basis of general rules and teacher seniority rights rather than schools' needs. Schools are now nodes in a larger bureaucracy; their instructional methods, equipment, and staffs are all chosen for them. Under the proposed contracting system, school boards would oversee a portfolio of diverse schools, each operated by a private group composed of teachers, parents, social-services providers, educational entrepreneurs, or combinations thereof. School boards would still be elected locally, but the fact that board members would not control jobs or details of school operations should attract a different sort of candidate—one more concerned with school quality and less with patronage or political opportunities. Schools, not district-wide school boards, would employ teachers, and unions would represent teachers in their relations with individual schools, not with entire school systems. Schools would be real organizations, not subordinate nodes in a larger bureaucracy, subject to constant tinkering from outside. They would be in charge of budgets, buildings, investment funds for staff development and other improvements in the instructional process, and responsible for performance.

Changes such as these could not be made overnight. Public officials would have to learn how to identify good providers and make sound contracts, and groups of educators and other professionals would have to form new organizations capable of operating whole schools. In many localities, contracting would start small, perhaps as an effort to provide new schools for neighborhoods and groups that the traditional public school system has served badly.

Principles Motivating Our Proposal

Throughout America, school boards, teachers, parents, and university faculty are collaborating on school projects intended to create exciting and effective learner-centered education. The Accelerated Schools Project, the Effective Schools Project, and the Coalition for Essential Schools all started at major universities and are examples of school reforms that are improving instruction. More recently, the New American Schools Development Corporation (NASDC), with the support of many leading corporations, has commissioned a number of innovative whole-school designs. There are also many high-performance independent and religious schools.

Regrettably, few public schools can take full advantage of these efforts. Schools that can fully implement a new instructional principle or theory are nearly always exceptions, somehow exempted from the rules and restrictions that govern the vast majority of public schools. Most have foundation grants, high-energy principals who can terrorize or work around the central office staff, or special support from businesses or foundations. Many draw on the resources of major universities, resources that are unavailable to the majority of public schools. Schools that gain great reputations are admired and publicized, but school systems seldom try to reproduce them. The annual spectacle of parents camping overnight, in lines, to enroll children in popular magnet schools exemplifies this problem. School systems can create good schools, but few see it as their job to duplicate successes or create for all schools the conditions that enable some to succeed.

Some argue that the reason schools seem impervious to change is the lack of agreement on what constitutes a good school. Differences do arise, for example, in debates between religious organizations and professional educators over issues such as prayer in schools, outcome-based education, and collaborative learning. For the most part, however, research and conversations with teachers and parents reveal a remarkable amount of agreement on the attributes of good schools. We believe, in other words, that there is a broad-based consensus about what it takes to provide high-quality education. The problem is that the current decision-making structure for public education makes it impossible to do what we need to do to have good public schools.

We have read many books and articles on successful schools and have asked hundreds of teachers, administrators, parents, and students about what kinds of schools they hope to have. While the words are often different, the underlying themes and principles are consistent:

- *Schools should be focused on student learning.* Schools should be organized around the needs of children. The question is, how would you organize a school if you wanted to enhance the learning of every student? Schools should be more personalized, encouraging long-term relationships between teachers and families. Schools should also be relatively small so that students and teachers get to know each other, and students and parents feel comfortable when they enter the school. Schools should be places where every student is known, and schools should do whatever is necessary to help every student learn.

- *Schools should be whole organizations and true communities.* Schools should act like serious enterprises that have definite goals. Like business firms and goal-driven nonprofit organizations, schools exist because their is work to do what individuals alone cannot accomplish. Whether it is a Montessori school, a cooperative learning school, or a school organized around themes, it is important that everyone in the school be committed to its goals and one another. Parents, teachers, staff, and administrators should maintain a shared interest in the overall performance of the children and the school. In order to do this, the school must have control over key resources, especially for staff selection and rewards, and for investment in school improvements.

  Schools, however, should be more than a businesslike organization. They should also be communities. Schools form a bridge between families and the larger society. They must serve both the interests of the parents and children in the school and the interests of the broader community. In order to do this schools should build bonds of trust between parents and teachers, teachers and students; and schools and their communities and trusting relationships can be sustained only if there are shared values.

- *The school building should be the basic management unit.* Teachers and building-level administrators should be in charge of their schools. Most decisions should be made at the school level. School staffs should have opportunities to learn what has worked elsewhere and have time to try out new ideas and to learn from failures. Teachers should be encouraged to work in teams to provide a total education— an education that ensures that every student in the school learns. When management is shifted to the school level, schools can be responsive to parents and truly put the education of children first.

- *Schools should treat teachers as professionals.* If teaching is to become a true profession, teachers have to be given much more responsibility in schools. Teachers should be considered a part of school management. They must have greater opportunities to collaborate with colleagues and have more say over the selection of other teachers in the school. If teaching is to become a profession and be attractive to able people, salaries paid to teachers have to be comparable with salaries in other professions. This might mean that teaching should become a full-time occupation (rather than a nine-month job). Most importantly, teacher compensation should be more closely tied to performance. Those who get better results, who offer rare or indispensable skills, and who work longer hours, should be rewarded for their efforts.

- *Teachers, principals, and parents must have confidence that their school is equitably funded.* The quality of a child's education should not depend on the level of funding available to the school she attends. Today, we tolerate great resource disparities, even among schools in the same district, largely due to a district's policies permitting senior teachers to cluster together in the "nicest" schools. All schools should start with comparable facilities and equal or near equal funding based upon the number of students enrolled in the school. At a minimum, schools should start out with comparable facilities and more or less equal operating funds based on the enrollment of the school.

- *Schools should be open to parents and welcome their participation.* Parents should be recognized as collaborators in a child's education. They should also be able to learn in advance what different schools offer and what they demand of children and families. Having made a choice, parents feel some responsibility for ensuring that the family fulfills its part of the bargain; they also will have a framework of expectations on which to judge the school. Not all parents can spend great amounts of time in schools, but some can be invited to contribute to the real life of the school, serving as aides and assistants, taking attendance, supervising study sessions, monitoring the lunch room, supervising play activities, or helping with health screening. Some parents can provide individualized instruction in the uses of technology and foreign languages, or participate in career education programs. Parent participation can also be encouraged through community education activities at the school. Parental commitment through choice and presence in the school links school with home, and makes it an extension of the family rather than a remote institution or a rival.

- *Schools should be organized to encourage high performance.* In most school districts today it makes almost no difference if a school does well or if it does poorly. They are assigned the same number of students, receive the same budget, and are subject to the same rules regardless of performance. This must change. Highly effective teachers should be paid more than less effective teachers. School budgets should be tied to enrollment so that schools that gain reputations for results and attract more students can obtain more resources. High performance should be a criterion for the right to operate a school. Principals and teachers who fail to achieve high standards should be replaced by those who can.

- *Schools should be given incentives to use resources efficiently.* Just as there are few rewards for high performance, schools today have few reasons for being efficient. In fact, schools are likely to receive more resources if they are inefficient. Putting more students in special classes not only reduces class size but also increases allocations for special education teachers and supplies. Efficiency can be improved by giving school administrators and teachers control over the use of the school's total budget. If schools could keep money saved by being efficient, they might explore less expensive staffing patterns, or ways of using technology that enable individual teachers to be more effective. If a school and teachers, for instance, could benefit from reducing sick leave and absenteeism, teachers would be less likely to take advantage of those benefits. Schools in the South have been able to recarpet schools with the savings from turning off air conditioners when classrooms were not in use.

In themselves these principles do not constitute a reform, but they establish the requirements that a successful reform must meet. They are extremely challenging, requiring large numbers of people to develop and use advanced skills and to expend intense effort. No system of governance can absolutely guarantee that we will have schools that meet all these requirements. The system of contracting we propose is only a framework for action, not a device that will automatically and without human effort meet these requirements. In the chapters that follow, however, we will show how a public education system based on contracting is a better match for these requirements than any other.

Why Such a Dramatic Reform Is Necessary

Most Americans want an excellent education for their children and are willing to spend time, energy, and money to achieve good results. Almost all of us have gone to some kind of school and know how a school operates. We also try to teach our own children and we have an intense interest in their personal success. Yet many Americans are frustrated and angry with public schools. They are not comfortable with what goes on in schools, are disappointed with the results schools are achieving, and feel that they have almost no voice and little control over the education their children receive. This is true of laypersons and educators alike: public school teachers and administrators are at least as likely as other parents to send their children to private schools.

Dissatisfaction with public schools is apparently not due to a lack of commitment among educators. The private schools to which some parents flee are staffed by teachers and administrators with training similar to that of those in public schools, and there is considerable circulation of staff among public and private schools. Even the ablest and most dedicated superintendents and school board members are unable to bring about improvements they seek, as the rapid turnovers in their jobs attest. In a situation in which many people share goals but all are thwarted, problems must run deeper than personalities.

What has gone wrong? We spend a great deal on public elementary and secondary education in the United States. Nationwide, per pupil revenues have risen over the last forty years at more than twice the rate of inflation. On a per pupil basis, the United States spends more than Canada, England, Germany, France, and Japan. More money might solve some school problems, but there is no reason to think that declining public confidence is caused by a lack of funds.

There is every reason to think that the problems of public education are rooted in the basic arrangements by which we as a society provide public education. In our efforts to help public schools respond to the needs of an increasingly diverse population, we have made public education more rule-bound, rights-driven, and divided into specialties; we have removed decision-making from the school level and centralized it in district offices, courts, and state departments of education. Hence, we have weakened schools as organizations and blurred their focus on the core mission of teaching. We had reasons to do these things but the results have not been good.

Presidents, even those calling themselves "education presidents," have discovered, to their dismay, that they can do little to affect the educational system. Powerful special interests spend millions on federal, state, and local political campaigns to protect the prerogatives and privileges created for them within the educational system. Major federal government education programs such as Title 1, special education, bilingual education, and even many research programs have become entitlements that threaten the coherence of schools and benefit provider groups as much or more than the children they were intended to serve.

States are responsible for education, but much as with the federal government, powerful education lobbies with large campaign war chests and strong delegations of their own members elected to the legislative bodies repeatedly stifle efforts to reform public schools. In many state legislatures, no one interest has the strength to make a significant change in policy, but all can and do veto changes proposed by others. Legislatures therefore focus on smaller matters, not fundamental reforms, micromanaging details as petty as the number of minutes per week a child must participate in physical education, or the national test scores and grades required of teachers to be state-certified.

The stalemate in state legislatures is particularly apparent in the area of school finance. For over thirty years reformers have attempted to reduce revenue disparities between property- rich and poor schools. Despite Herculean efforts, legislatures frequently lack the independent freedom of action to overcome interest-group politics and implement constitutionally required mandates for "uniform and general," or fair, financing of schools.

Local school districts are responsible for managing public schools, but few can pursue consistent improvement strategies. School board members continually find themselves in awkward and conflicted positions. Their powers are both legislative and executive: they make policy and then often take responsibility for administering it. Board members are elected to represent the interests of a public that is paying the bills for and expects to obtain the highest-quality education at an affordable price. This means that school boards must spend their time seeking a balance between the quality and quantity of education, and the tax price of those services. On the other hand, school board members are also employers of school administrators, teachers, and many other staff. As employers, they are expected to protect the interests of their workers, which usually means increasing budgets to provide higher salaries, more benefits, and better working conditions, regardless of the preferences of the public, the quality of instruction provided, or the community's ability to pay. As both policy makers and public employers, school board members face conflicts about whom they should serve.

This role conflict is most severe in heavily populated cities where school board members are elected from wards or single-member subdistricts. In such cases, board members must represent both their immediate geographic constituents, residents of their subdistricts, overall or districtwide interests, and the employees of schools. Narrowly defined constituency decision-making contributes to legislative gridlock in which no single group can generate a majority for its proposals yet groups can join together to defeat another constituency's wishes. Simple matters may get resolved. However, important and politically controversial policy questions such as teacher evaluation, achievement or performance testing, busing, student suspension policy, and student assignment often get bogged down in conflict and are not resolved.

Individual schools are also bogged down by lack of clarity about mission and locus of decision-making. Too often good principals and teachers are discouraged from making changes by rules and regulations issued by state or district bureaucrats. But an even bigger obstacle to change is that no one knows who can make a decision to do something differently. Everyone points a finger at someone else as the reason so little gets done. People who create successful schools and programs are lionized as heroes, but their success can seldom be duplicated because it is based on heroic personal effort, overcoming all the obstacles the system erects. Even when great successes occur, they are isolated; many successful schools and programs, in time, regress to the mean.

We paint a dismal picture of American public education. It is a venerable system that in too many districts has virtually creaked to a halt. From the federal government to the local school-house, decisions that are important to the nation and its citizens are not being made. The current governance of public education makes effective action at the school level almost impossible.

The Inadequacy of Current Reform Proposals

Most of the current proposals for reforming public education either do not tackle the bureaucratic gridlock that has stifled reforms in the past or fail to ensure an adequate supply of high-quality education for all children. Vouchers and other choice plans say how parents can get the resources to demand better public schools but not how public or private agencies will develop the capacity to provide them. Charter schools reduce the burden of regulation for a few schools but leave the vast majority of them under the current rule-driven governance system. School-based management changes decision-making at the school level but does not change the mission and powers of the central office, and it does little to reduce the constraints imposed by federal and state regulations, categorical program requirements, and union contracts. School board reforms urge an end to micro-management, but they do not relieve members of the need to resolve complaints and conflicts by making new policies that apply to all schools. The various systemic reform proposals such as Goals 2000 and the new standards projects try to align the different parts of public education through mandated goals, tests, curriculum frameworks, and teacher certification methods, but do nothing to eliminate the political and contractual constraints that create fragmented, unresponsive schools.

None of these reforms offers a complete alternative to the existing governance structure. Because all of the reforms, except vouchers, leave the structure's core intact—the commitment to governing public schools by politically negotiated rules that apply to all schools—they are much more likely to be transformed by the system than to transform it.

Hypothetical Contract Schools

What might schools be like under this proposed new system of contracting? No one answer is possible because the agreements or contracts negotiated between school boards and individual contractors will be different in different communities. We are reluctant to speculate for fear of vastly misportraying the creativity of parents, policy makers, prospective contractors, and others. Indeed, there are many remarkably creative contractors who will view schools in a very different way than they have previously been seen, and will draft proposals accordingly.

Nevertheless, out of a desire to display some of the ideas that become more widely possible under a contract school-management plan, we present a hypothetical example of a contract elementary school.[2]

WASHINGTON ELEMENTARY SCHOOL

It was 6 A.M., and Washington Elementary School principal Linda Verdin parked her car in the school lot. Usually she did not arrive until an hour later, but she had decided to come early on this particular morning to assist the newly engaged preschool subcontractor. The food-service staff, also a subcontractor employed by her company, had already opened the kitchen, and Verdin could smell the results of their breakfast preparations. Parents would begin dropping off their children at 7 A.M. Many would come in, have breakfast, talk to one of the day-care workers about their children, or perhaps meet with the county health nurse, whose office was located next to the school cafeteria, before leaving for their own work. Verdin asked that her school staff keep brief but accurate accounts of such parent visits and conversations. She knew that satisfied clients were a part of the con-

2. Appendix A presents two more hypothetical examples of contract schools, a middle school and a high school.

tract renewal discussions that she and her company representatives would have later that year with the district school board.

Verdin had been a public school principal for ten years prior to becoming head of a small nonprofit corporation that won a contract from the local school board. She and a group of good teachers with whom she had worked throughout her career decided to bid to operate Washington School. Their successful competitive proposal was the high point of her professional career, and many of the teachers in the group felt the same way. Here, at last, was a chance to operate the school they had dreamed about for so long—the school they had talked about for many hours in teachers lounges, homes, and at summer in-service education workshops. Though some members of the original group had left the school, disappointed that they could not have total personal autonomy in a school that was accountable for results, a solid core had stayed together.

Verdin had confidence that their operating contract with the local district school board would be renewed. After a tough year in which student test scores seemed unwilling to budge, results had now improved for many students, and parent-satisfaction survey results, as conveyed to her by the independent evaluation company, seemed high. Reports from middle schools indicated that her school's graduates were better prepared than most. Because enrollments were up slightly from last year, her budget was larger.

Her school's parents had recently voted to extend their voluntary donations for the enrichment programs that she had proposed for the forthcoming year. Donations were purely voluntary, and many of the low-income families whom Washington aggressively recruited were able to contribute nothing. But fund-raising among parents and community members, plus savings from the school's operating budget, were enough to paint a portion of the school two years ahead of schedule, and all major maintenance was now up to date. Verdin was especially satisfied with the work of a business manager she shared with two other contract elementary schools, one in her school district, another in a nearby district. The three principals had each felt personally burdened by the need to coordinate maintenance and keep school accounts, and they decided to join together to contract out the work. The move saved their sanity and led to a much higher level of maintenance and service than the schools had ever before experienced. The business manager had a plan for financing new landscaping and redoing the playground next year.

Verdin and parent council members were communicating smoothly. After a rocky first year in which seemingly no two people in the school had the same idea about student deportment and school authority, the parent council had approved the new discipline policy Verdin had proposed last year. Three parents had withdrawn their children from the school, saying the new standards were too demanding and arbitrary. But they were replaced quickly, as information about discipline standards spread and the student waiting list grew. Teachers and students seemed to like the discipline policy a great deal. Teachers in particular knew exactly when the principal would back them up and when she wouldn't.

Verdin had arranged, at her teachers' requests, a week-long workshop on cognitive instructional strategies which would take place during the three-week break between the first and second quarter. Her only immediate worry was the conversation she would have to have on Friday with one of the associate teachers, who simply did not seem able to relate to the older students. She and her lead teachers had agreed to extend the associate teacher's probationary period and, at the quarter break, to exchange his duties with a teacher who worked well with younger students. Verdin thought the teacher was promising and hoped he would stay with the school, but she knew that he had been contacted by a K–4 contract school, where he might fit in more easily.

Verdin was paid $80,000 a year as principal and contract director. Three-quarters of this amount came from overseeing the elementary school's instructional program—the core program, as it was called. The remaining $20,000 was paid to her annually for managing the school's subcontractors who provided food service, day-care, recreation supervision, foreign language instruction, and other supplementary instructional programs. The total financial package was a handsome amount for an elementary principal but not excessive, given the spectrum of her responsibilities and the $2 million annual budget for her school. When she went to the Rotary meeting each week, Verdin was proud to consider herself an executive as well as an educator. Like many of her peers as leaders of small enterprises, she knew that her total compensation was excellent but that her hourly rate of pay was modest.

By 7 A.M. Verdin was ready for her weekly meeting with the school's four master teachers. These were seasoned professionals with whom she had worked in other school settings, and the first individuals with whom she had spoken once she began to contemplate bidding on a school operation contract. Indeed, all four of them had contributed their own financing for a fund to cover start-up expenses of the new school. Each of these lead teachers held national certification through the Detroit-based National Board of Professional Teaching Standards, and each had also, in addition to his or her instructional responsibilities, supervised the three associate teachers in their learning groups, or instructional communities.

Washington School was divided into four such groups (sometimes referred to as learning "pods"). In effect, these were groupings of students and instructors by grade level or age. Kindergarten through second grade students were in one or the other of two groups. Third through fifth grade students were also assigned to one of two upper-grade groups within the school. Within a group, students were taught by a team of four instructors and two teacher aides. There were 70 to 80 students per group. However, all four teachers were responsible for all students in a group, and the students stayed with this team of teachers for the entire three-year period. Later, when they entered the third grade, students would be assigned to a new group and would have another team of teachers and aides until they completed the fifth grade and went to middle school.

Many parents contributed to the school, some as volunteers in a variety of areas. Others worked a specified number of hours each week in order to contribute their portion of the voluntary tuition for electives voted for by the parents at the school.

Verdin had made many efforts, which now were paying off, to engage senior citizens from a nearby retirement community to act as tutors, playground supervisors, cafeteria aides, and "big brothers" for Washington School students. During any particular day, there were as many as a dozen such volunteers on the school grounds. The result of all these efforts, when woven together, was an unusual school organization in which there were many adults each day to assist teachers and others in the work of the school.

Not all contract elementary schools in the district were organized in the same manner as Washington School. Some schools were operated by providers who stressed a particular academic or instructional theme. For example, there were three science-oriented schools in the district. Another school advertised itself as a Montessori School. Still another concentrated on environmental ecology, a theme around which all instruction was oriented. Parents could choose any elementary school in the district. Some schools grouped only 12 or 15 students with a self-contained classroom teacher. They were able to afford such small classes by selecting relatively inexperienced teachers and not having to pay them the higher salaries offered to Washington teachers. Verdin had no quarrel with any of these approaches. Indeed, there were parents who seemed to select happily from among each of them. However, her philosophy for Washington was that it would concentrate on academic fundamentals such as reading, mathematics, science, history, literature, and geography. She and her staff would strive to make all of these as exciting as possible. Each pod included a number of adults, some experienced and quite highly paid and others less professionally qualified, and less well paid.

Verdin believed that the master teachers brought an unmatched tone and instructional effectiveness to the school. She was reinforced in her approach, as more students applied each year to enroll at Washington. Each of the four lead teachers was paid well: between $50,000 and $70,000 annually, depending upon their specific agreement with the principal contract coordinator and the specification of their responsibilities. Associate teachers were paid less: $25,000 to $35,000 annually, again depending upon the amount of time they were expected to work during the year and their responsibilities. One young associate teacher was proving indispensable, and Verdin expected to offer her lead-teacher status within a year. She was determined not to let this gem get lured away by one of the many new contract schools forming in the district.

In addition to the lead teachers, associate teachers, and teacher aides, Washington School was always alive with teacher trainees from several local teacher-education colleges, community volunteers, and tutors. These trainees and volunteers sometimes burdened the senior teachers, but they provided an excellent pool of new hires. As Verdin explained, Washington School could try out potential teachers in real jobs, rather than just accepting anyone the central office sent out. The trainees were paid intern-level wages, not a large amount, but fair compensation for a job in which they were both providing services and learning their craft. Verdin carefully scrutinized trainees' performance and, in cooperation with the faculty of their college of education, gave them a thorough evaluation. She had hired three past trainees once they had completed their apprenticeships, and they were now proven members of the Washington instructional team.

All teachers, indeed all school employees, had an opportunity for an end-of-year performance awards. Principal Verdin's organization, "Instruction Associates," held a 501 (C) (3) status with the Internal Revenue Service. As such, it could not make a profit. However, end-of-year awards were possible if two conditions were met: the school had to achieve the performance and service expectations held for it contractually, and all costs had to be at or below the contract-specified total amount. If Verdin and her staff operated the school at less than the annual budgeted amount, any overage was split in half. One portion reverted to the school for instructional or facilities improvement, or student-related added services in the next operating year. The other half was allocated among school staff as one-time-only performance awards. Because Verdin's team-teaching arrangements had virtually eliminated the need for substitute teachers and teacher aides, and because the staff had been particularly conservative in the use of energy for heating and air conditioning, she was sure that there would be money for performance awards at the end of this operating year.

Another use of the savings from economies in staffing and other spending was to extend the school year. Washington School operated year-round with four ten-week quarters. Students attended school for 200 days. This was 10 percent longer than before the new public-school contract system was inaugurated. It was still shorter than the year-round schools attended by youngsters in other countries such as Japan and Germany. Nevertheless, the schedule accommodated the needs of parents and permitted free time for teachers to upgrade the curriculum and hone their instructional skills.

Each school quarter was separated from its successor by a three-week break. During the break period, the school's child-care services still operated. Teachers at Washington School generally were on year-round contracts. They had a month of total vacation time each year. They could also arrange to take an entire quarter (twelve weeks) off unpaid, if they had a need for a longer period of downtime. Otherwise, teachers were expected to work, even when students were not at school. There was always much to be done: learning how to incorporate new technology into their instruction, revising the curriculum, and providing parents with guidance about their children's learning and the next steps the children should be taking in their homework assignments and out-of-school experiences. Teacher aides, some of whom eventually pursued teacher training and advanced degrees and became apprentice and associate teachers, were paid an hourly wage.

By the time the 8 A.M. school-opening chimes had sounded, Verdin and her lead teachers had reviewed the business manager's monthly accounting reports; agreed upon the purchase of a new, experimental, mathematics-instruction software program; agreed to give one last chance in the school to a child who was becoming an increasingly serious discipline problem; and reviewed the schedules of associate teachers and teacher aides for the week. Verdin had also briefed lead teachers about the midyear performance results which the third-party evaluator had conveyed to both the school and the district board of education on the preceding Friday.

Lastly, they made plans for the end-of-quarter testing which would soon be scheduled with the third-party independent evaluation contractor.

Classes would start at 8:10 A.M. Students were now lining up on the playground with learning-group partners and teacher aides. All students wore the Washington School uniform. Verdin had proposed a uniform policy to the parent advisory council, and it had initially been a point of controversy. After two meetings, however, parents voted to experiment with a uniform dress code based upon the school colors. The plan began in the fall quarter and had proved a huge success with parents, who now knew exactly what their child would be expected to wear to school. No gang colors or personal competition over expensive shoes or other articles of clothing distracted from school activity. Local merchants who sold such uniforms liked the extra business.

Verdin had, through both education and experience, developed a three-pronged pragmatic philosophy regarding instruction. First, she did not put all of her faith in any specific way of teaching. Indeed, she was wary of true believers who thought there was one way, and only one way, to teach reading, mathematics, science, or whatever subject was at hand. It was true that phonics worked well in teaching some students to read. However, Verdin had also come to see that some teachers were gifted at using a whole-language approach, and their students also learned well. From experiences such as these she concluded that more important than having an agreed-upon school-wide instructional approach, was having an eclectic outlook that permitted each individual teacher or teaching team to develop a strategy they believed in or were excited about. She had come to see that many different kinds of teaching could be effective in the hands of a motivated and able teacher. She also had come to learn that no one method would suffice if the teacher was bored with it or was simply incompetent. Thus, she avoided being overly prescriptive and, instead, encouraged her teaching teams to explore strategies that made sense to them and about which they were enthusiastic. If a parent was intensely opposed to whatever strategy a learning pod was relying upon for a subject area, then the student could be transferred to the other pod for that grade level. Choice within Washington School was certainly possible

A second component of Verdin's strategy was that if a student was not reacting well to any particular strategy, then the teachers should try to reach him or her in some other way. Sometimes this meant transferring a student to the other pod—always with a parent's permission. Sometimes it simply meant one of the associate teachers or teacher's aides trying something new with the child.

The third prong of Verdin's strategy involved adults as role models for students. Verdin was eager to see the school filled with adults who offered nurturance to students, and adults who displayed a wide range of successful role models. Toward that end she had purposely recruited a racially and ethnically diverse staff. She had also recruited male teachers heavily. Washington's teachers were almost one-third male, two or three times the ratio at most elementary schools. However, Verdin thought this was an important component of what her school could offer, because such a large proportion of the students lived in single-family homes where the father was often not present. The desire for adult role models also fueled Verdin's continued efforts to recruit and involve school volunteers.

After school had begun, Verdin began her morning tour of the facility. She noticed that one of the upper-grade groups was using the school's science facility that morning. Another group was taking a field trip to a local aquarium. Field-trip buses were already present. Such scheduling matters fell to the school business manager, Mr. Bowman. He also negotiated subcontracts for food service, day-care, after-school recreation activities, grounds-keeping, and maintenance. Bowman was also responsible for keeping the school's overall set of accounts—an important task. Washington School had an annual budget in excess of $2 million. Cost overruns and deficits were intolerable, and a prudent reserve against unpredicted conditions had to be maintained. Verdin herself negotiated contracts for all personnel, including lead teachers, as well as for providers of supplementary instruction such in foreign languages, music, art, and physical education. Washington School was proud of the full range of such additional services; parents had voted to impose a tuition upon themselves in order to be able to offer these kinds of activities. Verdin was pleased to arrange for the services.

Each child was supplied by the school with a notebook computer which he or she could take home. These computers were purchased from voluntary parent contributions and fund-raisers. Under the public school system's rules no school could charge tuition, but parent contributions were permissible as long as donations were purely voluntary. The local public school board oversaw the student admissions process to ensure that students were admitted at random from among the whole pool of applicants.

Young students had "pen books" in which they could hand-print or write in script. Older students had keyboard powerbooks. Analytic assignments were routinely given, both to be completed in school and at home, beginning in the earliest grades. Students were expected and were helped to learn how to use computers and other technology as a regular part of their instructional day. Verdin's initial fears that students would lose their computers had proven unfounded. In the past year, only two computers had been lost—one by Verdin, who had it snatched at an airport security checkpoint. Washington School did not have a computer laboratory. There seemed no need to devote a separate room to technology. Doing so implied there was something special about it.

The only really special equipment at Washington School was the workstations in the science rooms. Here upper-grade students were introduced to analysis programs and activities such as computer-assisted designing. These workstations were also used at night by the adult education courses, which were offered by the school district at Washington School. Verdin leased the computers and space to the district for these evening activities. This seemed like a good way both to have the school serve as a center for much of the community and to gain added revenue for use of the school itself. These added revenues had defrayed discretionary tuition last year, and the school's parent council was deeply appreciative of Verdin's entrepreneurial efforts.

The lower-grade curriculum was covered in a slightly different way in each group but still followed the state-prescribed frameworks. Students learned reading, writing, and mathematics. Reading was taught with interesting stories. Young students were often read to at school, and were expected to be read to at home. Then they were introduced to fundamental concepts in science and geography.

The curriculum differed somewhat for the upper grades. State guidelines were adhered to, but there was more. Specifically, in the third grade history was introduced into the curriculum, and science started to be upgraded substantially. Two other components were added by what conventionally would be the fifth grade. A government component was introduced into the curriculum, and students began to learn fundamentals of civics. A health unit was also presented during the student's last year of schooling at Washington. This covered basic information about substance abuse, nutrition, exercise, and human reproduction.

Washington School also provided extra services for handicapped students. Generally these were youngsters who needed a little extra help in order to succeed in school. Severely handicapped youngsters who could not be integrated into regular classrooms attended a special school operated by a contractor for the County Board of Education. Each of the handicapped students received extra funds in the state school-finance formula. Thus, Washington School provided the contractor with added per pupil funding for such cases. These funds covered the added services such youngsters received.

The early grades ended their school day at 2:30 P.M. Many of these students stayed on for a variety of recreational activities provided by the local YMCA, a subcontractor with the school. These ended at 4 P.M. Following that, day-care was provided until 5 or 6 P.M. for those parents who desired it.

Verdin left Washington school at about 4 P.M. On her way home she stopped briefly at a student's house and delivered class and homework assignments. This student had been in a bad automobile accident, and Verdin was eager to assess his recuperation and appraise the extent to which he was able to stay abreast of his academic assignments. As she drove, she realized that even though the regular school and after-school programs had concluded, Washington School would still be operating. The after-school recreation activities would still be in progress, and after-school day-care would still be open. Later that evening, under a separate subcontract, the adult school would begin offering night courses to parents and other community members. It had been a full day for Verdin. Still, she felt secure about the entire school operation. There was a lead teacher assigned to stay until 6 P.M. each day, and that person was sufficiently experienced for Verdin to realize she was quite capable of running the school.

WHAT THE EXAMPLE ILLUSTRATES

Many things about Washington Elementary School make it representative of the schools that would arise under a contracting system. Washington is operated by an independent organization that obtained its contract by responding to a formal RFP (Request for Proposal) from the local school board. The contractor submitted a bid to operate Washington, and it remains free to bid for additional contracts.

Washington Elementary controls its own budget, which is based on a per pupil allowance guaranteed under the contract. The dollar level per student is the same for all schools in the district, except that special-needs students may bring some additional funding. (Some local school boards might choose to allow higher per student funding for high schools, but Washington's did not.) Washington can use its budget to employ individuals to perform some key services, and it can subcontract with specialized firms to provide others.

School contractors remain independent organizations; neither they nor their teachers and administrators are employees of the school board. Contract school employees have all the rights to job security and fair treatment accorded other American professional workers. But unlike teachers in traditional public school systems, they are free to seek and accept jobs in other local schools, unconstrained by a district-wide seniority preference system.

School operators enjoy great freedom of action, as long as they respect the terms of the school's contract with the local school board, which obligates the school to follow the statewide curriculum framework and participate in statewide testing programs. Like managers of other small professional enterprises, the managers gain their freedom by taking responsibility for attracting and retaining a high-quality staff, investing to strengthen weak spots in the school's instructional program, preserving safe and attractive facilities, maintaining parents' confidence, and demonstrating that student outcomes meet the terms of the school's contract. These are significant burdens, which educators in traditional public schools do not have to bear.

School operators know that Washington is evaluated through four principal avenues: (1) the ability of parents to exit and choose another school if they desire; (2) the results of a third-party, outside professional appraisal team which, among other features, ensures that the contractor is complying with provisions of the agreed-to contract; (3) the satisfaction expressed by parents in an independent polling effort; and (4) academic achievement results and other school performance measures established by the state education department.

The Organization of This Book

The book is divided into two parts. Part I, consisting of chapters 1 through 4, makes the theoretical case for contract schools and places the reform in the current education conversation between extreme private and public poles. Part II, chapters 5 through 7, focuses on the nuts and bolts of contract schools, and what would have to be changed to bring such schools about.

Chapter 2 explains why the current public education system is inadequate to meet twenty-first-century expectations for schools and how it inhibits education reform. Chapter 3 provides an in-depth discussion of contract schools, the principles underlying them, and the major features of the system. Chapter 4 compares school contracting to other reform proposals, especially privatization proposals such as vouchers and the Clinton administration's Goals 2000.

Part II begins in chapter 5 with a discussion of the operational dynamics of contract schools. Chapter 6 describes the changes that would be required in the way schools are financed. Chapter 7 focuses on the politics and pragmatics of establishing a system of contract schools. It discusses the politics of establishing contract schools at the state and local levels and examines changes in state law and local practice required to implement contracting.

The book also has three appendices. Appendix A provides hypothetical examples of contract schools, Appendix B provides a primer on the current public education finance system, and Appendix C asks and answers many questions citizens will have about contract schools.

A Critique of the Current Public School System

B y many standards, public education is one of the great tri-umphs of American society. Earlier in this century, public education provided the United States with the highest literacy rate in the world and, combined with the higher-education opportunities created after World War II by the G.I. Bill it supported unprecedented economic and social mobility. In the years after *Brown v. Board of Education*, public education also became the leading edge of a broad effort to eliminate racial segregation and race-based economic inequality. Though the latter efforts are still incomplete, the results are in the right direction. Many minority students' achievement levels still lag significantly behind those of whites, but the gap has narrowed measurably (Grissmer and Kirby 1991). Many African-American students still attend largely segregated schools, but the number attending integrated schools has increased dramatically. College attendance among blacks, Hispanics, and Native Americans is still far lower than among whites, but it is at least increasing. Minorities still earn less than whites in the same occupations, but the gaps have narrowed steadily (Smith and Welch 1986).

Despite these gains, public education receives constant criticism and is subject to successive waves of reform. As some have suggested, any society is bound to worry constantly about the arrangements it has made for the education and protection of its children, so that scrutiny of public schools is inevitable. There are, however, reasons to think that current worries about public schools are well grounded. As Peter Drucker has argued (1994), the era of stable and highly paid blue-collar jobs requiring only modest levels of education is over; stable industrial firms are almost a thing of the past, and people will be forced to choose between lower-paid service jobs and relatively better-paying "knowledge worker" jobs.

Knowledge workers will, by definition, have to master specialized skills, and they will have to be extremely adaptable. They will seldom work in assembly lines, and the organizations that employ them will themselves be lean and quick to change. Knowledge workers will have to shape their own skills and work to the current needs of an unpredictable economy. They will also have to manage their own careers, understanding the environment in which they work well enough to know when to develop new skills, when to leave one job for another, and when to start something new on their own.

The supply of such "knowledge worker" jobs may be highly elastic, depending on the skills and imaginations of the workforce. A nation in which skilled, adaptable, entrepreneurial workers are plentiful will have a booming economy and ample employment opportunities.

No one can assert with precision what the economy will demand in twenty years (just as no one twenty years ago could have predicted exactly what is happening today, with corporate downsizing and mergers, movements from in-house employment to contracting out, growing reliance on computer technology, economic growth fueled by software industries and their consumer product spin-offs, and the shrinkage of the defense industry). Whether or not Drucker's prediction is correct in every particular, it is clear that the future demands on education will be high. All graduates will need skills that build on but go far beyond the basics; they must also have the capacity to analyze their own situations and to understand how they fit into larger systems.

Because the entire economy, not just its low-cost production sectors, will face competition from lower-paid but highly skilled foreign workers, virtually everyone will need the kind of education that allows them to continuously learn new skills and develop new lines of work.

The current debate about whether public schools are better or worse than in the past (e.g., Bracey 1992; Berliner and Biddle 1995) is hardly relevant to the question of whether they are adequate to the needs of the future in which today's students will live. Putting aside relative performance levels, what does seem clear currently is that unacceptably large numbers of American school-age youth are insufficiently equipped with the skills and knowledge to enable them to acquire additional education or employment, or to lead fulfilling personal lives. This is true in all sorts of schools, including those in the wealthier suburbs. But it is particularly true in inner-city schools serving minority pupils, where barely half the students who enroll in ninth grade ever attain a high school diploma, and where even those students who persist in school long enough to be tested as seniors exhibit strikingly inferior levels of skill and knowledge (Miller 1995).

None of this is news. Recognizing it, educators and researchers have tried for years to develop new curricula and approaches to school management that will help develop higher levels of student understanding, performance, and motivation. There are many promising exemplars, including Ted Sizer's and Deborah Meier's "Essential Schools," the Paideia and International Baccalaureate schools, schools based on "constructivist" approaches such as those pioneered by Eric Schapps and developed further by several design teams funded by the New American Schools Development Corporation, and more traditional schools such as the "Roots and Wings" schools developed by Robert Slavin. These innovations, however, remain isolated, and efforts to "scale up," making more demanding and effective schools available throughout the public education system, have been dismal failures. As Seattle teacher union chief Roger Erskine has noted, we are not yet able to turn "random acts of innovation" into widespread school improvement.

Though there can never be enough good ideas about how to teach and motivate students, such ideas are not scarce now. Nor is there a shortage of exemplars of excellent practice. Virtually every major public school system has its own version of New York's Central Park East Secondary School or Indianapolis' Key School, which successfully educates the whole range of public school students, rich and poor, minority and majority, all within a normal public school budget.

If good ideas and reproducible examples of good practice exist, why are schools, especially those in the lowest-performing districts, so slow to change? Schools still look and perform much as they did a hundred years ago. Students go to school nine months a year, have summer vacation, attend fifty-minute classes from eight in the morning to three in the afternoon, take the same subjects, and graduate after twelve years of school.

Part of the answer is that bureaucratic systems, like our current public school systems, are not very good at change. Bureaucracies are set up to provide stable, reliable service. The goals of bureaucracy are fairness and predictability, not change. Teacher habits and training also mitigate against adaptive behavior on the part of schools. Adults in the schools have spent their careers working in particular ways, and many have difficulty imagining alternatives. However, as Muncey and others (1993) have shown, many adults in schools, often those with the most extensive experience and training, refuse to change the way they work even in the presence of training and help. In schools, as in virtually all organizations public and private, the most important explanation for organizational inertia is a lack of real incentives for change. (See Hardcastle 1994 for a case study of comparable inertia in a private sector industrial firm.)

Though the authors of this book believe strongly in development of new instructional methods and teacher training, our core assumption is that significant change in public education requires more: it requires a change in the fundamental incentives and structures that govern local school districts and public schools.

Three kinds of evidence support the proposition that current governance arrangements militate against school quality and prevent change. The first is that effective practice is difficult to reproduce. Public schools that provide rigorous instruction and help students succeed despite poverty and social turmoil are nearly always "special" in some way. Most have foundation grants, strong business supporters, or unique "magnet" status. Many such schools can gain access to needed resources and hire teachers who complement others already in the school. Being treated as exceptional means that teachers and principals in other public schools seldom use outstanding schools as examples. The conventional wisdom, that excellent public schools require charismatic leadership, is a tacit admission that the governance structure is hostile to quality.

A second indicator of governance problems is that school systems seldom have any free resources to invest in major improvements or to intervene in desperately failing schools. Competition for resources has created an overconstrained system in which every dollar is allocated to teacher salaries or to existing programs. New funds, e.g., from tax levy increases, are spoken for before they arrive, usually to fund deferred maintenance or roll back increases in average class size. Even the supposedly flexible categories of funds, such as staff development, are committed in advance to separate categorical programs or to programs selected by central office administrators.

The third and most devastating indicator of governance problems is the persistence of school failure. Every major city has schools in which dropout rates and other indicators of student failure have been high for decades. Though some such schools have suffered consistent neglect, many have been objects of repeated improvement efforts. These efforts, however, are largely piecemeal additions, such as counseling and self-esteem interventions, intensive health-care programs, and even day-care for students' babies. They are too small and do not affect instructional programs in ways to reduce school failure. The fact that failure persists despite turnovers in superintendents, school boards, and central-office leaders indicates that the lack of capacity is built into the system.

The Meaning and Significance of Governance

Reduced to its lowest terms, public education is education paid for and provided by local school boards and other instrumentalities of the state, fulfilling their responsibilities under state law.[1] Subject to the provisions of state and federal laws and court orders (defining student eligibility for free public education, the rights of students, and the rights and obligations of teachers and administrators), any arrangement made by a duly constituted local school board for the education of children can be considered public education.

How is this enormous enterprise governed? For the purposes of this book, public education governance is broadly defined to include all activities and institutions that set goals that publicly supported education is to meet, what persons and organizations may deliver public education, how publicly funded schools are to be administered, who is to take part in internal decision-making and what roles they are to play, what students can receive public education, who may instruct students, what funds and other resources schools and other institutions receive, what services teachers and others must provide, how resources and services must be allocated among students, what courses students must take, and what students must be able to demonstrate before they can be recognized as graduates. There is a vast list of decisions to be made about public education and about the actors who are to take part in the decisions. In the American tradition, power is widely diffused. Not one of the agencies, actors, or power centers that make decisions about public education is, by itself, capable of improving a single school. They must all work together. But any one of them alone can stop reform.

---

1. The term "public education" is widely used but seldom carefully defined. It certainly includes all forms of instruction in schools operated and funded from tax revenues by local public school boards. But there are many instances in which activities people call public education lack one or more features of the foregoing definition. Public education students frequently receive instruction outside of publicly owned school buildings, at museums, concert halls, theaters, zoos, and public and private colleges and universities. Some public education services are also delivered by independent organizations, including private providers of special education and remedial services, language, science, and mathematics courses and enrichment, and public and private colleges. Some public education services are also funded entirely or in part through private donations, fundraising, and parental payments for extracurricular activities and instruction. Public school boards also place some handicapped students in privately managed facilities and pay tuition, and some privately run alternative schools are funded entirely through contracts with public school boards.

The most obvious sources of prescriptions about public education are the laws and regulations enacted by Congress, state legislatures, and state and local school boards. But others play a role in school governance. In many localities, court orders determine how much schools will spend; whether students will attend school in their own neighborhoods or elsewhere for racial balance; what services parents of children with disabilities can demand; and whether or not local districts can offer special programs for particular groups of youngsters with particular needs, e.g., young African-American males. In many places, especially big cities, labor contracts—not only with teachers but also with administrators and custodians—determine when schools will open and close, who will administer them, who will teach in them, and what minimum standards of diligence adults must meet in order to keep their jobs.

None of these groups want schools to be hopelessly tied up in rules, mandates, and limitations; each thinks the requirements it imposes will make schools better. In the aggregate, however, the constraints imposed by this complex governance system are the sources of many school problems and roadblocks to improvement. Though none of these agencies, actors, or power centers is, by itself, capable of improving a school, virtually any one of them can put obstacles in the path of reform.

As school systems have become ever larger, their centers of control—school boards and central offices—have become ever more remote and distant for clients and employees. The sheer scale of large districts makes it difficult, if not impossible, for parents to participate in decisions affecting the education of their children. Many superintendents are too busy at the central administrative office to make routine visits to the schools. Parents and citizens have responded to this formality with apathy and special-interest representation. Each of these avenues reinforces the other. The greater the degree of parent and citizen apathy, the more withdrawn and alienated those concerned for the well-being of the entire organization become. This allows narrow and self-serving interests to wield great influence and makes schools constrained, beholden, and ineffective.

How Current Governance Burdens Schools

The governance arrangements sketched above have the following adverse effects on schools:

- Schools have become formal agencies of government, not intimate and personalized community resources for nurturing children.
- Schools are operated directly by political decision-making bodies, and

they reflect those bodies' preoccupation with standardization, avoidance of scandal, and symbolic deference to group demands.

• Teachers and principals have become preoccupied with compliance and avoidance of controversy, even at the cost of ineffective instruction.

• Schools are dominated by concern for jobs and other adult issues.

• Due to inequitable and unstable funding and shifting mandates, schools are often unable to pursue consistent instructional strategies.

• Schools practice "defensive education," avoiding charges of discrimination and negligence but not accepting responsibility for tailoring instruction to the needs of individual students.

Schools as Instruments of Government

When school districts were established, good-government advocates believed that the professional bureaucracy possessed the necessary information and technical expertise to run schools fairly and efficiently. Public schools were to be owned, financed, and operated by a local government agency. Decisions about educational policy and practice would be made by an elected school board. The superintendent and central staff would be the administrative arm of the school board and help it carry out its policy-making and guiding responsibilities.

This is not how most school districts work today. The school board and central administration are often at odds with one another. School boards are criticized for micro-managing the system, interfering in the day-to-day administration of schools. Central administration is accused of making policy by withholding information from the school board or giving up matters of policy to the unions in collective bargaining.

The major reason we have this conflict is that public school districts combine the functions of policy-making and service delivery. School districts not only collect taxes and decide how those dollars are spent, they also operate schools and many auxiliary activities for the schools. School districts hire most school personnel, dictate what activities will occur in the schools, build and maintain facilities, operate a bus system, provide food services, offer special programs, and handle community relations. The day-to-day burden of managing a large government enterprise overwhelms the job of making decisions to improve education. Not only are the superintendent and staff swamped with administrative detail, but school board members get dragged into solving administrative problems.

In order to operate such a broad array of programs and services, districts must adopt formal rules and procedures. Once adopted, bureaucratic rules are hard to change, even if they are shown to inhibit effective schooling and student achievement.

Huge organizational scale has driven American public education to be viewed in "systems" terms. This is the organizational frame of mind which has evolved in an effort to cope with the management of hundreds of thousands of students, tens of thousands of teachers, billions of dollars in resources, and multiple layers of governmental responsibility.

Student-assignment practices also consider the convenience of the system over the needs of parents and students. Almost all students are assigned to schools on the basis of where they live. It is an American tradition that students should attend school in their own neighborhoods whenever possible. In urban areas it is almost universally true that students attend elementary classes in their own neighborhoods, although their older siblings may have to travel much farther to their middle or secondary school. Even at the elementary level, however, there are important exceptions to the general practice.

Some students in major urban areas are bused out of their neighborhood attendance zones for purposes of racial integration. Individual students are also allowed to attend schools outside their neighborhoods for purposes of special education or to take part in unusual instructional programs, e.g., at a science and mathematics or performing arts magnet school. School systems occasionally develop magnet schools in order to keep middle-class students who might otherwise leave for private schools, or to create oases of integrated education in a school system that is geographically divided by race.

Though public school systems occasionally relax the connection between residence and school assignment for reasons of their own, they do so only reluctantly. If parents want a child to attend a school outside the neighborhood, they must often make the case that the local school lacks some program the child needs. Parents' requests are frequently denied if a transfer would adversely affect the racial balance of the sending or receiving school.

When families relocate, even within the same school system, children normally change schools. Midyear transfers can have a dramatic effect on the population of a school. Many schools in low-income and immigrant urban neighborhoods experience more than a 100 percent annual turnover in their students. Occasionally, these students move only a few blocks, continuing to believe they live in the same "neighborhood," but they are forced to change schools.

Such student attendance policies make parents feel powerless in the face of the school system. Children are too frequently assigned to distant schools to which they are bused at the direction of remote bureaucrats. Parents are invited to attend PTA meetings, work at the Christmas fundraiser and contribute to the school booster club, but they are not consulted on the most important question about their child's education, which is what school he or she will attend.

Schools Operated by Political Decision-Making Bodies

Schools are operated directly by political bodies—elected local boards, which are themselves instruments of state legislatures. Schools are thus subject to those bodies' need to respond to pressures, take actions that symbolize the importance of all groups, and act like they intend to find a universal solution to every problem.

At the state level, many independent organizations can make policies that affect schools: state appropriations committees, legislative authorization committees, state boards of education, state superintendents and assistant superintendents, job-training agencies, community college and higher education boards, and state courts all create programs, regulations, or mandates that schools must respond to. State education agencies, operating under legislative guidance, set requirements for the length of the school year, credits required for high school graduation, and teacher and principal certification. In theory, such state mandates are meant to ensure high-quality and professional oversight of local school systems. But many decisions are made or influenced through political processes, whether in the state legislature itself or in negotiations among interest groups. Several state legislatures, for example, have responded to popular discontent about education by imposing new standards and mandates without allowing for their cost. One state's "omnibus reform bill" was drafted by legislative staff under instructions to pick out the best ideas from several national reports, under the constraint that none could increase state funding for education. Moreover, many curriculum reform efforts have been forums for contention among interest groups about the content of multicultural curricula, the definition of sexist language, and the need to give equal attention to the histories and views of all groups.

In the grand tradition of American government, all the state-level agencies that have powers relevant to schooling are sovereign in their own spheres of action. Each has its own constituencies, powers, resources, and decision-making processes, and few have any need to coordinate their actions with others or to count the costs, in money or staff effort, at the school level.

Local school districts try to help schools by interpreting state mandates and advising on compliance. But the school district itself is also a source of fragmenting mandates. School boards resolve issues seriatim, and expect schools to find ways of adapting to them all, even the ones that may be contradictory or require multiple uses of the same resources.

Local board members are responsible to the constituents that elected them, both in making general policy and in listening to requests and resolving disputes. Whether they are elected or appointed, board members seek office in order to improve the schools. They attempt that by making policy. Scandals, constituent complaints, and disappointing test scores all put pressure on the board: they must do something. In most cases that "something" amounts to enacting a policy that constrains all schools. Though some school board meetings focus on important issues, time is regularly given to the small annoyances that vex any organization: a student who broke his ankle while away from school grounds at lunchtime, a dispute over whether a faculty member kept proper accounts of the proceeds from a school fund-raiser, or a charge that a student was improperly suspended from school due to misbehavior.

Because such matters get dealt with by the most authoritative body in the school system, their resolution affects all schools. If the resolution of an issue is encoded into district policy, all schools must take immediate account of it. Even if the resolution affects only one school, personnel in other schools know that they can be sharply criticized if a similar incident occurs in their school and they have not taken account of the board's precedent. The result is that all schools must be attentive to board actions, and over time the number of board policies and precedents that schools must observe becomes very great. In Dade County, Florida, twenty-five schools were identified for a "site-based management pilot," which exempted them from many existing district regulations but not from future ones. After three years, the principals in the twenty-five schools reported that board actions taken since the pilot began had severely eroded the freedoms they were originally promised.

Central administrative offices are also organized into multiple assistant-superintendencies, and each assistant superintendent is independent in her own sphere of activity. There is no incentive for the district director of federal programs to clear her actions with the directors of staff development, curriculum, personnel, or facilities. Like branches of the armed services, central office directors are capable of unilateral action, and understand that joint action takes time and dissipates their power. They, like state agencies, impose requirements on the schools separately, and leave it to teachers and principals to make the pieces of the school fit together.

The apparently sensible idea that schools should be accountable to public needs has had the practical effect of shaping schools in the image of the political arena and that arena's goals (satisfying as many as possible, injuring as few as possible, protecting traditional constituents, and responding to new claims as they arise); and this has led to reliance on politically negotiated settlements, deal-making, and logrolling.

The effort to govern schools through political processes inevitably makes them the focus of community conflict, conflict about values, individual morality, civic responsibility, respect for minority needs, and the imperative to distribute economic opportunity. Resolution of these conflicts—through negotiation, the creation of group rights, and straightforward horse-trading—creates regulations that shape the conduct of today's schools. And they threaten daily to displace the goal at the center of schooling: producing competent graduates.

Americans quite properly seek public schools that both respect the rights and values of a diverse population and make the most of the talents and initiative of individual students and teachers. Unfortunately, the rules, regulations, and bureaucratic machinery created to attend to the first of these goals threatens to overwhelm the second. The result: a system that works for very few.

Politics in such situations is neither good nor bad; it is inevitable. When decisions about the education of millions of children are centralized in one legislature or task force, agreement often can come only through two processes: the first is known as compromise. It involves the search for an inoffensive middle ground that gives each group as much of what it wants as possible and splits irreconcilable differences. The second process is fragmentation: each group is given a specific benefit or entitlement—a guarantee that schools will always provide a course that one group considers important, a week dedicated to its cause, or a special assembly or extracurricular event. Such concessions are usually minor, but they add up. Over time, such state actions accumulate into a highly limiting set of demands on students' and teachers' time and on how needs that are not formally recognized by the legislature can be met.

Local school boards can also narrow schools' choices among the alternatives set by the state, designating just one textbook or set of filmstrips and workbooks. Local boards can also have a strong effect on how teachers teach. They, and the central-office administrators who work under their direction, establish methods and standards for teacher evaluation, and determine what kinds of in-service training teachers will attend. School boards also affect pedagogy in the way they resolve everyday conflicts and scandals. School boards are frequently asked to decide whether a particular way of grouping students constitutes discrimination, whether teachers can punish or evict students from their classes, and whether all students have fair access to valued instructional programs. The cumulative effect of such decisions is to give teachers quite a detailed picture of what they must and must not do in the classroom.

Schools Preoccupied with Compliance

Teachers and principals who want to comply with all the mandates and expectations imposed by their governmental superiors have a daunting task. External mandates come from many sources and affect so many aspects of schooling that a sincere bureaucrat can be challenged to find a way of complying with them all. Those that do find a way to comply also find that they have limited options for responding to school-specific needs. Some teachers and principals despair of staying in compliance, believing that in a bureaucracy it is possible either to be effective or to follow the rules, but impossible to do both. But most, afraid that good motives are no defense against charges of noncompliance, choose to avoid trouble. This means that their actions as teachers and principals are influenced more by the desire to stay in compliance than by judgments about what will work best for students.

Educators' habits of operating as bureaucrats under regulation are deeply ingrained. Central-office administrators are afraid to devolve power to the schools, and many teachers and principals are afraid to accept it when offered.

Even those school boards and superintendents who support school-based management approaches have delegated only minor amounts of authority to the school site. The most important decisions—who gets hired and what is taught—are seldom made at the school level. Central administrators are afraid real delegation will reduce their power, and that someone in a school will violate a rule or procedure that will get the central office in trouble. With few exceptions, most schools feel powerless to make the changes that will help their children. Principals are expected to carry out central-office plans and procedures rather than act as academic leaders for the school.

Yet few schools can operate successfully by adhering to the rule-driven, civil-service-like procedures of most large districts. The sheer volume of requirements, created by well-meaning people, is inimical to effective schooling. Principals who want their schools to work for children are forced to react to local situations and ignore rules. They develop the art of creative insubordination, giving the appearance of being a team player by following rules when doing so doesn't hurt anything, and hiding or keeping quiet when school needs require that rules be ignored or directly violated.

Teachers are caught in much the same dilemma. As in many other areas of public service, following every rule exactly as it is written is a way to ensure that nothing gets done. Some public sector unions, including air traffic controllers and police, as well as teachers, can effectively strike while on the job by "working to rule." Anyone who has been delayed for hours at an airport while air controllers are performing such a job action will know how ineffective work under those conditions can be. Strict compliance with all applicable local, state, and federal guidelines can take all of a teacher's time. Even those state requirements intended to structure and discipline instruction can, if slavishly followed, make teachers' work ineffective. Effective teaching is more than transmitting a predetermined sequence of information to a group of receptive students. Good teaching requires engaging students in the discovery of knowledge for themselves, knowledge that expands and enriches what they already know about a subject. The learning process is different for each student, and an effective teacher is someone who can help every student become a learner, even when such activities deviate from state and district curriculum guidelines.

Process requirements can also be time-consuming and detract from good teaching. Taking attendance, monitoring student immunizations, grading papers, filling out reports, and attending staff meetings may all be important activities, but they take time. Teachers, like principals, learn which rules and activities are important and which are not. They learn that once they close the classroom door, they must choose between the requirements of the system and the requirements of their children. Most teachers choose the needs of children over bureaucratic busywork. But unless a teacher is secure and confident about her role, the conflict between process requirements and student needs can be highly stressful. And teachers are expected to handle the stress without the support of other teachers or the school principal.

Schools Preoccupied with Jobs and Other Adult Issues

Schools are intended for children but run by adults. Adult issues, about who will teach in schools, what income and other benefits they will receive, how much money will be spent on the school and who will decide where the money goes, have extremely strong effects on what students experience in school and what they will ultimately learn.

The teacher hiring and placement system is indistinguishable from civil service hiring and placement procedures at the federal, state, or local levels. It has real advantages, including protection against blatant patronage and efforts to fire teachers whose views are unpopular with the school board. But teacher hiring and placement has all the drawbacks of a civil service system, i.e., teacher placement based on seniority not the needs of the school, low motivation among some senior teachers who have gained tenure, and difficulty in replacing unproductive teachers and restaffing schools whose needs have changed.

In American public education, school districts, not schools, employ teachers. A school with a teacher vacancy cannot simply hire the best person it can find. Vacancies are filled by new hires only if no teacher currently working in the school system has claimed the job. In general, junior teachers have virtually no choice about where they will teach, and senior teachers have a great deal. Though most state laws prohibit collective bargaining over instructional issues, they do allow bargaining over working conditions. Because working conditions include teacher assignment, working hours, maximum class sizes, nonteaching duties, and teacher evaluation methods, collective bargaining can have a profound effect on how schools and classrooms are run. As McDonnell (1988) has shown, school boards made major concessions on working conditions in the 1980s, when they could not afford to meet union salary demands. The result, in most big cities, is that the teacher union is a virtual partner with the school board, determining who will teach and where, for how long, and to what standards.

In recent years, the most important teacher-assignment decisions have been prompted by declining enrollments and fiscal cutbacks, and very few members of the public are conscious of the staggering effect this can have on school operations. If a school's enrollment declines during the school year, it can lose teachers. Schools in the poorest areas, with the highest rates of student absenteeism, transiency, and dropout, are most often affected. Inner-city high schools can lose 10 percent of their teachers or more in early January, when midyear enrollment figures are assembled. When this process starts, it launches a civil-service-like procedure of "bumping rights" based on seniority, a procedure that rumbles throughout the school system.

Teachers who leave a school (or administrators with teaching certificates who are removed from their central-office jobs) need to find work elsewhere, and they do so on the basis of seniority. A teacher qualified to teach a particular grade or course can "bump" a less senior incumbent. The bumping chain can be long, and only ends when the last person bumped is too junior to possess any bumping rights.

One result of the seniority system is that the staffs of most schools are assembled through formal allocative processes, not selected by the incumbent staff or principal. Though some senior teachers choose to work in the most demanding inner-city schools, most can avoid doing so if they desire. The result, in virtually all big cities, is that the most experienced teachers cluster around "desirable" schools in low-stress, safe, middle-class areas. As the Los Angeles court case Rodriguez v. Anton has shown, this means that schools in the poorest areas, with the most unstable populations, are left with a disproportionate share of the youngest, least experienced, and, frequently, least qualified teachers.

Procedures for assignment of teachers and administrators emphasize equity for adults, but they reduce school flexibility. Senior teachers can decide where they will work regardless of whether they fit the school's needs. Literally every public school principal interviewed in five years of RAND urban schools research complained about deadwood senior teachers who did not fit the school or sympathize with the problems of the students, but would not leave. Rapid student turnover is part of the problem: within the working lives of older teachers, many urban school populations have changed completely, from white to African American, and often again to Hispanic.

In cities such as Houston, Los Angeles, and Miami, with large immigrant populations, the dominant ethnicity and language of a school's student body can change completely within three years. In those cities, some teachers expressed hostility to "those kids" who had turned a familiar situation on its head, requiring changes in pedagogy that teachers were unwilling to make (McDonnell and Hill 1993).

A further implication of public schools' concern with jobs is that spending priorities focus on hiring and paying people, thus shortchanging efforts to evaluate or upgrade their performance. School systems hire teachers centrally to ensure that all new recruits have degrees from accredited institutions and are eligible for state certification. Central-office units also design programs of staff development to ensure that teachers are aware of new techniques. Some try to upgrade their whole teaching forces by introducing everyone to promising new concepts like cooperative learning, or by training all teachers to use a new set of textbooks or curriculum materials. The larger districts maintain specialized central office units for staff development by curriculum area. These units also provide school specialists with refresher courses and introductions to new approaches.

Despite all this activity, school systems' training and technical assistance capabilities are small. Due to the politically competitive nature of school system budget-making, virtually all funds are allocated to existing commitments, especially employment contracts with teachers. The most important limitation on quality improvement is the school systems' lack of uncommitted funds to invest in staff training and improvement.

No major public school system has a staff development budget as large as 1 percent of its overall operating budget. (Business leaders, by contrast, report spending 3 to 4 percent of operating funds on training.) Training teachers and administrators is expensive: substitute teachers must be paid when teachers are pulled out of the classroom for training, and union contracts require stipends for weekend or summer training. Even the most efficiently run training or staff-development program is unable to assist more than a small fraction of a large district's schools in a year. Control of staff development programs is also fragmented. Though most districts have staff development directors who employ trainers and consultants, each federal or state categorical program has its own staff development budget, which is administered separately.

In many school systems, the teacher training activity that receives the most funding is controlled unilaterally by individual teachers. Teachers who attend graduate classes leading to higher degrees receive automatic wage-step increases with each small increment of graduate credit. Teachers, not principals or department heads, decide what they will study. Teachers usually pay their own tuition, but their wage-step increases usually reimburse all their expenses within a year. Because the step increases are permanent and become part of the base salary determining the size of future wage increases, the value of the raise, over the years, is typically many times the cost of tuition. A recent Booz-Allen study of Chicago public school expenditures (1992) estimated that the annual cost of such training-related wage increases was several times the district's staff development budget.

Most local public school systems gather and analyze measures of school output, e.g., student test scores, rates of dropout and graduation, and credit completion rates. Aside from annual publication of such measures, few school systems have management processes intended to target trouble spots and produce improvements. Principals in many cities con-

41

sistently reported that the central office rarely intervenes just because a school's performance data are poor. According to the principals, a school without financial irregularities, civil rights complaints, or incidents involving violence or racial tension is unlikely to be considered a problem for top management, even if its performance is low.

Schools Hamstrung By Low and Unreliable Resource Levels and Shifting Mandates

Funding for public schools comes from many sources. Most school districts have the authority to raise local revenue, usually from local property taxes. They all receive a substantial amount of money from state government. The average state contribution varies widely, from 20 to 90 percent of total per pupil expenditures. The average local contribution just about equals 40 percent. Small amounts (usually less than 10 percent) also come from the federal government under formula-driven programs that target funding for special services to low-income, low-achieving, handicapped, or limited-English-speaking children. Foundation grants and discretionary awards from state and federal governments seldom amount on average to even 1 percent of any local school system's income.

A significant amount of the funds available to school systems is spent outside the schools. All urban systems have large and complex central offices dedicated to accounting, purchasing, auditing, monitoring school compliance with mandates and court orders, hiring teachers, analyzing school and student performance, and providing technical assistance to teachers and schools. These offices can be large in absolute terms—New York City's, the largest, once employed nearly 6,000 people and even after rigorous downsizing still employs more than 3,000.

Analyses of the shares of public education funds spent on central-office administration, and on school-level administration required for compliance rather than instructional management, vary widely with the authors' assumptions. Analyses by Booz-Allen and Hamilton (1992) and Cooper (1994) estimate that big-city school districts spend approximately 20 percent of their funds on central-office activities, including centrally provided services to schools and school-level spending on compliance activities. Analysts who produce lower estimates of central-office spending normally count all staff present at the school site as instructional staff, and count the value of central-office services to schools as school-level spending. (For a range of estimates based on a variety of assumptions and methods, see, for example, Odden 1994b and 1995, Lankford and Wyckoff 1995, Chow et al. 1991, Walberg 1994, Raywid and Shaheen 1994, Robinson 1988, and Hanushek et al. 1994.) A recent paper by Allen Odden (1996) suggests that most urban schools would experience significant surpluses, in the range of $500 per pupil, if they received real-dollar lump-sum budgets of $5,000 per pupil, or slightly less than the nationwide average for per pupil expenditure.

Though most state and federal funds are allocated to school districts on the basis of student enrollment, schools themselves to do not receive funds on a per capita basis. In fact, schools are not funded but "resourced." Local school boards create formulas that determine, separately for grade schools and high schools, the number of teachers and administrators a school is entitled to claim. As Cooper (1993) has shown for New York City, a school is guaranteed a base-line level of administrative personnel—typically a principal, assistant principal, and secretary—and gains an additional teacher for each increment of 20 to 25 students. Schools also obtain desks, furniture, lab equipment, and other capital assets on a rough formula basis. Paper, books, and other instructional materials are allocated by formula. Repairs, remodeling, and utility bills are usually paid directly by the school district.

In light of the huge amounts spent on education nationally, newcomers to education are frequently surprised to discover that relatively little cash actually reaches any school. School principals frequently administer small discretionary budgets, normally in the range of $40–$75 per student, to be used for activities, field trips, minor repairs, and hiring consultants and speakers. Most principals, when asked about the budget for their school, respond in terms of their discretionary account, not the entire amount required to operate the school, including funds for teacher salaries, supplies, and repairs. That explains why real annual operating costs of a city high school can range up to $10 million or more, and are rarely less than $1 million; but in the course of four years of RAND fieldwork, no principal ever claimed to have a budget over $90,000.

Even federal and state categorical funds reach the schools in the form of specific resources, not flexible cash. In most districts, the central office hires a group of teachers who will be paid from funds from a specific grant, and sends them to schools according to the funding source program's rules. School principals and regular instructional staff may be able to request supplementary teachers with particular training, but the assignments such teachers can accept within the school—what subjects and students they can teach and where—are determined by the funder's regulations and district policy.

For the past thirty years, states have struggled to reduce per pupil spending disparities among school districts. Many books, starting with Arthur Wise's *Rich Schools Poor Schools* (1970) and subsequent court decisions show a clear pattern of inequitable school funding among districts in wealthy communities and those serving low-income populations.

Until recently, however, school finance reform has concentrated on inequalities among school districts in states. Few school finance reform lawsuits and studies have addressed funding inequalities within local school systems themselves. These spending inequalities among schools within a district are inevitably a consequence of local governance processes. State-level litigation has supported big-city and poor rural school systems' efforts to increase their gross income. It has ignored the fact, demonstrated in such local lawsuits as *Hobson v. Hansen* and *Rodriguez v. Anton*, that schools suffer most directly from the results of local governance processes, creating vast resource inequalities between schools and forcing schools to adapt to ever-changing levels of staffing and funding.

Local inequities in resource allocation interfere with the effective operation of schools in three ways. First, they create such low levels of funding in some schools that their staffs have great difficulty delivering a high-quality program. Second, they weaken staff members' sense of personal responsibility by providing a ready excuse for low performance, i.e., the school is entitled to more resources. Third, they force continuous shifting of staff members and other resources from school to school, making it nearly impossible for school leaders to deliver stable programs or hold anyone responsible for the results.

Low real resources. Resource disparities within school systems are masked by the summary figures used to describe resource levels. System-wide per pupil expenditure figures do not describe every school's actual funding. Even after adjusting for expenditures on central-office functions, per pupil spending averages are misleading.

Within some school districts per pupil expenditures can be twice as high in some schools as in others. Three factors lie at the root of the differences. First, school boards make conscious decisions to spend more on particular schools, e.g., to create lower pupil/teacher ratios in junior highs than in grade schools, or to provide extra aides for schools serving large numbers of special-education students. Overcrowding is a second contributor: due to immigration or other population movements, some schools become overcrowded, such that student/teacher ratios and other measures of resource concentration are badly distorted. The third factor is teacher placement on the basis of seniority. Senior teachers, who have first call on teaching vacancies, tend to avoid "problem" schools in turbulent low-income areas. Because senior teachers are often paid more than twice as much as junior teachers, school systems can wind up spending nearly twice as much per pupil in some schools as in others.

Under most public school districts' allocation formulas, a school has a certain number of slots for certified teachers, and it does not matter whether they are the most or least senior of the eligible individuals. A school can have all senior teachers (making, on the average for big-city systems, in excess of $55,000 per year) or all entry-level teachers (making on average barely $20,000), and the school system's accounting practices cannot tell the difference.

The resulting inequalities affect schools' real capabilities. Better-staffed junior high schools are bought at the cost of less well-staffed elementary schools. Overcrowded schools or those with very high pupil/teacher ratios have less opportunity to deliver imaginative and flexible instructional programs. Schools hamstrung with large numbers of inexperienced teachers, including teachers with provisional certificates because they have failed key courses or examinations, are inevitably less capable than schools with concentrations of better-trained and more experienced teachers.

Resource instability. In the past decade, big-city school systems have experienced constant reallocation of their resources. The worst cases occurred in Los Angeles, Chicago, and New York, where declines in state and local revenues forced midyear reductions, often as great as 10 percent, in overall system budgets. But even in cities with stable total-funding, student population movement forced continual midstream changes in school staffing.

In most city systems, schools receive an initial allocation of staff members in September, when the first counts of school enrollments are available. These numbers are typically adjusted in October, when student attendance figures start to fall due to dropouts, transfers, and low daily-attendance rates. Surprisingly, the figures are often adjusted again in January and March. In some big-city high schools, the only thing certain about teacher assignment is that no student will have the same teacher for longer than one semester at a time.

Turbulent resource allocation interferes with schools' ability to deliver consistent programs and to take responsibility for the progress of individual students. It can destroy any relationships formed between students and teachers. To support the kinds of high-quality schools discussed above, school systems must be capable of stabilizing their schools, either by guaranteeing fixed minimum-staffing levels despite student turnover, or by permitting students to remain in the same school even when they move to new neighborhoods.

Teachers and principals are always keenly aware of the hand they have been dealt. Many understand that no public school system can supply all the people and equipment for an optimal school, and most do the best they can with the cards they have. However, the belief that the deck has been rigged so that "our" school got lost in the shuffle while others drew a full house, has a profound effect on motivation. When the worst-funded schools are, as they are invariably, those in the poorest areas, struggling with the most oppressive social problems, how can staff be asked to take seriously more rigorous standards and expectations?

A system that creates palpable inequalities among its schools fosters cynicism and diffuses responsibility. Some schools obviously have first pick at the best teachers, new equipment, up-to-date texts, and sound, well-maintained facilities. Others are forced to make do with the teachers left over after the "bumping" process has run its course, to improvise around used textbooks and patched-up equipment, and to make sure that aging facilities are not, at the very least, hazards for the children in them. Slogans such as "All children can learn" and "high expectations for all" have a hollow ring under these circumstances.

Even fair allocation decisions can diffuse responsibility, if made secretly or in ways that signal concern with goals other than educational effectiveness. The fact that the most important assets of the school system—teachers—are allocated to preserve individuals' seniority rights rather than to maximize school effectiveness is counterproductive, whether or not it creates inequalities. The belief, widespread among school staff members, that staff development time, new equipment, maintenance and renovations—not to mention the assignment of promising new teachers—are allocated according to mysterious processes including the "pull" of individual principals and neighborhood groups, often reinforces cynicism and passivity.

When a school system's resource allocation process is not transparently fair, it encourages virtually all teachers and principals, including those who may in fact be getting more than their share, to suspect they have been somehow deprived. With that suspicion as a base, the next step is easy: failure is not my responsibility.

Shifting mandates. Uncertain resource levels are not the only causes of turbulence in the work of schools. Schools are also subject to constant changes in the rules under which they operate and the priorities advanced by the board, superintendent, and central office.

Instability of rules has two main sources: the fragmentation of administrative responsibilities and authorities in the central office, and the constant effort to improve the schools through new programs initiated by the superintendent and board.

The fragmentation of central administrative arrangements creates a complex and shifting set of requirements. School district central offices are traditionally organized into many specialized units, each responsible for some aspect of school operations—management of federal and state grant programs; improvement of curriculum in some particular area, e.g., science or English; selection and upgrading of school personnel; allocation of supplies and repairs; evaluation of overall school performance; and so on. Each of these units has its own staff and funding line, and though the superintendent of schools is nominally superior to the heads of central-office bureaus, her influence is limited. Most superintendents have time to supervise only a few central-office activities. The result of central-office fragmentation is that bureaus operate independently of one another and seldom coordinate the demands they make on the schools. Though a change in school staffing or teacher training or evaluation methods may affect all aspects of a school's program, those implications are seldom anticipated or worked through at the central office. Changes are left to be reconciled at the school level. As many principals and teachers report, the result is that they spend a great deal of time deciding how to reconcile central-office directives and calculating the risks of noncompliance.

In addition to these structural sources of instability, the school reform process itself is a source of great turbulence. As Elmore and MacLaughlin (1988) note, "School reform has proven to be steady work: no one has found a single-factor solution to all the schools' problems, and many bold reform strategies dissolve into tinkering at the margins." Discontent with school performance has produced constant pressure for reform. But instability of board coalitions and superintendents' tenure have led, in many school districts, to a succession of incompatible reforms. Top-down reforms in teacher training, testing, and curriculum have been succeeded by decentralization initiatives, followed again by efforts to tighten fiscal controls, standardize curriculum, and strengthen accountability based on student test scores. Further, as recent studies of reform processes in several big cities have shown, no reform gets enough time or money to work out. New initiatives are announced, put into place in several schools, then subjected to budget cuts, and finally succeeded by other reforms that experience the same cycle. The succession of conflicting initiatives has made school staffs cynical about the motives and competence of their superiors and tentative in the implementation of any particular reform.

Schools Practicing Defensive Education

Today's public schools are not required to do whatever is necessary to make students succeed. The school's responsibility for student success ends, for all intents and purposes, with the obligation of delivering instruction and seeing to it that students are not impeded from access to it. Like defensive medicine, i.e., the practice of selecting tests and procedures to avoid charges of medical malpractice rather than to meet individual patients' needs, public schools are often driven by the need to avoid blame, not to do the best possible for students.

Though several states guarantee every student (in the words of the New Jersey Constitution) "a thorough and efficient education," public school systems are designed to manage institutions, not to ensure individual benefits. Only handicapped children are guaranteed an education that is appropriate to their needs (originally under P.L. 94–142, the Education for All Handicapped Children Act and now under the Individuals with Disabilities Education Act). If a neighborhood school does not provide what a handicapped child needs, the parents can demand a new program, transfer of the child to another school, or public payment for private education.

But about 90 percent of all children are not covered by P.L. 94–142. For these youngsters no mechanism exists to ensure they get what they need. Parents can obtain action if they demonstrate that their child's school has been starved of resources, and they can petition for a transfer to another school. The school system, however, enjoys great discretion in responding to such petitions, and parents must be prepared to devote a great deal of time and energy pursuing them. For all practical purposes, the public school system is not designed to ensure that the individual student gets what he or she needs.

In any human organization, performance varies and unpredictable problems crop up. Yet the obligation of school systems to both identify and solve problems is particularly high, because the people who most directly observe its performance, children, are not qualified to judge its quality. Moreover, students are required to go to school and cannot object to poor service by quitting or going elsewhere.

The fact remains that some groups of students are highly likely to fail.

In many urban school districts, African-American students are as likely to drop out of high school as to finish, and those who do finish school and take the Scholastic Assessment Test (formerly Scholastic Aptitude Test) are likely to average below the 25th percentile for white students. Much the same is true for the U.S.-born children of Hispanic immigrants. As the plaintiffs in lawsuits such as *Rodriguez v. Anton* have demonstrated, the public school system delivers less to them—less money, more dilapidated school buildings, fewer and more poorly prepared teachers, and fewer books—than to other students.

No one with any firsthand knowledge of how schools serving these youngsters operate, or with direct responsibility for their quality, has ever argued that these schools are adequate. When challenged about the adequacy of the services provided in such schools, administrators invariably fall back on the defense of process, procedures, and compliance with applicable rules and regulations. They make no claim that the system is structured to ensure that these students succeed in school.

As long as school boards, superintendents, and central offices concentrate on protecting the entire system and its institutions from as much disturbance as possible, in part by permitting marginal improvements here and there, public schools will not change. A good governance system for public education would attach far greater importance to intervention on behalf of children whose schools have failed them. It would display the same passion for achievement that most systems already demonstrate for student safety. It would attack school failure just as it now attacks school violence.

Conclusion

The system sketched out above is not aesthetically pleasing. Rule-bound, it discourages initiative and risk-taking in schools and systems facing unprecedented problems. Politically driven, it substitutes decisions reached by elected officials and central administrators that satisfy as many people as possible for professional judgment and initiative on the part of competent, caring professionals in the school and classroom. Emphasizing compliance, it defines accountability as adherence to process, when results are the only appropriate standard. Organized to manage institutions and minimize conflict, it ties up resources on permanent staff and the management of routine operations.

Under the current system, schools have few incentives to make pledges about what students will experience or attain, or to critique their own performance. When schools succeed they are seldom reproduced, and when they fail they are seldom closed or restaffed. Few staff members benefit greatly from being in an excellent school or suffer much from working in a mediocre one.

Despite the critical nature of the analysis in this chapter, however, the current system has a major advantage: it exists. It collects and spends public funds, manages schools, and processes students through them with minimal interruptions or uncertainties. It may not use funds efficiently or produce high-quality results for all students, but it does operate. In contrast, the alternatives defined in subsequent chapters do not exist on a large scale anywhere in the United States, and their capacity to provide stable and reliable school operations for thousands of students remains to be demonstrated.

Nonetheless, the dependency of today's public schools on regulators and overseers from the outside is evident from a principal's comment: "Nobody knows whether there is a problem in a school unless there is an overt conflict, or if test scores are bad. When those things happen, the superintendent comes to the school to meet with parents and staff. He promises that something will be done, and sends in a special program or additional staff members to solve the problem. Once that is done the school is presumed not to have any problems until the next time it comes to public attention."

THREE

A Contract School Strategy

The contract strategy we propose in this book would break up the public monopoly over the provision of public education and devolve responsibility for operating schools to nonpublic entities, including groups of teachers, parents, social service organizations, and private firms. Contracting in public education is part of a larger reform movement to redefine the appropriate roles for government in American life. During the last fifty years, governments at all levels in the United States have grown dramatically. The reasons for the growth of government are many and complex. But clearly part of the reason, particularly in the early years, was to correct for inequities and imperfections of the expanding, private, capitalist economy. Now many believe that government has grown too big and inefficient. In order to reduce the costs of government and improve the quality and efficiency of social services, citizens and politicians around the world are experimenting with ways of privatizing many aspects of public life.

Contracting-out is just one form of privatization, the one that retains the strongest governmental influence on service provision. Governments have shed services, as in the recent closure of the Interstate Commerce Commission. Governments, especially in Europe and former socialist countries, which operate large public enterprises, for example, have sold them to the private sector both to raise revenue and to improve service. Volunteerism, self-help, and user fees are additional ways to reduce the costs and responsibilities of government. In the field of education, deregulation and vouchers have many strong supporters.

Contracting, however, is the most common method of privatizing public services. Under this strategy, governments purchase services from the private sector, from either for-profit or not-for-profit organizations. As a strategy, contracting has been widely used in the United States for many years. Even in public education, most school districts have experience in purchasing noninstructional services like construction, repair, transportation, accounting, and legal representation. Some districts also have contracted out for some instructional services—foreign language, arts, and music instruction—and many have hired independent contractors to deliver federally required programs such as compensatory education and education for the handicapped. Sylvan Learning Systems provides remedial reading instruction in Washington, D.C., and organizations like Dialogos offer foreign-language instruction in public schools.

What is new in our proposal is that we propose to contract out school districts' principal activity or core service—the operation of whole schools—to private providers. Furthermore, most contracting in the public sector has been for services that public agencies have not provided in the past. We propose to take a very large and expensive activity that has been provided by publicly organized local school districts for one hundred and fifty years and shift it to private providers. This, of course, would be a major undertaking.

The purpose of this chapter is to provide a rationale for contracting out the provision of education. At the most general level, our argument is quite simple. As we enter the twenty-first century, the tasks facing public schools are daunting. Children entering schools are more diverse and many are poorly prepared to be active learners. At the same time, society expects more from schools. A higher proportion of students must achieve higher educational standards if they are to participate fully in a changing information-based economy. The current rule-driven, bureaucratic school system, described in the previous chapter, cannot meet these challenges. Despite decades of studies, recommendations, and reforms, it has been unable to create and sustain enough strong schools to educate American children for the twenty-first century.

We believe strongly in public education. We believe that there are important public benefits from education and that education through the twelfth grade should be required and paid for with public funds. There is no reason, however, why government also must provide that education. In fact, we believe the best way of preserving public education is to capture the creativity, incentives, and efficiency of the private market for the purposes of public education. A system of contract schools will regard students and parents, not regulators and bureaucratic overseers, as its primary customers. Each school will be a whole organization capable of building a sense of real community. The school will be the central unit of management, and teachers in the schools will be treated as professionals whose jobs and rewards depend on one another's performance. Because schools will be funded in real dollars on a per pupil basis, funding inequities will be obvious and pressures for equitable funding will be very strong. Because schools' survival will depend on performance, they will have strong incentives to operate efficiently. Schools will also have strong incentives to be open to parents and to be organized to encourage high performance.

The intent of contract schools is to create an alternative system for governing public education. Based on the proposition that public schools must be freed from micro-management by political bodies in order to be effective, contracting recognizes every school as an independent organization. These independent schools are free to focus on delivering a particular model of education and meeting the needs of a defined group of students. Teachers and principals in such schools can assume responsibility for what they produce; and the policy system and parents can hold them accountable for delivering the promised instruction and services, as well as for producing satisfactory student results. Under a contract strategy, all public schools, not just the select few, can have these characteristics.

The Definition of Contract Schools

Contract schools are publicly funded schools operated by an independent group of teachers and administrators under a contract with a public agency. Some of these schools could be run by the staffs and parents of existing successful schools: neighborhood schools with good reputations for serving students and their communities, and magnet schools with well-defined programs and histories of success. Other schools could be established through the issuance of public requests for proposals, or through direct negotiation with community groups or educational institutions. Public education authorities could set minimum requirements for potential contractors, but these would have to be broad enough to include non-educators. Contractors might include universities, teacher unions, ad hoc groups of parents and teachers, businesses, social service organizations, and private for-profit companies.

Contract schools would be individual legal entities (in most cases not-for-profit 501(C)(3) organizations) rather than administrative departments or units of a central public authority. This means schools would be capable of negotiating contracts, spending public funds, and hiring and firing staff members on the basis of performance and contribution to the school's overall success. Like any other publicly funded institutions, contract schools would be subject to audits by public authorities. But schools would also have the legal authority to defend their interests in court, a major change from current practice. For example, if a local school board tried to close a school that was meeting all the terms of its contract, the school could take the board to court. Current public schools, even charter schools that are exempted from most district regulations, have no such legal recourse.

A district would hold many contracts, each specific to the mission and instructional approach of the individual school. The school board would determine the district's need for certain kinds of schools. For example, a district with a significant population of Spanish-speaking children might decide to run a bilingual elementary school. The board would then invite independent organizations to submit proposals for operating a bilingual school and offer a contract to the group it deemed best suited for the job.

Standard to all contracts would be the basic requirements for student graduation and state licensing that now apply to private schools, including civil rights guarantees and health standards. In addition, every contract would outline the goals of the school and its basic instructional program, along with the kinds of student outcomes expected and the methods for assessing them. Outcomes could be linked to state or national standards, or established locally for all schools or for particular types of schools. Some contracts would resemble those under which many public magnet and alternative schools now operate—agreements that a school will pursue a defined mission and receive public support, as long as it operates as promised and gets good results.

Contracts could require all schools to cover the state-mandated curriculum or require that all students pass statewide minimum competency tests. However, school boards could not prescribe the curriculum in such detail that all schools would be forced to run identical programs. Districts would have to resist the tendency to re-regulate instruction through the contract document.

It is useful to put contracting into the context of other current reform proposals. Figure 3.1 arrays public school reforms of the 1980s and 1990s according to the location or the focus of the reform effort and the degree of public-private provision. Pure voucher proposals are not included here because they would completely eliminate public oversight of schools' performance. Our contracting proposal fits in the southeast quadrant. Charter schools, privately managed schools for the handicapped, and schools run under contract by private providers like the Edison Project and Sabis International also fall in this area because they all focus on the school (rather than the school system) and rely on independent (private or non-

MANAGEMENT RESPONSIBILITY

	PUBLIC	PRIVATE
REFORM FOCUS:	Traditional Public Schools	
SCHOOL SYSTEM	Goals 2000/Systemic Reform National Standards Movement	Contract management of whole district (eg. Hartford)
	University-based school reforms, such as Sizer, Comer, Levin	Charter Schools
	Magnet Schools	Private schools for the handicapped
INDIVIDUAL SCHOOL	University Laboratory schools	Charter Schools hiring private operators, e.g. Edison, Sabis
	School-based management/shared decision-making	School Boards hiring private groups to operate schools (contract schools)

Figure 3.1 Current Reform Proposals

profit) groups to provide educational services under the general oversight of a responsible public agency.

Before 1990, most of the reform debate dealt only with changes on the left-hand side of this figure. These were proposals for changing what goes on within publicly operated schools. They involved tinkering with the organization and operations of "traditional" public schools, or they sought to increase school staff engagement in decision-making through site-based management and shared decision-making.

Beginning in the early 1990s, the reform debate began to challenge the public monopoly of school management and operation. Since then much of the education reform action has been on the right-hand side of figure 3.1. Increasingly, school districts began considering or accepting the idea that parts of public education can be operated by others. Cities such as Baltimore, Maryland, and Miami, Florida, signed contracts with private companies to manage individual schools. Charter school laws in a number of states allow districts and other public agencies to charter public and private groups to operate individual public schools, some of which then hire private management firms like the Edison Project.

Charter school laws now in force in nearly half the states take the idea behind contract schools—public control but private provision—and create a small number of privately operated public schools. Much of what we propose is similar to what others would like to see in strong charter-school laws. The problem is that most charter laws strictly limit the number of schools that can be operated by private groups. They leave the vast majority of public schools within the public bureaucracy. Our proposal would change the entire system to create a system of policy incentives supportive of independently owned and operated schools.

The School as the Fundamental Unit of Management

A major premise of our proposal for a system of contract schools is that the school must be regarded as the basic unit of management. Though students learn particular bits of information in classrooms, the sum of their knowledge—the information, skills, habits, and values that they take to the next level of education or into their adult lives—depends on the ways in which their separate classroom experiences build on or conflict with one another. Teachers often work alone in closed classrooms, but their effectiveness depends heavily on the quality of students' prior preparation and on whether other classes reinforce or conflict with what is taught. Exceptional teachers can motivate and discipline the students they have before them, but students' overall attitudes and effort reflect the sum of their experiences in the whole school context.

Students succeed or fail because of the quality and coherence of instruction they receive and the reinforcement for consistent effort they experience in a particular school, not because of the district's capabilities or the performance of other schools. Parents judge public education on the basis of their own child's experience in a particular school, not on some average assessment of the performance of all schools.

Still, the dominant themes of contemporary educational research and policy ignore the school as a whole and focus instead either on its discrete components—techniques of instruction and classroom management, content of individual courses, methods of remedial instruction—or on the context of regulations, policies, group entitlements, and rules concerning use of funds that constrain schools' operation. In public education, broader systems of funding, regulation, training, and assistance are also important. Here again, however, far more depends on what happens within the school than outside it.

Much current educational policy and research treats the school as a black box: things are done to or for the school, not by it. Assets (staff members, equipment) are added to or subtracted from schools. Constraints in the form of new goals, performance quotas, testing programs, and regulations governing treatment of students and teachers are imposed on schools by school boards and funding agencies. Staff members and students are brought into the school or taken out of it in pursuit of district-wide priorities, such as fulfillment of union contracts and maintenance of racial balance. New curricula and staff training programs are selected for whole districts and then infused into schools. Budget shortfalls are met by mandated district-wide reductions in school staffing or services, and the use of budget increases is usually determined at the district level, in negotiations between the school board and the teacher union.

Such policies are always intended to make schools better, stronger, or fairer places. But, as decades of research in education and other areas of public service have shown, it is never safe to regard an organization as a passive material ready to be molded, or to assume that the results of policy will always match its intent. From the perspective of any one policy maker or goal, schools may respond inadequately or perversely, no matter how clear the intent of the policy.

The School as a Real Organization and Real Community

We also believe that schools need to be real organizations and real communities. What does it mean for schools to be real organizations? Such a school would be based on specific ideas about how instruction can be organized to meet the needs of a particular group of students; it would be an active organization, not a passive barometer of external forces. If a school were a real organization it would be in control of its funds and resources, including teachers, not a node at which a central administrative organization assembles a number of discrete instructional assets.

A real organization has clear goals and the capacity to organize and adapt its own activities in order to meet them. Such a school could invest in its own future by hiring, training, and developing teachers to work effectively within its specific context. A school that was a real organization would exist to teach and form individual students, not to provide comfort and political cover for school board members and superintendents. It would run on adult personal responsibility, ensuring that every teacher and administrator was rewarded for contributing to the students' instructional success; and it would not burden students with adults who cannot or will not help students learn. Such a school would also say frankly what it requires of students and their families, and it would not allow students to disrupt other students' learning or destroy the school's educational effectiveness.

In some limited respects schools resemble firms. Though they are not profit-seeking organizations, they are, as described in the economic theory of the firm, groups of people coordinating the use of their complementary skills toward a common end. Under the economic theory, firms develop because there are some ends that individuals cannot achieve alone. Though some products can be produced by individual artisans, others require complementary efforts, e.g., by people who can design products but lack the skills to manufacture them. Efficiency is another reason given for the formation of firms: some products can be made at lower cost or higher quality by people working together rather than individually. Firms can also assemble greater resources—more equipment, money for flexible investment, savings to tide the members over hard times—than can most individuals.

Under this definition, hospitals and social service organizations can be seen as resembling firms. So can schools. In all cases the firm exists to produce something that no person can do alone, uniting the efforts of many persons through a plan of complementary activities.

Integration, planning, and comparative advantage are at the core of the theory of the firm. People do not coordinate their activities to produce something that they can do better if left alone. Groups attempting to produce a joint product are more effective than groups in which people disagree on what is to be produced and how, or in which everyone tries to use the same equipment at the same time. Groups that cannot combine their efforts effectively dissolve, in part because other organizations can produce better results, and in part because group members who truly care about the task to be done depart for other, better-integrated groups.

The theory of the firm can provide important new perspectives on schools. It can help us clarify schools' purposes and understand the internal relationships among people who perform key functions, such as teaching, investment in improvements, quality assurance, and client relations. And, though few schools are organized to make profits, all are constrained to operate with the funds they have available, and all are threatened if others lose confidence in their performance or if more effective competitors emerge.

What does it mean for schools to be real communities? A community is a bridge between the most fundamental unit of society, the family, and the broader society, as defined by city, state, and nation. Schools assume responsibility for a family's most precious asset, its children. They also act on behalf of the broader society, to ensure that children learn enough to become informed voters, decent citizens, productive taxpayers, and full participants in a future economy. Because the hopes of parents and the broader society are not always identical, schools must deal with conflicting needs and expectations. They must do so with great competence and sensitivity, simultaneously maintaining parental trust and public confidence.

Trust becomes a moral resource to a school community when shared values, especially about the education and care of children, induce participants voluntarily to moderate their personal interests in order to advance such common goods. Teacher willingness to forgo seniority considerations and "share the load" in teaching unusually disadvantaged students, rather than opting to teach only those who come to school especially eager to learn, is one example of this phenomenon. Another instance would be a faculty's decision to extend the school day to provide more time for instruction and teacher development even though such actions entail a longer workday.

Real communities build unity without destroying individuality. They do so by developing basic agreements in principle about values, norms of behavior, and bases of reciprocal obligation. Though they cannot satisfy the needs of all members at all times, communities thrive by maintaining members' confidence that their shared norms and concerns are more important than their differences. To be a real community, a school must be free to engage parents and other adults about values, sometimes following and sometimes leading, but never automatically imposing formulas based on extraneous political settlements reached outside the school community.

Schools must be highly competent at recognizing the different desires of parents and the state, devising instructional programs that serve the purposes of both parties whenever possible, and resisting demands from either parents or the broader society that needlessly or callously override preferences of the other. To perform these functions, a school probably needs to have its own conception of the child's interests, one that is richer than a mere vector sum of the demands of parents and the state.

Treating schools as real organizations and real communities requires profound changes in the external institutions that govern, provide resources for, and assist schools. As real organizations, schools can no longer be regarded as subordinate nodes in a local district bureaucracy. As true communities schools must have the capacity to adapt to meet their members' needs and, accordingly, to differ from one another. If public schools are to be true communities, individual schools, not whole school districts, must be regarded as the primary unit of organization.

The fundamental challenge of school reform is to find means by which schools can accept government money and yet be both real organizations and true communities. Because traditional policy and research do not address this challenge, we must start pretty much from scratch to design public institutions for K–12 education. We can take nothing for granted about government's existing arrangements for controlling public schools.

Public and Private Purposes of Education

Contracting is a way of organizing public education that takes into account both public and private purposes, or benefits, of education. What are these public and private benefits? Schools provide a public benefit by preparing students for productive employment and participation in society and government. Everyone in a community benefits when schools do a good job and graduates contribute through employment and service to the community. Communities suffer when they must support the unemployed or pay the costs of incarcerating young people convicted of criminal acts. Schools also are expected to help each student reach his or her individual potential, the benefits of which accrue primarily to the individual and family. These private benefits of education are also important. Clearly, schools attempt to provide both public and private benefits, but not always in equal proportions or with the same understanding of those roles. A school's or school district's particular orientation to its mission will have much to do with how it sees its responsibilities. Should schools provide a sorting function for society by tracking and credentialing students into various occupations and career paths? Or should the focus be on ensuring that every child has a chance to develop his or her talents? These questions sound abstract but they affect daily decisions. Should difficult students be suspended? Should special-education students be included in regular classrooms? How do we assess student achievement—by standardized tests or by some form of performance assessment?

Some of the pressure for restructuring schools reflects a growing political sentiment that schools need to pay more attention to the public benefits of schooling. This is certainly the case in efforts to improve America's economic competitiveness by placing more emphasis on science and mathematics, foreign languages, and preparation for the workplace. The excellence movement of the 1980s sought to improve school performance by stating national goals and by requiring more rigorous national testing.

One of the consequences of this public-goods orientation has been an emphasis on service delivery rather than on successful learning. Accountability is seen from this point of view as offering the right courses, having well-equipped laboratories, integrating computers into the classroom, and so on. Success is measured in terms of meeting standards of good practice, often established by professional organizations or the state education department, instead of by determining whether children are actually learning something.

Many parents and members of the public, however, distrust this focus on professional and bureaucratic standards. They see too many children either failing in school and falling through the cracks in our educational system or being taught things that seem to threaten community and family relationships. Emphasizing new technologies and world-class standards in mathematics and science, for example, concerns parents who want their children to remain in a small community and take over the family farm or business. Families with strong religious beliefs complain that the more secular approaches of most schools will drive a wedge between themselves and their children and possibly reduce the childrens' commitment to taking care of them as they get older. These parents care little about national rankings and professional standards. They want schools that will prepare children for successful jobs close to home.

Parents in urban areas want schools to be vehicles of social mobility, not institutions that warehouse, test, fail, and sort students and graduates. They want schools to play a role in creating a democratic community by reducing social and economic inequality and by instilling values of service, tolerance, and reciprocity. For many educators and inner-city students and families, promoting social equality is just as much a public benefit of education as increasing America's competitiveness.

The purpose of schooling, in other words, is multifaceted and often leads to confusion and frustration. A successful school reform proposal needs to help all the players in public education to clarify the school's mission. We need an educational system that enables all the participants to discuss these issues of public and private benefits and create schools with clearly stated and agreed-upon goals. In order to meet this variety of purposes and values, schools will have to differ in their goals and approaches. What is important is that each school knows where it is headed, and that the families and children in those schools support their goals and programs. One thing we do know is that schools with clear missions and with programs and tests that support those missions are more successful than schools that are confused about their direction. A central tenet of contract schools is that every school should have a clear and specific mission. This enables parents to choose a program they believe best serves their children.

Market-Oriented Public Schools

Like vouchers and other privatization schemes to improve schools, contract schools use competition to improve their effectiveness and efficiency. But unlike vouchers, and like charter schools, contracting creates competitive markets within the public sector. Contract schools are market-oriented public schools rather than schools that operate in a private market. This is an important distinction because it affects who chooses goals and makes decisions about schooling. In a private market, consumers are sovereign. Private schools are largely autonomous and accountable only to consumers, usually parents who pay the school tuition.

In a market-oriented public system decisions are shared by the community, providers, and consumers. The community, operating through a local school district or another public agency, helps determine how much schooling it wants and how to pay for the schools. Community representatives participate in determining the kinds or range of schooling options to be available in the district and in setting standards and expectations that schools receiving public support will have to meet. Providers then compete with other providers for public resources by offering an educational program that meets these standards and expectations. The focus of public attention is on the goals of education, the supply of schools, and school funding, leaving control over how schools are organized and run to providers. Consumers—parents and their children—then choose the privately provided education program that best serves their needs. Providing choice for parents restructures the market for public schooling in a way that permits parents as consumers to have some control but not "sovereignty" over the operation of schools. Parents are able to influence public schools both by influencing community standards for the schools and by choosing among schools. By creating competitive markets within a public system, contract schools attempt to change the incentives that drive the participants within public education.

The use of competition and markets within the public sector is not a new idea. Most of our public utilities, such as natural gas, electricity, and telephone service, combine elements of public control, competition, and private provision. In most of these cases, the government could not afford to provide these services by itself. Yet there continues to be a compelling public need to ensure that the services are available at reasonable cost to the public. Consequently, government uses its power to structure markets so that private businesses and individuals have an incentive to meet the public's needs for these necessary public utilities.

Government does the same thing in other areas of activity. Recent debates about health care focused on how best to restructure the market for health care so that it would provide the public purpose of near universal coverage. Few propose having government provide health care; the costs would be too high. The question is how best to structure incentives so that private providers will serve those who cannot afford the current high cost of private care.

Government has also successfully used new market mechanisms to deal with problems of environmental protection (the Clean Air Act of 1990), child care, and job training.

Heretofore, market principles have not been applied extensively to public education. Contract schools, charter schools, and other recent proposals share the belief that schools can be improved by breaking up the public monopoly over the provision of public education, and by introducing new markets and private providers into the system. Just as one would go about analyzing market failures in the private sector, we attempt to analyze how markets (the system of incentives) need to be changed in public education. Who are the important participants in a market for public education? How should a market be established? Who should have control over what sets of decisions? What needs to change in order for schools to serve children? What other public systems that affect public schools need to be changed? Finance systems? Personnel systems? Accounting systems? All of these topics are taken up later in the book.

Caution is called for when introducing market ideas and competition into public education, however. There is obviously a demand for and supply of public schools. Schools produce services that are highly valued by most citizens. Voters regularly approve or reject school levies depending on whether the perceived value of the proposed service is worth the projected tax cost. There is one important way that the market for education is different from most markets for consumer goods. When consumers buy clothing or food items, they have a great deal of information about the products and they know their own tastes. Information about the products is transparent and neither the producer nor the consumer has a particular information advantage. In education as in health care, consumers do not have as much information as the professionals, and are therefore at a disadvantage. Most parents know very little about curriculum and educational strategies. Information is, in these cases, asymmetric. And under certain circumstances asymmetric information can greatly weaken a market. This is particularly the case when consumers believe the producers with the information advantage are acting in their own self-interest.

The only way markets work effectively with asymmetric information is when consumers trust that suppliers are likely to act in the consumers' interests. There must be a relationship of trust created by personal relationships and shared values. Governments can pass rules prohibiting parties from exploiting each other, such as laws against fraud and insider trading, but these are a good deal more costly and cumbersome than when the parties are operating under conditions of trust.

Contracting, we believe, will help build trust markets for public education. By participating in public debates about education and having a choice among schools, parents not only will have more information about their children's education but will also be able to select programs based on shared values. Relationships of trust between parents and teachers, and students and teachers, will replace the suspicion and conflict characteristic of many schools today.

Choice and Competition

In any market-oriented approach to school reform, choice and competition play essential roles. A market exists when suppliers and consumers have choices that influence others' behavior. Efficient or effective markets exist when choices are well informed and do not adversely affect others. Contracting is a system of public education designed to encourage educators to provide high-quality education programs that meet both community and individual needs, and to enable parents and children to find programs that serve their interests.

Part of the challenge of creating an effective public school system is to provide the right mix of educational opportunities for the needs of a particular education community, and then getting the right children into the specific programs they need. No one would assume, for example, that there is one car that would satisfy all the drivers in a city or school district. Consumers have a choice of many models of new and used cars, and there is a system that makes it possible for consumers to find the cars they want and companies that sell them. The same is true of education in most communities, especially large urban districts. The population of potential students is increasingly diverse. Many students come from immigrant families that do not speak English. Students enter schools with different levels of school preparedness and with different experiences with adults and organizations.

The essence of contract-based public education is that it requires local public education agencies to make decisions on a school-by-school basis. Under contracting, the school board need not ask whether a school concept is right for all the students in the district, or whether some stakeholder groups would dislike a particular school. All the board need ask is whether there is a demand for a particular kind of program, whether there is reason to think the proposed academic program can be effective if it is well delivered, whether the people proposing to run the school have plausible credentials for doing so, and whether the options available in the district satisfy the full range of demands and needs there.

Contract schools must attract students if they are to survive over the long haul. The pressures on schools to offer something that makes them stand out—a distinctive curriculum, social climate, or extracurricular program—will be strong. Only by distinguishing themselves from run-of-the-mill offerings can schools hope to attract the interest of potential students and their parents, a prerequisite for persuading them to enroll.

Schools must deliver on their promises if their reputations are to survive. In addition to maintaining a distinctive and consistent program, a contract school must develop a reputation for quality, such that parents expect their children's opportunities for employment and higher education to be increased, not compromised. They must deliver on their promises well enough to keep current students from transferring out, create "brand loyalty" among families with several children, and attract enough new families to fill the entering class each year.

That is a demanding set of requirements. Most of today's public schools would feel intimidated by these expectations, which are regularly met by schools outside of public education. Private and most public colleges and universities meet those criteria every year. Private elementary and secondary schools of all descriptions—inner-city parochial and wealthy preparatory schools—-meet the challenge of establishing an identity, building a reputation for quality, and maintaining consumer loyalty. Even religious schools, which often benefit from parents' attachment to the institution sponsoring the schools, can live and die on their reputations for consistency and quality. As Celio (1994) has documented, many Catholic schools that closed in the 1970s did so because their traditional clients concluded they offered little to set them apart from public schools and produced little better in the way of results. Conversely, Catholic schools that survived were those with well-grounded educational traditions and the skills to maintain quality.

The need to build identity and reputation encourages a number of school staff behaviors that "effective schools" advocates consider essential. School staff must articulate a mission for the school and work hard to make sure all elements of the school contribute to attaining school goals. Under contracting, administrators and teachers have strong incentives to do just that. The mission should be easy to communicate and meaningful to parents; it should focus on what children will experience in school and what they will be able to do upon leaving it, not on subtleties of educational technique comprehensible only to professionals. Contracting puts a premium on meaningful communication with parents and prospective parents.

"Effective Schools" advocates believe teachers need to work in teams and to be concerned about the overall effectiveness of the school. A mission stated in terms of the desired attributes of students leaving the school helps teachers understand how their particular class or subject matter contributes to the school's final product. As studies of "special" public schools have shown, this focus on mission makes teachers understand how they depend on one another and encourages efforts to identify the school's deficiencies and help remedy them (see Lipsitz 1983; Hill et al. 1990).

The demands of sheer economic survival also encourage teachers to be concerned about the performance of the school as a whole and about the contributions of their peers. In a contracting system, when a school is forced to close because too few students want to attend, or the district decides performance does not meet promises, all teachers and administrators have to find new jobs, no matter how well they taught their own classes. Staff members therefore have strong incentives to help one another, identify weaknesses, and ensure that variations in teacher performance do not harm the school's ultimate product and reputation.

Accountability

With contract schools, accountability to parents is provided by their right to choose a school for their children. If a school fails to deliver on its promises, parents can move their children to another school along with the money supporting them. As with parents who choose private schools, these parents will not be eager to disrupt their children's education or to change other arrangements like day care and transportation. Parents can express their opinions, knowing that the school staff has made promises to them, and that the staff have freedom to adjust the school's programs and policies. The volume of movement from one school to another might not be large; in private education, it is not. But parents who think their children are ill served by an existing school will have a ready option, and schools that lose the confidence of large numbers of parents will have trouble surviving. Under contracting, parents will have the option of exercising all three of Hirschman's options of exit, voice, and loyalty. As one of the present authors has argued elsewhere, each of Hirschman's options is strengthened by the availability of the others (Hirschman 1969).

Schools also need to be accountable to the larger community through the contracts they have with public authorities. A contract is a promise to deliver quality education for children in return for public funds and a warrant to operate a school for some period of time. Some procedure is needed to make sure the school lives up to that promise. Relying solely on parent choice only holds the school responsible for the private benefits of education. The public authority awarding the contract needs a way to hold schools accountable for the public purpose of education.

We believe the ultimate measure of school performance is student learning. Are all children in schools learning as much as they can, and learning those things that will enable them to succeed after school, in their work and in their communities? This, of course, is a hard question to answer. In the past most of the accountability approaches emphasized controlling the inputs to the education process. It was assumed that if the inputs to schooling were carefully regulated, then student achievement was guaranteed. Consequently, schools were and still are constrained by a plethora of rules dictating how schools are organized and operated. Legislation in most states requires teachers to be certified and administrators to have teaching experience and additional college course-work. Laws establish the length of the school year, the length of the school day, the number of minutes per class period, the time required for each subject, the size of facilities, and the curriculum to be taught. All of these rules were established to ensure that students received a good education. Accountability is achieved, according to this line of thinking, if the rules are followed. Or put another way, if the rules are followed, children will learn.

Disillusionment with this regulatory approach to accountability has led to demands for assessment and evaluation. Sometimes assessments are made on the inputs to the educational process and sometimes on test results. Both have their problems. Numerous efforts have been made to evaluate teachers and teaching. Standards are established for effective teaching, and then teachers are evaluated against those standards. It might be a test, such as the National Teachers Examination, or it might be a performance-based assessment in which teachers are evaluated while actually teaching. Again the implication is that if teachers pass an exam at a certain level or do certain activities during a classroom observation, then children are learning. There have been few efforts to tie classroom teacher evaluations with student achievement.

Testing students moves in the direction of holding schools responsible for student learning. Students now undergo a continuous and exhausting regime of testing. Every class has its test. There are district-wide and state-wide subject matter tests at periodic intervals of a student's career in public schools. Many states now have competency tests for graduation. Schools are said to be accountable to the extent that teachers and students are frequently tested and the results are made public. However, disappointing SAT scores and middling standings among other industrialized nations on standardized achievement tests have caused national concern. For many the issue is not that schools give tests, but rather that parents and the public are dissatisfied with the results.

Incentives for High Performance

Under the current publicly controlled and publicly operated system of schools, educators face mixed incentives, not all of which focus their attention on student learning. Laws that require mandatory attendance, that give local school districts a monopoly over public education, and that provide per pupil funding ensure that the jobs of school administrators, teachers, staff members, and suppliers are protected whether or not students learn. Even within school districts, a school whose students achieve in the bottom 5 percent of the district gets the same level of resources as a school whose students are in the top 5 percent. Required attendance areas make it almost impossible for parents to voice dissatisfaction by changing schools. Where there are no consequences for teachers and administrators if students do not learn, there is no accountability, no need for standards and evaluation. Teacher evaluation and student testing become largely symbolic. They don't make any difference.

Accountability only means something if there are consequences when children do not learn. This is what a system of contract schools will do. It rearranges the incentives within the public education system to reward schools that improve student learning and penalize those that do not. Incentives are established by creating markets for both providers and students. School district boards will be able to reward high-achieving contractors by extending their contracts to operate schools. They will also be able to contract for new schools to replace failed ones. Parents can affect the resources available to the school by their choice to enroll or transfer their children to another school. The jobs of administrators and teachers will not be guaranteed. They must provide a high-performance program in order to continue employment. Only when there are consequences, when whether a school opens and remains open depends on the performance of students, are standards and evaluation meaningful and accountability present.

A system of contract schools forces schools to say exactly what they hope to accomplish with their students, and it creates strong incentives for school staffs to assess their own performance and make a public case that they have succeeded. Parents and local public authorities need not always accept schools' assertions at face value, but they can make school-provided information an integral part of the accountability process. Local public authorities will also need to develop their own measures of school performance and ensure that parents have a full range of performance information for all schools. The result should be that everyone involved in public education—parents, school staffs, the public, and public education officials—will know much more about individual schools than they do now.

Holding school contractors accountable to government standards will take some effort, but, we believe, less effort than holding today's public schools accountable. As we have pointed out, there are now few incentives for public schools to comply with government regulations. Private suppliers of education, on the other hand, are more likely to comply because renewal of their contracts depends on it. They also have less political protection than bureaucratically run schools. James Q. Wilson in his book on bureaucracy (1989) gives several examples of cases in which private providers were more accountable than public bureaucracies:

When Washington decided to increase the proportion of female workers in shipyards, it obtained more compliance by far from private shipyards doing business with the government than from shipyards operated by the U.S. Navy. When state regulatory agencies began urging electrical utilities to encourage conservation among their customers and to develop alternative energy sources, investor-owned utilities did more than municipally-owned utilities serving comparable markets. For many years the Environmental Protection Agency had more success in getting private power generators to reduce pollution than it had in getting the

69

Tennessee Valley Authority to do so. . . . [Public] agencies enjoy political protection denied to most firms. (p. 359)

Quality Assurance

Once every school has a contract with tailor-made performance expectations, public education authorities have real leverage for quality assurance. The local public education authority fulfills its responsibility for ensuring that all children get a quality education by maintaining a portfolio of contracts serving two objectives: first, ensuring that the local system as a whole offers a range of approaches and services that matches the diverse needs of local children; and second, ensuring that no child receives a low-quality education.

Contractors who failed to provide instruction as promised, or whose students' outcomes were low and not improving as anticipated, could be fired or given an ultimatum to improve or be replaced. Parents could also take their children out of low-performing schools at any time, and move them into better-performing schools. Local public authorities would be under an obligation to warn parents that a school had run into trouble. Authorities would also be obliged, by constant attention to their portfolio of contracts, to see to it that children leaving a failing school had a better place to go. They would also continuously evaluate contractors' performance, both to prepare for negotiations around contract renewal and to identify contractors not delivering on their promises and failing to produce positive student results.

In communities where parents are intensely interested in choosing among schools, private organizations might make money selling information about schools. (One national information service, School Match, now offers data on school systems to business people thinking of relocating.)

However, as Chubb and Moe (1990) argue, public authorities must ensure that all parents, not just the ones able and willing to pay, get such information. They suggest that the state fund independent parent-information centers. Local public authorities would also need assistance in identifying needs for new types of schools, identifying promising potential contractors, and monitoring contract performance. Many of these functions could be performed by contractors, though not the same ones that operate the schools. But the evaluation and contractor identification process could not be neglected or performed for free; these functions would be the main mechanisms by which the public would be assured that its children were being well cared for and its money carefully used.

Equity

Defenders of the present system argue that market-oriented reforms, such as charter schools and contract schools, would increase inequalities in public education. This is an important concern, but not a well-founded one. Despite state constitutional provisions requiring states to establish "uniform and general" or "thorough and efficient" systems of public education, there is little equality in the current structure. Average expenditures per student vary dramatically between rich and poor districts in many states. The situation is exacerbated within districts in which the average expenditure often masks wide variations between schools in the poorest neighborhoods of city school systems and schools in "better" city neighborhoods.

A system of contract schools would lead to a more equal allocation of resources among schools than the present system. Contracting allocates cash in the form of a fixed per-student reimbursement payment from the local education authority to the school. A contract system is designed to ensure that virtually all the money available for the public education system is spent in the schools. Local education agencies would still exist and could claim some money, say 5 percent, for administration. But all remaining funds would go to the schools as cash, and the amounts received by individual schools would be matters of public record. Differences could not be hidden, as they are now, in district-wide accounting systems in which schools are not cost centers. Once schools received their cash budgets they would be free to buy whatever they needed in the open market. Most services provided by current local education agencies could survive only if they attracted voluntary customers.

The question of whether government or the market produces fairer outcomes is not always obvious. Government permits some people in power to make decisions for other people. That power can be used for good or for ill depending on the inclinations of those with the power and the political pressures on them. In contracting, political authorities would still have a key function, awarding contracts, but they would have strong incentives to make decisions based on explicit performance criteria and price, rather than on political considerations, which is the current situation.

Opening Up the School Budget

A major benefit of contracting is that it forces all school costs into the open. Most existing per-pupil expenditure figures are of little assistance in helping the public understand how much money is actually spent on teaching and learning activities per pupil. Existing expenditure reports reflect the costs of running the whole system, with all its attendant costs for servicing debt, paying salaries and fringe benefits, running a major transportation system, and, in most cities, providing more meals than the local restaurant industry. They do not distinguish the costs associated with instruction at the school level from the costs of district-wide administration. A contract strategy opens up the possibility of focusing public attention on expenditures per student at the school site.

Contracting requires each school to negotiate wage and benefit packages with its teachers or administrators. No entity other than the school itself could pick up "hidden" costs such as those for fringe benefits and retirement. Groups of schools might hire an independent organization to provide services ranging from staff training and recruitment to benefit and retirement packages. But these services would be funded solely out of the cash payments made by the public education authority to the schools, payments based solely on the per-student allotment.

Increasing Spending Flexibility

Contract schools would enjoy substantial freedom about how they used their money. State regulations or contract "boilerplate" language could set minimum qualifications for the school principal and a few members of the instructional staff, but few such prescriptions would be warranted. In general, schools would compete on performance and be free to configure themselves and select staff members according to a site-specific plan. Any other arrangement would make it harder to run distinctive programs, quickly returning school governance to the very problem it needs to avoid—bureaucratic standardization of structure and practice.

Contracting could create a much fairer distribution of staff among schools than the existing system does. As explained earlier, the existing system permits unilateral placement decisions by senior teachers to determine the distribution of resources among schools. This situation, and the fact that central-office services, including maintenance and repair, are typically allocated on a "squeaky wheel" basis, means that students in low-income areas often receive the benefit of far fewer real resources than students in more advantaged areas of the same school district.

Eliminating Inequalities Within and Between States

In order to provide equal opportunity among school districts in a state, most states would have to change their school finance systems. In chapter

6, we propose a system of full-state funding for schools that would eliminate most of the expenditure variations within a state. This could be done by using state-wide sources of revenue to support schools, and a distribution formula that allocated equal amounts per student to each district and required districts to pass through almost all of the state funds to schools on a per pupil basis. The problem of interstate inequality requires a different study (and book) on the federal role in public education. Clearly under the current fiscal constraints facing the federal government, there are not sufficient federal revenues available to eliminate or even substantially reduce spending inequalities among the states. The federal government could, however, use its substantial legal and regulatory powers, just as it has in the areas of health care, job training, and welfare reform, to create incentives that would lead to greater spending equality among the states. Interstate inequities are important, but they do not have to be resolved to implement a contract system for the provision of pubic schooling.

Efficiency

It is generally true that government bureaus are less efficient than private organizations. There are several reasons for this. First, public administrators must serve a variety of purposes and are less likely than private executives to pursue a core purpose efficiently. Second, public administrators have fewer incentives than their private counterparts to be efficient because they cannot personally benefit from any resulting savings. Third, most public officials have less authority to do what is necessary to be efficient, such as being able to hire and fire employees, set pay according to individual productivity, and purchase resources from low-cost providers.

Public schools are no exception. It is not that teachers are paid too much or that we spend too much on schools. In fact, polls indicate that many people would be willing to have their taxes increased to improve public schools, if the schools operated more efficiently. The problem is that there are few incentives for schools to be efficient, if by that we mean to allocate resources in ways that improve student performance without increasing costs. In fact the opposite is true. Schools are under constant pressure to add new programs and services, such as AIDS awareness and teen pregnancy awareness, that often reduce the time and resources available for the core education subjects. Public schools are now asked to do too many things other than deliver instruction to be the efficient learning environments they could be. There are political pressures to increase salaries of teachers, administrators, and noneducational staff, and to reduce the workload. Furthermore, current regulations, policies, and collective bargaining contracts give school boards and school administrators almost no room to make changes that would increase efficiency.

A contract system, in contrast, creates pressures for performance in the same way that it encourages initiative and responsibility among school staffs—through competition. The need to attract students encourages high performance. Contracting responds to a need identified by Albert Shanker, president of the American Federation of Teachers. Schools, says Shanker, are the only institutions that he knows of in which "If you do something good, nothing happens, and if you do something bad, nothing happens" (Shanker 1990). Contracting is a governance system designed to both reward schools that gain reputations for quality and punish schools with bad records.

Under contracting, schools that gain a reputation for doing a poor job of educating children are in danger of losing, first, their student enrollment and, ultimately, their public funding. The prospect of closing the school is a great motivation for teachers and administrators. Because teachers and administrators are employees of the school, not of the local district, they have no automatic reinstatement rights elsewhere.

Contract schools would also have the authority to use their funds more efficiently. Schools would be free to allocate their income as needed. If a contract school needed to spend less on driver-training, substitute teachers, or elective courses, and more to hire a highly qualified math teacher or to send an English teacher for retraining, it could do so. It would need permission from no one. Staff development would not be mandated from on high; schools would have the freedom to reallocate their budgets to buy what they need. Like private schools, contract schools would have responsibility for their own staff development and quality control. These services, which are now centrally administered and therefore unresponsive to individual school needs, would be purchased by schools on the open market. Though some cost savings related to the existing system are likely, contracts must include reasonable funding for staff training, self-assessment, and adoption of promising new teaching methods and technologies.

There is another positive benefit of contracting. Because the local school system's central office would be reduced to a contracting agency, schools should have more money to spend. School-level funding is now approximately two-thirds of total per pupil expenditure. If elimination of the large, central-office, civil service staffs saved only half the money now spent outside the schools, spending at the school level could increase immediately by nearly 15 percent.

Multiple School Providers

Contracting expressly allows for new kinds of nongovernmental institutions that can help schools maintain quality and may increase efficiency. Local public education authorities may not want to execute separate contracts with dozens, or in some cities, hundreds, of individual schools. They might prefer whenever possible to deal with organizations capable of running several schools under a master contract. This would simplify the contract negotiation and monitoring problems faced by local school boards. Organizations responsible for several schools would be the local board's prime contractors. They would also become mechanisms to ensure school quality.

Such organizations could be created by the local school board itself, by entering into contracts with teacher cooperatives, teacher unions, local colleges and universities, profit-making firms, nonprofit civic and religious groups, and other local organizations to run multiple schools. The board could also enter contracts with similar organizations established in other localities: a teacher cooperative in Minneapolis might agree to run some schools under contract with St. Paul. Ted Kolderie of the University of Minnesota has envisioned just such an arrangement as a long-term consequence of Minnesota's Charter Schools law, which lets a local school board designate existing school communities to "opt out" of the existing central administrative processes and labor laws.

As these locally based organizations developed capable staffs and managerial capacity, the ones with quality reputations might become regional or national in scope, offering to run schools in many school districts and providing assistance to other schools on a fee basis. At that point they would come to resemble existing contract-school providers, hereafter called Management and Assistance Providers (MAPs). One existing MAP, The Edison Project, develops curricula, trains teachers, provides quality control, and assesses performance for the schools it runs. Local school boards still make their own assessments of the schools' performance, but the basic work of maintaining product consistency and quality is done by Edison, much as it is performed by religious orders for Catholic diocesan school systems.

Organizations capable of running multiple schools can develop distinctive approaches to education and capitalize on the recognition and consumer confidence that a "brand name" engenders. They are also likely to benefit from economies of scale in designing curriculum and staff development. Stronger schools run by an organization can assist the weaker ones, and staff can be transferred from one school to another, both to shore up shaky programs and to increase exposure to high-performance organizations. Because of these advantages, schools operated by MAPs are likely to become major forces in a contract system.

The services of MAPs cannot be free. Their costs would be paid from contract funds received by the schools. A school might join a MAP for a fee, or a MAP running several schools could deduct its operating costs before sending money to the schools. Estimates of these costs vary. Catholic diocesan school systems typically assess schools between $10 and $25 per student to pay for testing, consulting, and financial management services. This compares rather favorably to $1,500 to $2,500 per student spent on most public school system central offices. MAPs could become large organizations, and they too might develop bureaucracies. But the need to maintain their schools' reputations gives MAPs strong incentives to control costs and avoid creating barriers to school effectiveness.

Assuming a school size of 500, a MAP charging $25 per student would cost the school $12,500. A secular organization might pay its employees twice as much and deliver more services than a Catholic diocesan school system, therefore requiring as much as $50 per pupil. If the average per pupil expenditure were $5,000, the school's overall budget would be $2.5 million, and the MAP's costs would be 1 percent of the total. Another cost estimate can be based on the Edison Project's rule of thumb that the corporate central office would have one staff member per 2,000 students. If the average school size were 500 students, that would make one staff member per four schools. If these staff members cost $100,000 each (salary, fringe benefits, and office overhead), the cost per school would be $25,000, again less than 1 percent of the school's budget.Public officials would retain ultimate responsibility for school quality. They can replace contractors who fail to deliver, or force a MAP to make substantial quality improvements as soon as performance falls below acceptable levels. A local public education authority can also continually "prune" its portfolio of contractors. When contracts come up for renewal, contractors whose schools fall below some set level of performance (say the 25th percentile of all local schools) could be eliminated from consideration. The contracting system, in fact, ensures something that is not now possible in public school governance: unrelenting attention to the quality of instruction and learning in the lowest-performing schools. Like any other arrangement in human affairs, contracting can be done poorly. But it creates incentives that should, over time, substantially raise performance in the weakest schools and raise average performance levels of all district schools.

A Professional Role for Teachers

Almost everyone, certainly almost every successful person, can remember the profound personal influence exerted by one or more special teachers. Regardless of the prospective instructional effectiveness of new technology, the power of new curricula designs, or advances in cognitive science, there will be a need for teachers, particularly outstanding teachers. It is difficult for a machine or technique to inspire, motivate, or act as a model in the same manner as a good teacher. Technology certainly has the power to enhance instruction, but we doubt that it ever will or should replace teachers.

Hence, attracting and retaining able individuals in education must also be a major objective of a contract school system.

Few understand the magnitude of America's current education workforce. Public schools alone annually employ more than 4 million individuals. Private schools employ another 300,000. More people are directly engaged in operating America's schools than in growing our food.

Thousands of new recruits are inducted each year into teaching. Studies suggest that approximately a third of new teachers (and almost half in some states) drop out of teaching in their first three years and pursue other careers. Some leave because they are unqualified to be teachers or cannot take the strain of classroom teaching. But most leave for better-paying and more satisfying jobs. The Shavian adage— "Those who can, do; those who can't, teach"—is a myth. The large number of former teachers now pursuing other careers testifies all too disconcertingly to the fact that these individuals can successfully do many other things. Also, the other careers they pursue often offer them the prospect of earning a great deal more money in the process. Lastly, many of the best individuals who do remain in education are drawn from classroom teaching into administration or other noninstructional roles, because this is how they can enhance their remuneration and prestige.

What would it take for contract schools to attract larger proportions of able individuals into education and enable them to pursue classroom teaching as a fulfilling professional career? There are at least three answers to this question. First, teaching will have to become seen as a professional career that one can pursue and in which one can earn, if not initially then at least eventually, an amount comparable to what an accountant, salesperson, business manager, government attorney, or other mid-level organizational professional earns. This higher level of compensation may well be stretched out over an entire work year. One of the reasons why teachers currently have limited income-earning capability is that they frequently are not employed for a whole year. Extending the school year, or at least teachers' work years, would be a good thing. It is time to acknowledge that America no longer has an agriculturally dominated economy, and that we seldom need to suspend schooling in order to harvest crops.

Second, teachers in contract schools must accept that not all teachers are equal. In most public school districts today, all teachers possessing similar academic degrees and years of service are paid the same. This civil service mentality discourages individuals who want to be regarded as true professionals and are willing to make the added effort necessary for high performance. It unfairly rewards those who take advantage of the system and ride the coattails of their harder-working colleagues. Also, the "all-teachers-shall-be-treated-alike" phenomenon probably does more than anything else to restrict public willingness to pay teachers higher salaries. To build a true profession, teachers will need to accept differences among themselves that are based upon legitimate measures of differential training, performance, or market demand.

In contract schools, some teachers, such as master teachers, will have more responsibility than others. Some will achieve better classroom results than others. Some will work longer hours than others. Some will obtain more training and preparation than others. Some will submit their instructional efforts to more assessment and evaluation than others. There is a long list of differences among teachers that contractors will have to take into account in compensating teachers in contract schools.

A third change necessary to convert teaching to a true profession is to enhance the autonomy of teachers. They must have greater discretion to achieve the expectations established by policy makers. It is altogether appropriate for policy systems to specify the outcomes they want the education system to achieve. It is not appropriate for the policy system simultaneously to prescribe the processes by which these outcomes will be obtained. When management engages in such micro-management and over-regulation, it simultaneously precludes real accountability. A person who dictates both what outcome is wanted and the means by which that outcome is to be produced has only herself to blame if results fall short of expectations.

If we as a society want to hold teachers "accountable" for results, then we must provide them with reasonable professional discretion in determining the manner for achieving the goals.

However, if teachers are to be provided with greater professional discretion and are thus deserving of greater professional financial compensation, they must simultaneously accept greater professional responsibility.

In short, teachers must begin to police their ranks, much as do many other true professionals, such as physicians, accountants, and architects. This means that teachers must begin the unpleasant task of appraising the behavior of their peers and assisting or eliminating those who perform below expectations. The need for contract schools to attract students and to meet the performance objectives in their contracts will provide a strong incentive for teachers to insist on high performance from their colleagues.

Stability of Rules

A major problem with the current education system is that it is constantly changing the rules for operating a school. Principals and teachers rarely have time to adjust to a new set of rules before they are again changed. The over-regulation of schools and the tendency for rules to change have paralyzed many schools.

It is paradoxical that a system that is ridiculed for its reluctance to change is subject to such rule instability. The reason this occurs is that school boards try to accommodate all of the diverse political and societal demands by adopting new programs and creating new rules for all schools. School boards do the best they can to accommodate and mollify each demand, even at the cost of constraining schools so much that they cannot do anything well.

A contract system will go a long way toward alleviating this problem. A school with a contract will have legally enforceable rights to continue operating and receiving public money, as long as it performs as promised. In contrast, schools operating under existing site-based management or magnet school schemes remain part of the school system bureaucracy and are therefore vulnerable to changes in administrative or political signals. They can maintain their independence and special character only as long as a majority of the local school board supports them. Site-managed schools like Chicago's depend on waivers that can be revoked at any minute. Even the charter schools recently established under state laws in Minnesota, California, Massachusetts, and other states have no legally enforceable rights. They can last only as long as a majority of the school board is willing to tolerate them, i.e., only as long as they are not controversial.

Legally enforceable contracts let schools that are performing well survive controversy. As a system, contracting also gives public authorities a superior means of handling political conflict. It assumes that conflict and diverse demands are inevitable. Its response, however, is not to satisfy every demand everywhere, but to make sure that the system accommodates diverse demands somewhere. It holds promise of protecting individual schools from the turbulence of educational politics while deflecting political pressures in a productive fashion. It does so by side-stepping the need for consensus on curriculum content and instructional methods and by consciously fostering diversity on the very issues on which Americans are most divided.

Contract Schools Accommodate Diversity

Contracting implies a commitment to diversity in educational offerings. Schools choose or are commissioned to provide particular kinds of services. Basic civil rights guarantees and employee protections would still apply, but a school would not be required to take actions incompatible with its basic mission or approach. For example, a school commissioned to provide bilingual instruction to Spanish-speaking immigrants would not be required to offer courses for Mandarin speakers, even though the school system might be obligated to create a school or program for that purpose elsewhere. A school offering a curriculum designed for African-American boys might be required to admit white girls if they applied, but it would not be required to change its curriculum to accommodate them. A community, parent, or educators' group that desired a particular form of multicultural curriculum or classes urging approval of alternative lifestyles might be able to obtain these things in a particular school. Nevertheless, the same group could not hope to have the services they want mandated for the whole school system, and would have few incentives to demand their duplication elsewhere in the system. Such diversity permits each school to focus on a defined mission and to differentiate its products from other schools.

If no one approach to schooling is universally required, there is little need to resolve educational differences through political means. Different tastes and preferences can find expression in different schools. It would be possible, therefore, for individual schools or groups of schools to adopt definite approaches to schooling and to become, in effect, fully aligned and standards-driven. The success of networks of schools connected with Montessori, Waldorf, Paideia, and religious groups attests to the power of such alignment.

Diversity is an inevitable by-product of any reform based on increasing schools' independence. If schools are independent, they will take on a character that reflects the needs and values of community, staff, or students, and will appeal to students and new staff members on the basis of affinity. Contracting accentuates the pressures for diversity by forcing school staffs to explain their assumptions and approaches to public authorities and to make specific claims about what students will learn.

Given the wide range of social, cultural, and language groups served by public education, public schools under a contract system will inevitably come to define different goals and pursue different approaches.

Diversity brings its own problems. Many fear that diversity encourages public support of schools run by hate groups and cults, or the teaching of dogmatic creationism or "flat-earth" theories in schools. Such problems may arise, but they may also be teapot tempests. It is not easy to run a school under even the best circumstances; fringe groups are likely to be discouraged by the problem of competing with high-quality "mainstream" alternatives.

Nonetheless, the very possibility that fringe groups might be encouraged to establish contract schools means that elected officials can face some difficult decisions. Should districts contract with groups propounding divisive ideologies or lacking any experience as educators? Local education authorities could resolve such issues by contracting only with organizations that have track records for running schools, including the staffs of existing public and private schools, teacher unions and teacher co-ops, higher education institutions, school reform networks, and school-management firms. More perplexing difficulties may arise about whether to contract for schools on the outer boundaries of traditional educational practice or content. Such decisions will inevitably involve balancing the interests of competing groups; that is, the decisions will be political.

The complexity of these decisions, however, should not be allowed to obscure the central points. These issues already consume time on the political agenda of local authorities. The issues will remain alive under contracting, but they will be easier to handle. Under contracting, the fringe groups will focus their demands on whether they get authority to run a particular school, not whether their views should be incorporated in the curricula of all schools. A state or local school board can, therefore, address such issues as boundary-setting questions, not fundamental ones. Political conflict might still be harsh, but the majority of schools will be unaffected by it. Virtually all of the educational approaches traditionally permitted in licensed private schools will be eligible for operation under simple contracts. Only educational ideas representing fringe interests hostile to major groups in society are at risk of being denied the opportunity to provide schools.

Conclusion

A system of contract schools has several major advantages over the current system. First, contracting focuses attention and resources on schools where the education of children takes place. Second, contracting creates incentives for schools to concentrate on high student achievement. Third, contracting increases educational options, thereby reducing conflict about public education.

Contracting treats schools as real organizations and real communities rather than as parts of a larger community. This permits each school to serve the students and the families in that school. Instead of being preoccupied with following district rules, contract schools focus on how the school as a whole helps students learn. Because schools are the basic unit of management in a contract school system, there are also pressures on public officials to place as many dollars as possible in schools and to limit the size of the central office.

Contracting creates strong incentives for schools to concentrate on providing high-quality programs. Because contract schools are schools of choice, they need to attract students in order to survive. They must also keep students, once they enroll, by establishing a reputation for quality. If parents are unhappy with a school, they can transfer their children to another school. The prospect of declining enrollment and the accompanying decline in resources provides adequate motivation to keep schools focused on teaching and learning. Meeting performance objectives is also required for contract renewal. Under contracting there are consequences for not performing well, and as a result there is real accountability.

Finally, a system of contract schools reduces political conflict in districts by providing more educational options. If groups can find or establish schools that reflect their interests, they have no reason to fight among themselves. Less time and resources are spent at all levels responding to disgruntled parents, and more time and resources are available for the core activity of schools, learning.

FOUR

Contracting and Other Reform Proposals

number of other reform proposals are intended, as is contracting, to focus resources and decision-making authority at the school level, so that schools can become truly productive and responsible organizations. Education vouchers, the most widely discussed of these proposals, would almost totally deregulate public education and make schools free actors in a market, competing for students. Site-based management leaves the existing public education governance system intact but tries to create greater school-level initiative by increasing teachers' and parents' involvement in decision-making and by allowing schools to request waivers of particular rules. Systemic reform tries to free schools of overly specific regulations by creating new systems of student performance goals, standards, and tests; by eliminating rules that do not promote attainment of goals and standards; and by coordinating all public investments in curriculum development and teacher training. The laws for charter schools allow groups of teachers and parents to operate schools free of many state and local regulations.[1]

These alternatives represent dramatically different reform strategies. Education vouchers is a pure demand-side strategy: it gives parents total freedom to select schools and guarantees that public funds will follow students to any school they attend. It assumes there will be an adequate sup-

---

1. Charter school laws, which have been enacted in various forms in twenty-four states, permit limited numbers of schools—-including existing public schools and new ones—to seek contractor status. There are two main differences between charter school laws and the contracting plan described above: first, few laws for charter schools establish as clear a contractual relationship as described in chapter 3 above; and second, all state charter school laws put strict limits on the numbers of schools that can be operated under contract, while the contracting proposal would eventually cover all public schools.

ply of public and private schools willing to compete for students and their vouchers. In contrast, site-based management and systemic reform are supply-side strategies. They sustain the current practice under which public bureaucracies operate all public schools but alter key supply conditions—in one case increasing the degree of freedom at lower levels of the bureaucracy and in the other clarifying and rationalizing the requirements all schools must meet. Charter schools follow a mixed supply and demand strategy, encouraging creation of small numbers of new schools under relaxed regulatory schemes and allowing some degree of parent choice. Contracting is also a mixed strategy that resembles charter schools in many ways; however, it would make schools completely independent organizations, bound to local school boards only by legally enforceable contracts and requiring conversion of entire local school systems so that parents would have the broadest possible range of choices.

All the foregoing reform strategies might improve on the existing system in some ways. Vouchers, like contracting and charter schools, would encourage initiative in schools and create strong pressures for school performance. Again like contracting, vouchers would create a situation in which all parties engaged in a school—teachers, administrators, and students—would be present by mutual choice. Site-based management creates some expectations that teachers and principals will try to tailor instruction to the needs of current students and solve problems that occur in their schools. Systemic reform clarifies schools' responsibility to emphasize student achievement over all else, and uses student achievement goals to discipline the actions of all the adults in the public education system. Charter schools would provide a limited number of schools the advantages of contracting. But all the approaches, including contracting, also have liabilities.

This chapter describes the strengths and weaknesses of all these proposals and compares them to contracting. The chapter starts with a discussion of potential problems with contracting. We do not repeat the extensive discussion of contracting in the previous chapter. Instead we focus on problems of contracting common to all education reforms and problems that may be peculiar to contracting. A discussion of the downside of contracting is intended to draw clearer distinctions between our proposal and the other major reform proposals. The chapter then goes on to describe and analyze vouchers, site-based management, systemic reform, and charter schools. Finally, it returns to the reasons we think contracting is a superior alternative to all the others.

The Downside of Contracting

When introduced to the idea of contracting for public schools, skeptics raise two kinds of challenges. The first is that under a contract system inequalities of educational opportunity might increase because sophisticated families will take advantage of the best opportunities, leaving lower-quality programs for the less informed and less motivated. Popular programs will have the most applicants and thus can be selective. The best students, teachers, and administrators will gravitate to these programs. Weaker and less prepared students and less successful teachers will be weeded out of the best schools. People who make this challenge are often sincerely concerned that disadvantaged children will not benefit equitably from a system of contract schools. They also assume that the current system prevents such abuses because it claims to do so.

This phenomenon—that the alert and aggressive get the best out of the education system—is endemic to all forms of public education, including the current system and all of the reforms discussed in this chapter. The major difference between contracting, vouchers, and charters on the one hand and the current system and systemic reform and site-based management on the other hand is that in the former group the phenomenon is more transparent. In bureaucratically run systems the most alert and influential families get their children into the best schools and programs, using less public and obvious methods.[2]

Under contracting, families choose schools and schools choose students; schools openly compete for teachers in a labor market, and vice versa. Schools say what they will provide students and how hard students must work to succeed. Families that do not take their opportunities for selecting a school seriously would end up with less desirable options than those who inform themselves and seek options.

Under the current system families are assigned to schools, but those who will press a transfer petition to the top of the bureaucracy usually get their way. Senior teachers can choose where they work and they usually cluster in the safest and most middle-class schools in a district. Schools say they are for all students, but low-income and minority students are likely to end up in lower tracks or less challenging classes.[3] Minority students (especially African-American males in big-city high schools) are

---

2. For a sampling of the extensive literature on this phenomenon, see Oakes (1985, 1995), Guiton (1995), Anderson (1994), Ogbu (1994), and Orfield 1994).

3. See Jeannie Oakes' work on tracking cited in note 2 above.

more than twice as likely as other students to end up in workbook-oriented remedial courses and separate special education classes. Aggressive and knowledgeable parents can get their children assigned to the "best" teachers in a school and to "gifted" or "enrichment" programs. Districts transfer bad teachers and disruptive students to other schools, so that nobody has to cope with any one problem for long. The current public education system as a whole tolerates a high student dropout rate, especially among male minority students.

No one knows exactly how much these phenomena contribute to differences in opportunity between advantaged and disadvantaged students. And because we have not had a universal school-choice program anywhere in America, we do not know whether the kind of choice that contracting would create might increase or decrease disparities in educational opportunity. We know that contracting, like vouchers and charters, makes self-seeking by parents and teachers more transparent. We do not know whether contracting, vouchers, or charters make such phenomena more or less prevalent. It would be important to monitor this issue closely in the early development and full implementation of a contracting system. But the monitoring must start from a good baseline, which reflects the current system's actual performance, not just its rhetoric.[4]

The second set of challenges is particular to contracting. How can school boards establish clear contracts and enforce them? How can they ensure an adequate supply of providers? What will a school board do if a

4. A serious discussion on this topic would require a baseline understanding of the sources of inequality in the current system. These would include the mechanisms mentioned above, as well as such well-documented phenomena as "tracking" lower-class children into nonacademic programs, discriminatory admission to gifted and talented classes, low "time on instruction" in inner-city schools, low teacher expectations for minority students, use of special education classifications to isolate African-American boys, lax disciplinary policies in minority schools, and efforts to encourage difficult students to drop out of schools. To the degree possible, these sources of inequality should be cataloged and quantified, so that the comparisons between bureaucratic and choice systems could be made on bases of fact, not rhetoric. A project now underway under direction of the senior author of this book will create a framework for fair comparison between educational choice proposals and the current system. It will do so by providing quantitative baseline estimates of inequalities caused or tolerated by existing education bureaucracies, and comparing these to inequalities reportedly resulting from choice programs. The project's primary method will be exhaustive reviews of all the available research on allocation of benefits within the current public school system, including school finance research and the literature on inequalities of access to quality education programs.

contractor-run school fails? What will happen if a contractor runs a school that parents like but that does not teach students anything? Many of these questions are addressed in detail in the second part of this book, but it is worth beginning to answer them here.

These questions arise from the contracting proposal itself. Under contracting, public officials cannot operate schools directly; they must hire independent organizations to do so. Public officials cannot dictate details of contract schools' staffing or operation, but they must hold schools accountable for performance. These facts raise important questions about the supply of school contractors, protection of the public interest, and school performance accountability. We cannot answer these questions definitively without the benefit of some real contracting experience, but we can suggest how they might be answered.

Supply of School Contractors

Policy makers, educators, and parents need to know what happens if:

- There are not enough good proposals to run local schools;
- Nobody offers to run a particular school, or nobody will do so at the level of spending offered by the school board;
- A particular district has trouble attracting contract proposals, even though neighboring districts have plenty;
- A local school board tries to load every new contract with provisions that virtually reproduce the whole precontracting state education code;
- A particular school is performing below expectations (or is not fully living up to its promises about open acceptance of minority students and assistance to them), but the board cannot find a more promising contractor.

In general, as later chapters will discuss in detail, to maintain a match between supply and demand for competent providers, states and localities would need to expand contracting gradually so that a supplier infrastructure could develop. States should provide investment capital to attract new providers and help good ones expand. Arizona, for example, now provides $100,000 in start-up capital for every new charter school. States will also need to track the contracting experience of local districts and require changes in contracting policy for those that drive away good providers. None of these responses will suffice, however, if school boards offer too few dollars per pupil for a contract school to operate. However, in states that have given charter schools the full funding to which their students were entitled, there has been no shortage of potential providers.

Protection of the Public Interest

Policy makers, educators, and parents need to consider what happens if:

- A contract school pursues educational, personnel, or student relations practices which, though not in violation of the contract, are offensive to some;

- Parents in a one school complain that another school offers something theirs does not (e.g., band);

- A school makes unusually high demands of teachers, and many are asked to leave;

- A local board gets a proposal from an extremist group that would preach discrimination or hatred, but is qualified to teach basic subjects.

Most of these issues are less difficult to resolve under contracting than in a conventional public school system because contracting promotes a diverse supply of schools. Contracting makes it unnecessary for any one school to please everyone. If a school satisfies no one it will fail, but if it does a good job serving a defined clientele, others have no basis to complain. No contract system can be entirely free of tensions about whether a given school should or should not receive public support. Local boards will be empowered to rule out proposals from "extremist groups" but the definition of extremism will probably differ from, say, San Francisco to northern Idaho. Under contracting, such issues will be resolved through community politics, just as they are now. Like the supply problems discussed above, these will become evident in new ways under a contracting system. They do not warrant rejecting the idea of contracting altogether, but they do require close attention as contracting schemes are implemented.

Performance Accountability

Policy makers, educators, and parents need to know how key issues can be handled, including:

- At the time of contract renewal, a school has a mixed performance profile, good outcomes on some measures and bad on others;

- A school is producing poor student performance reports but parents like the school and protest a proposal to close the school or assign it to another contractor;

- A school contractor claims that the standard district assessment underestimates its students' learning and proposes another set of outcome measures.

Most of these issues are impossible to resolve in advance of the establishment of a contracting system. Because the current system does not take schools seriously as organizations, little work has been done to hold whole schools accountable. The details of school accountability must be worked out during the development of a contracting system. Some things are clear, however. Parent choice will provide a separate barometer of school performance. School boards will need to use multiple measures of school performance. Schools must be held accountable for the value they add to student performance. Many school boards will also want to consider measures of school climate, parental trust, and teacher professionalism. Again, contracting will force new developments in this area of public education management.

Having acknowledged that our own proposal has liabilities and raises difficult questions, we will now turn to description and analysis of other competing reform proposals.

Vouchers, a Demand-Side Strategy

John Chubb and Terry Moe made the most complete case for demand subsidies in their 1990 book, *Politics, Markets, and America's Schools.* But theirs is only the latest and most complete in a series of books and articles that advocated replacing the present heavy reliance on bureaucratic management of public schools with a lightly regulated market. As early as 1970, the Office of Economic Opportunity (OEO) tried to mount an experiment with education vouchers (see Jencks and Areen 1970 and Doyle 1977). Since that time, lawyer John Coons and several collaborators have advocated introducing consumer choice and privatization into public education. (See especially Coons and Sugarman 1978). The immediate precursor to Chubb and Moe's book was *Winning the Brain Race* (1988), coauthored by Xerox CEO David Kearns and by the former OEO voucher experiment manager, Dennis Doyle.

In addition to these voucher-based comprehensive reform proposals, there have been some proposals for partial voucher programs that leave the public school system intact but provide limited payments (usually worth less than a third of public school per pupil expenditure) that parents can use to pay partial tuition in private schools. In recent years individuals, corporations, and philanthropic organizations have also set up numerous local programs that provide vouchers for limited numbers of disadvantaged children (see Moe 1996). The following analysis concentrates on proposals for complete voucher systems only, i.e., those that would put all public funds under the control of parents and voucher-redeeming schools.

Since the 1970s, the voucher movement has been led by Coons, Doyle, and Chubb and Moe. They argue that choice, which is the underlying mechanism in voucher plans, affects the motivations and performance of teachers, parents, and students, and can transform schools from indifferent providers of routine academic courses into communities that lead and develop students as whole people. As one of the authors of the present book has recently written, the argument for greater choice hinges on six propositions (Hill 1996):

- If all students have choices, schools will have to compete by offering clear and distinctive approaches to education.

- The need to keep promises made to parents fosters what the "effective schools" movement has worked so long to create, i.e., schools in which teachers and administrators are united by a common instructional mission, interdependent, and mutually accountable.

- Simply by choosing a school, parents convey an authority and legitimacy to the educational process that both motivates students and strengthens the school's ability to make demands.

- Schools of choice can influence students' attitudes, motivation, and effort in ways that other schools cannot.

- A chosen school is far more likely than a non-chosen school to be a community in which students learn by example how adults in the real world live and work together.

- Parents need not choose innovative or unusual schools for these advantages to apply. Nor do parents need to be able to find a school that they think is exactly right for their children. What matters is that parents consider the chosen school preferable to the available alternatives.

Contracting and site-based management can also provide for greater choice in education. What set Coons, Doyle, and Chubb and Moe apart was their emphasis on putting public funds in the hands of parents and on complete private control of schools. Chubb and Moe wanted more than choice among public agencies: they urged entrepreneurial freedom for private individuals and organizations to offer schooling in return for publicly paid tuition.

Chubb and Moe (1990) make a compelling case for removing schools from the dead hand of legislatures and government agencies. They envision a system completely divorced from public control. They write: "The schools' most fundamental problems are rooted in the institutions of democratic control by which they are governed; and despite all the talk about 'restructuring,' the current wave of grab-bag reforms leaves those institutions intact and in charge" (p. 216). They sketch out a publicly funded school system "that is almost entirely beyond the reach of public authority."

Under vouchers, a public school is any school that is eligible to accept students and receive public money, which it will collect from parents in the form of vouchers. By definition, any privately owned school that accepts public money becomes a public school. Schools would be licensed by the state, not the local district. Licensing criteria, according to Chubb and Moe, should be "quite minimal, roughly corresponding to the criteria many states now employ in accrediting private schools—graduation requirements, health and safety requirements, and teacher certification requirements. Any group or organization that applies to the state and meets the general criteria must be chartered as a public school, meaning it can accept students and public money." Local public education agencies could continue running schools, assuming that each school meets the basic criteria for a state license. Public education agencies would not, however, supervise the privately owned schools that operate in their localities.

Funding

The state would manage a "voucher office" in each district, which would distribute tuition funds directly to schools, based on the numbers of students enrolled and any "scholarship" factors that might apply. The state would pay to maintain the voucher office in each district. Local public education agencies might decide to stay in business, but they could not use any state or federal money to pay the costs of superintendents, central offices, or other trappings of bureaucratic control. Local public governance costs would be paid entirely out of revenue derived from the funds collected for students voluntarily attending publicly run schools.

Schools would collect public money only through voucher payments. The amount of money a school would collect for any one student would be determined by a number of factors, including the local average per pupil expenditure (derived from a combination of state core support and local add-on efforts) and "scholarship" allocations, reflecting students' special needs (e.g., low-income or minority status, handicaps, or language difficulties). State and local expenditures on schooling would presumably be set through political processes. Scholarship amounts for some students would also be affected by federal and state categorical programs that target funds to special populations.

Parents would be free to send their children to any state-licensed school. They would not, however, be free to gain admission to a school by offering personal donations above the voucher amount guaranteed by the state. No school that accepted public vouchers could demand extra payments from parents.

Schools would have a great deal of freedom in determining course content, schedules, and methods of instruction. They would be limited, as are private schools today, by state graduation requirements and competency testing standards. Grade schools would also be influenced by the admissions requirements of the high schools their students prefer, just as high schools today are influenced by college admissions requirements. But basic licensing would be the only constraint on institutional freedom. State and local education agencies could not try to influence curriculum and pedagogy by "back door" methods such as requiring particular staff development or teacher in-service training courses. There could be no universal requirements for such things as teacher career ladders, parent advisory committees, textbook selection, use of technology, or hours of homework.

School decisions about how courses are to be organized and taught, and instructional areas to be emphasized, would be driven by the market. Some schools might try to attract students with special curricula or other extracurricular or social climate features that might appeal to parents. Other schools might offer conventional instruction but try to distinguish themselves on grounds of high quality or rigorous instruction.

Teachers

The state would continue to certify teachers, but with minimum requirements—much like those historically used for private schools. This would widen the field from which potential teachers could be selected. Because schools would set their own teacher-hiring policies, the state would have no basis for requirements other than completion of a bachelor's degree from an accredited institution and evidence of good character.

Schools would recruit their own teachers and decide whom to hire. A school's overall staffing decisions would be constrained by income: the size and pay scale for teaching staff would be a function of the number of students admitted and the total income accumulated from student scholarships.

Teachers would be employed by individual schools. Schools would set their own pay scales and make decisions about teacher promotion, tenure, transfer rights, seniority preferences, and dismissal. The need to build the school's reputation by attracting and keeping a capable teaching staff would be the only real constraint on a school. Schools might offer merit pay plans, tenure, or other inducements to attract and hold good teachers. Teachers in a particular school (or in a network of schools) might organize for collective bargaining under private-sector labor laws. Public school systems might wish to maintain their current labor contracts, but those arrangements would not affect schools run by private organizations.

Schools would evaluate their own teachers, and make decisions on hiring, firing, retraining, and reassignment on the basis of each individual's contributions. Teachers would be evaluated in light of the school's particular mission and instructional strategy, not according to the more general criteria that now govern public school teacher evaluation.

Student and Parent Choice

A student would be free to attend any school in the state. The state might offer free transportation for students attending schools far from home, but it would have no obligation to do so. Student assignment would result from a mutual choice process—students choosing schools and schools choosing students. A school could establish minimum academic requirements and require student and parent commitments, e.g., to homework and volunteer work. It could also establish a minimum per pupil scholarship rate, thus favoring students with special needs or students from high-spending districts. The ablest students, and those who bring the highest tuition amounts, would presumably have a broader choice of schools than the less able or students from poorly funded districts.

To ensure that students and parents learn about and can pursue all school opportunities, the state would fund a parent information center in each district. This center would publish information on each school's mission, staff and course offerings, parent and student satisfaction, staff opinions, standardized test scores, and other data that would promote informed choice among parents and students. The center would also provide counseling for parents and children who want to explore alternatives, and would set up school visits and interviews for parents. The center would, in addition, manage the flow of applications to schools, to ensure that all applications are submitted at the same time and have an opportunity for fair review. It would also work directly with schools to place students whose parents could not decide on a particular school, or students who were not selected by the schools they initially chose.

Schools would make their own admissions decisions, subject only to nondiscrimination requirements. They would also be free to expel or suspend students (and to deny suspended students readmission) for cause. These actions must, however, be based on the school's experience with the child and its own needs as an organization, not on arbitrary or capricious motives.

Quality Control

Consumer choice would be the basic mechanism of quality control. Schools that gain negative reputations for any reason—poor instruction, low student outcomes, unpleasant social climate, arbitrary treatment of students, or poor labor-management relations—would risk losing current students and having fewer applications. Faced with the imminent possibility of operating at a loss, such schools must close or reform themselves. The state-run parent information center might discourage parents interested in particular schools, but it will not have the authority to close schools down or force specific remedial action.

Students finding themselves in failing schools or schools that did not meet their individual needs would be free to leave immediately. Any new school they chose would be paid their full voucher, prorated from the day of enrollment. The state-run parent information center might also help students find new schools if their first choice proved unacceptable or if it closed.

The state could hold schools accountable only for procedural requirements. It would ensure that each school meet the criteria spelled out in its license and obey nondiscrimination laws in admissions and other matters. Schools that did not operate as pledged could presumably be denied access to public funds. But although the state would gather and publish school outcomes data, it could not hold schools accountable for performance. In Chubb and Moe's words, "when it comes to performance, schools are held accountable from below, by parents and students who directly experience their services and are free to choose. The state plays a crucial supporting role here in monitoring the full and honest disclosure of information by the schools—but it is only a supporting role." The state may impose conditions for continuation of a school's license, but it may not intervene in a school's operation or require specific remedial actions.

Under vouchers, government agencies would have no responsibility for staffing, supervising, or guaranteeing quality control in the schools.

Market forces, and the self-interested initiative of people who own and staff the schools, are expected to ensure quality. Good schools would attract many students and make money. The best could not only sustain themselves but even expand or open new branches. Bad schools would attract few students and go broke.

Schools would be forced to attend to student needs and parent preferences rather than to the requirements of a centralized bureaucracy. Funding would be based on attendance, not on the placement preferences of senior teachers. Teachers and principals would have strong incentives to collaborate, press one another for good performance, weed out weak staff members, and work as hard as necessary to build their school's clientele. Teacher pay and job security would depend on contributions to school performance, not on longevity or accumulation of credits and degrees.

Schools would compete for students and, in doing so, they would be forced to differentiate their programs and products, both in quality and type. Some schools might try to be excellent in a safe, conventional way, while others would provide innovative services or appeal to particular tastes in subject matter or pedagogy. Product differentiation would help parents and students anticipate what to expect from a school. They would know whether they were likely to enjoy it and be willing to do the work it requires. They would also have little trouble knowing whether the school had kept its promises. Accountability would therefore be direct and immediate: Schools that delivered would keep their students; those that did not would be abandoned.

Problems with Vouchers

Vouchers offer a potentially strong remedy for educational failure: parents can withdraw their children from a failing school instantly and enroll them elsewhere. The value of this remedy depends on the availability of genuine choices.

The problems of vouchers derive directly from their strengths. Voucher plans expressly exclude public authorities from interfering with school operations or parental choices. That protects schools from the burdens of over-regulation, and it allows educators to implement innovative ideas without seeking sign-offs from cautious overseers. Vouchers also allow parents who have distinctive views about what and how their children need to learn can seek alternatives that publicly run systems might not offer.

The complete absence of public oversight can also be a liability for vouchers. A pure demand-side strategy privatizes all decisions about what schools will be offered and what schools students will attend. It either denies the importance of broader community standards for what students will learn, or it assumes that private decisions by school operators and parents will somehow automatically take account of those standards. It also assumes that schools will naturally adapt their programs to take advantage of new advances in educational methods and technology and to prepare students to meet newly emerging demands of the economy.

These assumptions challenge the justifications normally given for compulsory attendance and public investment in K–12 education. State laws requiring students to attend school exist because it is feared that some parents might not appreciate the value of education or might emphasize children's short-term earning potential over their long-term opportunities. States fund public education for a related reason—the fear that some parents would not willingly invest enough in their own children's education or that lower-income parents could not invest enough, whatever their preferences. States also develop standards and policies for public education on the assumption that local parents, educators, and community leaders might not fully understand the challenges that students will encounter in jobs and higher education.

Voucher plans do not privatize all educational decisions. They maintain the principle of compulsory attendance in some sort of school and guarantee continued state investment in K–12 education. They also create incentives for schools to compete on quality and to validate their performance by demonstrating that their graduates succeed in later life. But pure demand-side strategies take the state out of the business of guaranteeing an adequate supply of schools, protecting children against foolish parental choices, and changing standards to fit evolving needs.

Supply of Schools. Voucher plans assume that entrepreneurs, drawn by the possibility of income from tuition payments, would offer to run schools. But it is not clear where a large supply of privately run schools is to come from. Giving public school students access to the existing private and parochial school systems will not solve the supply problem. Even in New York City, where Catholic schools educate over 100,000 students and constitute what is, in effect, the twelfth largest school system in the country, there is no room for a million public school students, or even one-quarter of that number. Few other cities or states have that large a supply of privately run schools. During the 1993 debate over the California vouchers initiative, a survey of existing private schools indicated that they would be able, even with dramatic expansion of some facilities and staffs, to serve only 4 percent of the current public school population.

Starting a school is not cheap or easy. Aside from the capital costs of school buildings and equipment, the requirements of curriculum development, staff selection and training, and quality control are imposing. The Edison Project spent three years and tens of millions of dollars designing curricula and staffing and management plans for a new kind of school. Edison hopes to recoup its investment by opening a large number of schools, but the front-end costs are enormous. More evidence of the high front-end costs of new schools comes from the experience of charter schools. In Minnesota, Massachusetts, Colorado, California, and Arizona, groups of highly motivated parents and educators are experiencing great difficulty creating the shared vision and organizational arrangements necessary to start a charter school.

The strength of the supply response to vouchers might not be a serious problem in suburban and small-city school systems. Many such systems have essentially sound public schools that might prosper if they became independent. However, big cities might have a different problem. They have few schools that would be considered good, even by the standards of suburban and small-city public schools. Many more big-city schools are failures by any standard. Some big-city systems already have a form of choice in open enrollment policies that allow students to enroll in any school with room for them. Choice, however, in terms of demand for better schools has little meaning in the absence of a supply response. The demand for better schools has been apparent in big cities for a long time. But there is little evidence that the supply of good schools has increased at all. New York City's open enrollment policy is rendered virtually meaningless by the fact that the nonselective magnet schools to which all students may apply get ten to thirty applications for every seat. The majority of students who try to choose a school other than the one in their neighborhood end up back in the school they tried to flee.

The rigors of urban education are likely to discourage entrepreneurs. What profit-seeking entrepreneur could be confident of staying solvent running a school in an area burdened by violence, strikes, ill health, and family instability? What investor would choose to build a school in a core urban area when he might collect a similar amount per pupil in a far less stressed suburb?

Though many of the most insistent critiques of vouchers are stated in terms of equity and civil rights, they all reflect a concern for the supply problem. The fears that good schools will discriminate against the poor, and that children whose parents are not aggressive consumers will be consigned to the worst schools, are not figments of the public imagination.

Schools seeking to establish sterling reputations might well discriminate on admissions, grading, and teacher hiring, all to make themselves as attractive as possible to the middle class. Under demand subsidy, no administrative agency would exist to disbar a school that suffers a scandal or to force quick action to remedy a problem. The result is that scandals of discrimination or malpractice will end up in the newspapers, courts, or legislative hearing rooms.

Should the facts bear out any of the fears outlined above, a voucher program could be short-lived. Lawsuits based on unequal distribution of publicly funded benefits could lead to the imposition of new regimes of regulation. It is not far-fetched to think that schools accepting public funds would come under court-ordered regulation of their admissions, expulsion, grading, promotion, curricula, and teacher hiring and compensation. Chubb and Moe (1990) admit that a demand subsidy system entails these risks. They call for limited public regulation and oversight, including licensing of schools, to protect students and to avoid devastating scandals.

Parental Choices. Total reliance on parental judgment is a second liability of a pure demand-side strategy. Though most parents have strong incentives to make thoughtful choices for their children, some might be careless and some might misplace their confidence in schools that serve their children poorly. These parents, if they exist, might or might not prove to be less well educated and have lower incomes than average: as research on private voucher programs shows, when low-income parents have choices to make, most are highly attentive and demanding. John Coons (1978) is probably right in saying that the fear that parents will make poor choices for their children is far less well founded than the fear that bureaucrats will do so.

There are, however, examples of parent groups organizing to oppose district efforts to close or restaff schools that have consistently failed to teach students basic skills or prepare them for college. Long habits of collaboration with teachers or principals can, in some cases, encourage parents to place their trust where it is not warranted. Recognizing this problem, Chubb and Moe (1990) suggest that local public authorities provide student outcome information on the performance of all schools accepting publicly funded vouchers. Such a remedy might, as intended, drive wedges between low-performing schools and parents. However, it is unlikely to prevent newspapers and interest groups from demanding that public officials intervene in the operation of low-performing schools.

Standards. Rigorously implemented, a voucher plan would eliminate key roles now played by state boards of education, i.e., monitoring changes in society and making investments to ensure that public schools prepare students for the future. State boards now conduct studies and hold public forums to discuss such issues, and they try to create remedies in the form of statewide mandates and assistance efforts.

Voucher plans such as Chubb and Moe's do not provide for such state-level analyses and remedies. In their purest form, voucher plans would leave these functions to the market—schools might compete by providing compelling visions of what children will need to know in the future and by showing how their curricula match those needs. Think tanks, university-based policy analysts, and newspapers might also analyze the offerings of a state or district's schools according to alternative visions of future needs. There could be no guarantee, however, that schools or parents would pay attention to such independent analyses. State governments might seize the opportunity provided by their residual public information function to formulate school goals and student achievement standards. But the state's analysis and recommendations, like those of private parties, would have only persuasive authority.

Whether the absence of an authoritative state is a problem or a virtue depends on whether one believes states can perform such functions accurately or effectively. Few state boards of education have succeeded in articulating influential visions for the future of their schools, and many local school systems and schools safely ignore much of state policy. However, systemic reform programs in many states are creating more rigorous and credible standard-setting processes, particularly in less controversial areas such as reading, science, and mathematics. A pure demand-side voucher plan would dispense with state-standards programs, and thus lose any value they might have in setting student-outcome goals and providing frameworks for comparison of school outcomes.

A Supply-Side Strategy: Site-Based Management

Many school superintendents and teacher union leaders have supported site-based management, an effort to loosen the strings on schools through administrative action. Site-based management, in effect, maintains the vertically integrated character of the pubic school system but attempts to create more resource control and decision-making independence at the school-site level.

Site-based management (SBM) and shared decision-making (SDM) were the education community's response to the decentralization movement in American business. In the mid-1980s, businesses believed they were losing out to more flexible and innovative Japanese companies, which could produce high-quality products quickly in response to consumer demand. Businesses imitated Japanese management techniques, including increased worker control over some aspects of the production process and quality circles in which coworkers discussed possible product improvements. They also imitated some aspects of Japanese corporate structure which, relative to U.S. businesses in comparable industries, featured smaller corporate central offices, more reliance on subcontractors, and more modest investments in stockpiles of parts.

Following the lead of business, many educational policy makers proposed similar reforms for public school systems. The Florida legislature authorized SBM and gave local school boards new waiver authorities. School superintendents in Dade County (Florida), Rochester (New York), and Louisville (Kentucky), among others, led local movements for site-based management. Again in imitation of industrial practice, the Dade and Rochester superintendents sought to involve union leaders as partners in increasing school staffs' freedom to innovate. Unions understood the new movement as an opportunity for greater teacher influence at all levels of the school system. At their leaders' urging, shared decision-making, meaning the use of formal decision-making processes in which teachers and principals bargained as equals, was soon paired with site-based management.

By permitting teachers and principals to make their own instructional decisions, SBM/SDM was expected to promote new creativity and improve the morale of teachers. Though it was expected ultimately to lead to improvements in instruction and student achievement, the effects of SBM/SDM were expected to be evident first in teacher morale and retention and, in teacher shortage areas like Miami, in the number of people seeking teaching jobs.

Some SBM initiatives create opportunities for increased school-level freedom of action without prescribing the processes by which decisions must be made. These initiatives can strengthen the principal's role as the school CEO without necessarily increasing teachers' or parents' roles in decision-making. In most localities, however, SBM is paired with provisions for shared decision-making, which require specific decision-making processes intended to "empower" teachers or parents, or both, relative to the school principal.

Funding

Site-managed schools are usually funded under existing school district allocation methods. Though pilot schools in early SBM/SDM efforts were offered small start-up grants for staff planning time, funds were still controlled by the district central office, and the assets bought with those funds were allocated to schools according to formulas and teacher contract provisions. Some SBM/SDM schools attracted foundation grants, and some local school boards discussed the possibility of giving schools lump-sum funding, but only one district in the country, Moses Lake Washington, ever allocated more than a fifth of its funds directly to schools.

Teachers

Site-managed schools were expected to work with the teachers they already had. Some districts (e.g., San Diego and Salt Lake City) allowed teachers and principals to select new teachers when vacancies occurred but did not give SBM/SDM schools any new powers to fire or discipline incumbent teachers. The teacher union in Dade County did agree to work with the superintendent's staff to review schools that were experiencing principal-teacher conflicts over roles and powers in shared decision-making, and the union waived contractual provisions to allow some involuntary teacher transfers.

The Cincinnati teachers union proposed a new labor/management process for review and retraining of low-performing teachers, which led to a modest number of teacher reassignments and firings. But centralized teacher contracts and allocation processes remained intact under SBM/SDM.

Student and Parent Choice

Site-managed schools were expected to draw students by the same processes as traditionally run schools. Schools that served geographic areas before SBM/SDM continued to do so, and magnet schools continued to attract students in the same ways. Some site-managed schools adopted new instructional approaches and petitioned for magnet status, and some asked for relief from student busing processes, but most continued to serve the same student groups.

Parent groups demanded to be included in shared decision-making. School systems that were among the first to adopt SBM/SDM adopted some new requirements for parental involvement in school planning and decision-making. School systems that initiated site-based management in the late 1980s and early 1990s made more explicit and ambitious provisions for parental involvement. Chicago's reform law created a very strong place for parents and community members, who were to constitute a majority of the school site councils. These councils had little control of funds or teacher staffing, but they could and did hire and fire principals.

Quality Control

Some school system central offices were to evaluate site-managed schools just as they evaluated regular schools. In Miami, however, the central evaluation unit conducted a special three-year assessment of the first twenty-five schools to try SBM/SDM. The results were mixed, showing a small average improvement (and great variability) in teacher morale and other school-climate measures, and no consistent change in student achievement. Other evaluations produced similarly modest results.

Most school systems adopting SBM/SDM expected to assess student outcomes and to offer staff development assistance or to replace key staff in failing schools. The Louisville superintendent offered to pay independent assistance organizations to help troubled schools, and a Kentucky statewide reform law promised to pay for staff development and put especially troubled schools under the guidance of "distinguished Kentucky educators."

Few school systems were able to provide much help to schools shown to be performing poorly under site-based management. But disappointing evaluation results strengthened the hands of skeptical school board members and central-office administrators. Site management plans were curtailed in Columbus (Ohio), and Los Angeles, and SBM/SDM pilot schools in Dade County came under increasingly strong regulation from the central office. Site-based management advocates in some communities were able to build special school-assistance organizations that operated independently of the central office. Louisville and Cincinnati set up private, independent teacher-training centers with mixtures of private and public funds, and teacher unions set up their own SBM/SDM-oriented education renewal centers in New York, Miami, and Chicago.

Problems with Site-Based Management

Efforts to improve education through marginal changes in governance are attractive to people with stakes in the current system. However, because such marginal changes leave intact the mandates, civil service system, and labor contracts that constrain schools, they have produced little in the way of school-site initiative and accountability. Superintendents have proven unable to keep their own assistant and associate superintendents from imposing new restrictions on schools; school boards have been unable to resist solving problems with new mandates; school district financial officers cannot find ways to create school-site lump sum budgets; and teacher unions that will permit school-level decisions on filling staff vacancies cannot agree to site-level teacher evaluation, salary determination, or firing (see Hill and Bonan 1991; Malen et al. 1990; Murphy and Beck 1995). Even in Chicago, where site-based management is backed up by locally elected school-site councils with the authority to fire the principal and request regulatory waivers, far fewer than half the schools have been able to make significant changes in staffing, staff training, or instructional methods.

SBM/SDM is the educational establishment's effort to accommodate the general trend toward reduction of bureaucratic controls on activities that require discretion and judgment. Superintendents and school boards from cities as distant as Miami and Los Angeles, and as unlike as Prince William County, Virginia, and Bellevue, Washington, have all tried it in some form. In virtually all cases, SBM/SDM is carefully hedged to avoid threatening or upsetting major actors in the current education system. The basic functions of school boards and central offices are left alone. Teacher-union contracts, state and federal program regulations, and other mandates are left intact. Senior teachers still have the right to teach in whatever school they choose, and schools must still get their supplies, equipment, and repairs from central-office units. School evaluation is still done by a central-office unit whose measures and methods were designed for a uniform school system, not one in which schools are expected to use diverse instructional approaches.

When they were first proposed, SBM/SDM plans looked like they might encourage school innovation. Schools participating in SBM programs were urged to reassess their own performance and consider alternative ways of serving their students. School staffs were urged to suggest how district-controlled staff development programs might serve them better, and many were allowed to select new teachers when vacancies occurred. Schools often got small amounts of money (seldom more than $10,000) to pay for extra teacher-planning time and were occasionally able to keep and reallocate savings from energy conservation and reduced use of substitutes. School staffs were promised a hearing if they proposed waivers from state or local regulations or, on occasion, from teacher-union contract provisions.

In practice, however, these new freedoms proved less significant than they appeared.[5] School boards and associate and assistant superintendents

---

5. Sources for this and other criticisms of site-based management include: Malen and Ogawa (1988), Malen (1990), Hill and Bonan (1991), Wohlstetter (1995), Wohlstetter and Odden (1992), Murphy and Beck (1995), Mohrman and Wohlstetter (1994), Hannaway and Carnoy (1993), and Bimber (1991).

remained in control, and many schools found their freedoms short-lived. Schools in Dade County were discouraged from requesting waivers affecting bilingual education programs, an area where a strong central-office faction was opposed to change. District staff development units in many cities explained that they had to serve the most numerous schools, not just the privileged ones in the site-based management programs. School boards that had promised schools freedom from mandates continued to issue new policies in response to new problems, and principals in SBM schools soon reported that their promised freedoms were eroding daily. SBM schools were required to take their fair share of tenured teachers who were at loose ends after being pushed out of their former schools. Supplies and repairs were hard to get and slow in coming. Perhaps most importantly, school boards that had endorsed decentralization while under the leadership of SBM advocates like Joseph Fernandez often went back to their old ways when new superintendents took office.

Some teachers and principals seized the opportunity to transform their schools. But many more recognized SBM as yet another short-lived initiative, and continued to act as if the prior centralized governance structure was the permanent one. Many adopted the forms of SBM/SDM, creating school-site councils and building school-wide improvement plans, but did not make substantial changes in curriculum or teaching techniques.

Site-based management has failed to bring about the hoped-for increase in school staff initiative for two reasons: first, it did not make a profound enough change in district management to convince teachers and principals that it was here to stay. In many cases, the schools that most readily adopted the forms of SBM/SDM did so expressly in order to comply with the wishes of higher-ups, not to seize real control of their own affairs. Second, SBM/SDM plans did not include the incentives and assistance necessary to guarantee that teachers, principals, and parents would focus their attention on the quality of instruction and other services to children. Teachers and principals who chose business as usual lost nothing. Those who took initiatives accepted the risks that their actions would be reversed and they might be punished when the old regime returned to power.

As is now evident, a decentralization plan means little unless it includes a way of changing the incentives under which teachers, principals, administrators, and board members work. Behaviors will not change unless poor performance is penalized and different behaviors are rewarded. If school staffs are supposed to take initiative and responsibility, there must be strong rewards for those who do and penalties for those who do not, and the same must be true for administrators, who must be faced with the choice between helping and getting out of the way. Organizations whose very purpose is contrary to decentralization inevitably interfere with it. Because site-based management plans were initiated from within the educational establishment as a primarily defensive measure, they did not and could not be bold and fundamental enough.

Another Supply-Side Strategy: Systemic Reform

Systemic reformers compare the existing public school system to a business firm that has been poorly managed and needs to rationalize and integrate its parts. Its advocates say there is nothing inherently wrong with a public education system that is controlled by policy-making boards and administered by a traditional bureaucracy: today's problems can be solved by re-engineering the system so its parts are correctly aligned.

Perhaps the most influential proponent of the systemic reform concept is David Hornbeck, who formulated a strategy for statewide governance reform in Kentucky, based on the concept of a rationally linked system of statewide goals, performance standards, examinations, and rewards and penalties for students and schools. Other important contributors to the concept are Marshall S. Smith and Jennifer O'Day of the Stanford University School of Education, advocates of "systemic school reform," which would re-engineer all parts of a state's education system to support a new statewide curriculum.[6]

Hornbeck begins with statewide goals and deduces what is needed in curriculum, measurement, and accountability. Smith and O'Day take a statewide curriculum framework as their foundation and induce a system of governance and technical assistance to ensure its implementation. Despite different points of origin, however, Hornbeck and Smith and O'Day come to very similar conclusions. Both assume that low school performance is caused by the diversity of goals, means, and constraints that have emerged from multicentric political and administrative processes. They assert that a more definitive set of goals, whether stated in terms of student outcomes or curriculum content, is the starting point for education reform. Once the goals are sharply defined, the other elements of the governance system can be aligned with them.

Systemic reform would not change the current definition of a public school as a school operated by a local public education agency. It contem-

---

6. In 1993, Smith was appointed undersecretary for the U.S. Department of Education in the Clinton Administration.

plates the continuation of a system of schools managed and staffed by civil servants working under the supervision of elected state and local boards of education.

Funding

Systemic reform advocates do not directly address the issue of funding. Aligned systems assume that schools receive their money, teachers, and other key assets from the state or local education agency, as they do now. The idea of increasing school-level initiative by allocating budgets as lump-sum cash amounts (rather than as packages of predesignated people, services, and equipment) is not incompatible with alignment, but it is not an explicit part of the systemic reform proposals.

Systemic reform advocates generally steer clear of the fiscal equality arguments advanced by school finance litigators. They focus instead on equality in provision of specific services. They prefer to set standards for equality of services and facilities, called delivery standards, to ensure that all students get access to (in the words of the Chapter I Commission), "pre-school programs, reasonable class sizes, and teachers who are experienced and working in the areas in which they received training."

Smith and O'Day write approvingly of national groups that have recommended "school delivery standards . . . that include inputs as well as outcomes and that would . . . establish criteria for determining under what conditions students might legitimately be held accountable for their performance." These standards would "provide operational specifications for assessing whether a school is giving its students the opportunity to learn."

A re-engineered system would be driven by a clear and demanding vision of what students should know. In practical terms, this means that content and student mastery standards for any discipline are set by experts—academic and intellectual leaders in the field, successful teachers, and business and professional people who know what graduates need to know in order to work for them.

At present there is no complete, definitive set of such standards, but groups at the state and national levels are working to create them. The one universally admired set of content and performance standards is the high school mathematics standards set by the National Conference of Teachers of Mathematics (NCTM). NCTM's ambitious efforts to define a national curriculum framework are now being imitated, equally ambitiously, by professional groups in the natural sciences, social studies, music, and English.

Once standards are established by professional organizations, they will be translated into curriculum frameworks, specifying what students at different grade levels should know and suggesting how related materials can be taught together. The actual textbooks and instructional materials are not to be developed by any authoritative group: materials will be left to publishers, school designers, and to school staffs themselves.

Teachers

Systemic reform implies no changes in the school staffing practices of the existing system. Local public school agencies will hire teachers from a registry of certified teachers, and will base pay and job rights on master contracts negotiated with local unions. Supporters of systemic reform do, however, worry about whether today's teachers can deliver the new, more demanding curriculum. Teacher training, therefore, is the central method by which new standards and curricula are to be introduced into schools. Teachers are to be trained, both in schools of education and during inservice efforts, to follow the mandated curriculum frameworks. Training programs in schools of education would be changed in two ways: First, the state legislature, as part of its endorsement of instructional goals, performance standards, and curriculum frameworks, would require state-supported teacher training programs to bring their programs and methods into line. Second, teacher examinations and certification procedures—hurdles that stand between a teacher's graduation from a school of education and entry into a teaching job—would be made more rigorous and aligned more closely with the curriculum frameworks. At least two national organizations are working to create standards, examinations, and methods of teacher evaluation for states to use in certifying teachers.

Student Assignment

Systemic reform would not change the basic methods now in place to assign students to schools. Though most students would presumably attend schools on the basis of geographic proximity, nothing would rule out the use of magnet or special-purpose schools, either to meet demands for special instructional programs or to desegregate school districts.

Systemic reform does not rule out student choice among schools, but it does establish explicit pressures—in the form of general standards, aggressive state monitoring, and teacher training—likely to make schools more uniform, not more diverse. Though some schools would undoubtedly try to run special programs and set themselves apart, the vast majority are unlikely to differ enough to make much of a difference in terms of creating a great demand for student mobility.

The lone exception to the norm of geographic-zone assignment of students occurs when individual schools consistently fail to meet standards for service delivery or student outcomes. As Hornbeck's Chapter I Commission report specifies, when the state determines that a school has consistently failed its students and has not improved despite receiving assistance from the state, its students should be free to enroll elsewhere. Student funding will follow individuals to new schools, and the former school's budget will be reduced accordingly.

Quality Control

The primary strategy for guaranteeing quality is maintenance of high standards for inputs. If curriculum, teacher training, and service delivery are all governed by consistent high standards, proponents reason, school failure should be rare. High levels of spending on teacher in-service training and technical assistance should also maintain school quality and prevent failures. Hornbeck's recommendations for the reauthorization of Chapter I, and the several state reform strategies built on his ideas, set aside major parts of state and federal education program budgets for teacher training and for school staff planning time. Recognizing that investment in continuous quality improvement is often halted by budget crises, these reforms try to segment the state budget to guarantee a steady rate of investment in quality assurance.

The use of student testing programs linked to curriculum frameworks is expected to contribute to quality assurance in three ways: first, these programs put school staffs on notice about what is expected of them; second, they give parents the information they need to press school staffs and school boards for improvements in particular schools; and third, they help target state quality reviews and possible interventions in failing schools.

Smith and O'Day also propose that states and local systems support informal networks of teachers to break the traditional isolation of schools from each other and encourage professionals to share their experiences about how best to implement new curriculum frameworks. They also suggest routine on-site monitoring of schools by teams of experienced teachers drawn from other districts, and a professional inspectorate staffed by experts who can both judge schools and provide technical assistance.

Systemic reform supporters generally advocate establishment of local training and technical assistance centers to which schools can turn voluntarily for help. Funded by special government or foundation grants, such centers are expected to respond to school requests for tailor-made staff training and technical assistance. This arrangement frees schools from the pressures associated with training provided by the school system's central office, which may not correspond to schools' peculiar needs but must be accepted whether the school wants it or not. The arrangement also fosters some sense of school initiative and independence in a system that is otherwise highly regulated.

A rigorously aligned system of standards, curriculum, and testing will allow state and local authorities to identify failing schools promptly. States will also have a repertoire of rewards, assistance, and sanctions that they can use in improving failing schools and protecting children.

School staffs will also be closely monitored. Student testing is to be frequent, exhaustive, and closely aligned with instructional goals and the curriculum frameworks. State officials should, therefore, be able to identify any school's strengths and deficiencies. Parents can also peruse school outcomes reports and insist that school staff members make improvements.

Schools whose students are failing their performance examinations can be quickly identified and investigated. The first step, presumably taken by the state government, will be to determine whether the school meets service delivery standards and to supply whatever is needed—funding, advice, training, staff supplements—necessary to bring the school up to standard. Schools that failed despite meeting (or being brought up to) the delivery standards would be candidates for more drastic action, possibly, in Smith and O'Day's words, involving efforts "to reconstitute the school—i.e., replace all the instructional staff including the principal, and engage a new faculty with the responsibility for bringing the school up to standards." The Texas state accountability program includes similar provisions.

Hornbeck advocates nearly identical measures but also calls for state-mandated remedial assistance for schools in trouble. Schools failing to meet performance and delivery standards must seek the advice of organizations specializing in school improvement (e.g., Larry Lezotte's Effective Schools organization). In the Kentucky state reform, failing schools must seek and follow the advice of a distinguished educator. Schools that fail despite this assistance may be restaffed and redeveloped, and their students are free to enroll elsewhere at the expense of the local school district. These provisions presumably supersede teacher job rights established by contract. Some systemic reform proposals also put a remedy in the hands of individual parents. Parents who believe their child's school did not meet the delivery standards would have standing to sue in federal court. The courts would have the authority to mandate appropriate remedial placement for the child and to order improvements in the school and in the district policies deemed responsible for school failure. Though this method of protecting children is subject to great delays in particular cases, it is intended to help children by sensitizing school staffs to the risks of ignoring performance and outcome standards.

Hornbeck and Smith and O'Day favor school site-based management. They expect systemic reform to focus, but not control, the efforts of local teachers and school administrators. To paraphrase Hornbeck, a system aligned according to student outcome standards specifies ends, not means. Successful schools today use a wide range of methods, and there is no reason to think that will not be true in the future. To paraphrase Smith and O'Day, a curriculum framework and associated teacher-training and testing help set priorities among the things that might be taught but does not ordain one as the best.

Though systemic reform is a simple idea, its implementation can be complex. It is accomplished in part by training and socialization of teachers, ensuring that their knowledge and professional values are consistent with the idea of a rich and challenging curriculum. It is also accomplished in part by enforcement, ensuring that poorly performing schools are readily identified, and that the state has the leverage to change a school that is not operating under standards set by, respectively, student outcome goals or the basic curriculum frameworks.

Problems with Systemic Reform

Systemic reform sustains current governance arrangements that treat the school as the lowest-level unit in a large hierarchical organization. The hierarchy of goals, standards, curriculum frameworks, and tests is intended to inform local professionals about what must be accomplished and to guide individual schools in setting improvement priorities. The school is governed by rules and standards, and is a franchise of the system's central office, not an enterprise of the teachers and administrators in it.

Systemic reform motivates school staff effort by improving the specification of goals and creating outcome measures that are harder to fake. It also tries to unify schools by creating overarching curriculum frameworks and by aligning pre-service and in-service teacher training to the basic curriculum frameworks.

The standards and curriculum frameworks are not supposed to be so specific that all schools become alike. However, as some participants in the standard-setting processes have commented, the competition for "air time" among different disciplinary groups and subject matter specialists can lead to a very full curriculum with little flexibility left for the schools. "Think about it," said the Business Roundtable's Christopher T. Cross (now president of the Council for Basic Education) in the April 21, 1993, issue of *Education Week*, "As standards in each of the disciplines are published, reality will hit. . . . teachers now have a hard time getting through the material they are expected to cover." He concluded, tongue in cheek, "One can imagine the theoretical school day growing to about 18 hours and the school year to about 500 days!" As vocational education administrators found, raising content and course completion standards in one subject area (e.g., college preparatory English or mathematics) can reduce the time available for other subjects.

Systemic reform is, moreover, unlikely to encourage a great deal more responsibility and problem solving at the school level. Uniformity of training for teachers and principals might lead to greater integration of effort within schools, but schools will still be driven by the need to comply with mandates created elsewhere. The main premise of an alignment-based system is that schools will adhere to fixed curriculum frameworks and will prepare students to pass examinations written to reflect national goals and standards. Although, in theory, there may be room for instructional innovation, schools whose students have trouble passing key state and national examinations and obtaining proposed "certificates of initial mastery" will have little choice but to concentrate on the materials covered by the examinations. Indeed, as Koretz has shown (1992), teaching to the test always narrows the range of what is taught, even if the tests cover important materials. Schools confident of their students' ability to pass high-stakes tests can afford to spend time on information, issues, topics, and themes they consider important, whether or not they are part of the test. Other schools do not enjoy that freedom.

Civil rights organizations and groups concerned with the education of disadvantaged students objected to the testing and certification required by a standards-based system, pointing out that all students will be held accountable for identical performance standards regardless of the quality of education they receive. Students in low-income areas and low-quality school systems, they argued, will have less opportunity to learn what is required to pass the tests and will suffer when test scores are used to control access to jobs and higher education. Service or delivery standards have been proposed as the solution to this problem. If all schools are required to deliver instruction that meets the same minimum standards (stated in terms of the methods and levels of instruction, student exposure to factual material, and practices using higher-order analytical skills) all students should have equal chances of passing high-stakes examinations and obtaining "gateway" certificates that lead to valuable opportunities.

Delivery standards will inevitably direct teachers' and administrators' attention to compliance issues. Schools whose students are in danger of failing key examinations will be forced to prepare a defense, and the only sure defense is the traditional one: compliance, i.e., our instructional services meet the standards, and if students fail, it is not our fault. The pressure for compliance behavior is likely to be intensified by any legal provision that would allow parents to enforce delivery standards by suing in federal court. Courts would, therefore, be asked to rule on which services met which standards, and on what exceptions to the norm were impermissible. State education agencies and enforcement units like the U.S. Department of Education's Office for Civil Rights would inevitably adopt court-developed standards as the basis for their own actions. Such a development might make good law, but it is hardly likely to lead to good educational practice. School staffs anxious to avoid litigation or administrative penalties would be handed the strongest possible incentive to follow what had been blessed in adversarial judicial processes and to make sure their services passed legal muster. (See Hill and Madey [1982], for a discussion of similar processes occasioned by judicial decisions under the Education for All Handicapped Children Act.) There may be quicker ways to strangle school initiative in the cradle than formal adjudication of students' rights to particular services, but if there are, they have not surfaced yet.

No one can be against clearer and more articulate goals and standards and a serious commitment to ensuring that all students get an education that can prepare them for the modern world. Taken in conjunction with genuine institutional changes, new goals, standards, and curricula could lead to real improvements in the performance of many schools. But grafted onto the current system of governance—as is now proposed—systemic reform further centralizes control of schools in the hands of state officials and courts. It is a step backward.

Systemic reform does not, in the words of Chubb and Moe, "attack the institutional causes at the root of the problem." Taken to its extremes, as in current proposals to reform the federal Title I program and to redefine the federal role in education, systemic reform includes tightly enforced service-delivery standards and legal determinations about individual entitlements to particular kinds of educational services. These governance features are incompatible with the core goal of governance reform, i.e., encouraging initiative—taking and responsible schools.

Systemic reform leaves many elements of the existing system intact (i.e., rule-making on all matters concerning schooling by school boards, other legislative bodies and courts, and detailed inspection and compliance processes administered by permanent school system bureaucracies). It depends on a framework of goals and related curricula that translate official objectives and performance standards into guides for classroom practice. To be a system-wide reform, such a framework must be universally applicable. It must also be specific enough to guide all schools to pursue the official objectives and work to attain the standards. The curriculum framework is, therefore, official public policy and so must be sanctioned by high-level elected officials.

The curriculum framework need not be set in stone for all time: the legislature will almost certainly permit refinements to reflect new developments in science and other branches of scholarship. But it will always be subject to definition in the legislative process. The conflicts about curriculum that now fracture communities can still rage. State legislatures will still be called on to resolve issues about the teaching of scientific principles that some think deny the existence of God, or to blunt the curriculum's treatment of such issues as ethics, birth control, multiculturalism, or acceptance of alternative lifestyles. The fact that the curriculum framework is uniform and mandatory means that issues about it will inevitably become politicized. The framework is, in a sense, an official mandate. Even if its design is delegated to groups of specialists working with the public and educators in an effort to frame consensus, its authority will ultimately depend on legislative action.

Faced with the demand either to mandate or forbid teaching of some set of ideas, legislatures will be forced to choose between burdening schools with many requirements or finding verbal compromises that eliminate controversy by creating ambiguity. Legislative negotiations produced today's fractionated and misaligned public school system. Schools operating under an official curriculum framework may be able to define specific missions and take distinctive stances in the beginning. Sooner or later, however, political pressures are likely to erode the curriculum framework, and the forces that now dominate public education governance will soon return it to its current form.

Systemic reform begs the question of how the political forces leading to fractionation are to be controlled. Smith and O'Day, for example, show how "a common vision and set of curriculum frameworks establish the basis in systemic curriculum reform for aligning all parts of a state instructional system," but do not show how that common vision will be created or stabilized in the face of diverse public ideologies, aspirations, and interests. Brandon (1993), writing of the difficulty of maintaining such a system, notes that "each component presents . . . a moving target. . . . While a small group of reform leaders or coordinators will be examining the changes and interrelationships among all these moving components, most policies in each area will be determined by active and committed individuals whose attention is focused on one part of the picture. While they may be aware of the overall educational policy context in which they operate, it is difficult to conceive of a workable centralized process which would keep them all working within a coherent set of time-frames and limited missions."

Systemic reform presumes a consensus on what is to be taught, something Americans have not reached and are unlikely to reach soon. It is desirable to remove inconsistencies based on accident or habit rather than carefully worked-out settlements of political disputes. But the consensus for a fully standardized, rationalized, and coherent educational system is not likely to arise, and, as Brandon writes, "If there is no consensus there is no reform."

Charter Schools: A Mixed Supply and Demand Strategy

Charter school statutes now in force in nearly half the states offer private persons the power to control decisions about an individual public school's educational program.[7] In return, charter school operators accept an obligation to deliver a specified program of instruction and remain accountable to state government as an institution carrying out a public trust.

Charter schools laws vary dramatically from one state to another. Some legislatures clearly intended charter schools to be only incrementally different from other schools operating under waivers of a few rules, while others apparently hoped to create a set of fully autonomous schools that could compete with, and possibly force changes in, the existing public school system. Some state charter school statutes make local school boards, which often oppose charter schools, the sole government agency authorized to grant charters; others allow a variety of state institutions to grant charters, including state colleges and universities and specially constituted state agencies. Some laws give charter-authorizing agencies extremely broad discretion in the decision to grant a charter; others strictly

---

7. For detailed discussions of these issues, see Millot (1994, 1995a, 1995b).

limit the scope of charter schools' autonomy, limit the term of the charter to only one or two years, put a cap on the number of charter schools allowed in the state or any school district, limit the charter school operators' authority to hire and fire staff, require that charter school personnel be members of the local district teachers' union bargaining unit, and guarantee charter schools substantially less than the full per capita costs of educating a public school student. The idea of accountability to government is also compromised in some state charter school statutes that fail to include a requirement that definite student performance standards be established in each charter.

Charter school supporters hope that successful charter schools will influence other public schools and force changes in operation of local public school systems, by:

- Creating demand for ever-increasing numbers of charter schools

- Providing examples of innovative instructional practices and resource use that other schools might imitate.

- Creating competition for students that might force existing public schools to become more innovative and flexible.

- Creating a cash drain from local public school systems that will force reductions in central-office functions and a movement toward real-dollar per pupil funding for all schools, forcing, in the long run, a movement toward an all-charters public school system.

As a result of the differences in state and local programs, charter schools differ. Millot (1995a) and Bierlein and Mulholland (1993) have analyzed the differences among charter school programs. Some charters are existing public schools that have adopted new instructional themes or methods but still employ the same staff members, serve the same students, and occupy the same buildings. Others are brand-new schools developed from scratch to deliver a particular instructional program and serve only those students who choose to attend. Some charters follow the same rules as all other public schools, except for specific and very limited waivers. Others have almost total freedom from state and local regulations and union contract provisions. Some charters are owned and operated by the local public school system. Others are private nonprofit organizations authorized to receive public funds.

In theory, such schools will attract many students away from district-operated public schools, thus creating an economic threat and forcing existing public schools into instructional and staffing innovations that would not occur if public schools remained monopolies. Again in theory, once charter schools exist, both charter and district-run schools are accountable to the market for survival. If either fails to attract an adequate number of students—because their educational program does not meet local needs or their cost structure is unsound or inefficient—they will go out of business.

Competition is the core value of charter schools, but most charter school advocates agree that charter schools' educational practices and competitive behaviors should be kept under some constraints. As publicly funded agencies, charter schools are obligated to protect the civil rights of students, parents, and teachers, remain ultimately accountable to elected public officials, and operate under open meetings and freedom of information requirements. Charter school statutes also require charter school programs to be approved by agencies of state government, and they reserve to government agencies the ultimate right to terminate the charter of a school that misuses public funds, mistreats staff, or fails to educate students.

Funding

Charter schools are funded on a per pupil basis. Depending on state law, charters either receive the entire state per pupil contribution or that amount plus some share of locally raised public funds. Most districts can retain some funds for central-office costs and services to schools, though some schools can negotiate additional funding if they decide to pay for their own transportation needs or food service.

Charter schools generally do not receive any public funds until students are in attendance, and changes in enrollment have immediate effects on school income. Start-up costs are borne by school organizers, not by the local public school board.

Teachers

Under most state laws, charter schools can be either entirely new organizations or converted public schools. New charter schools have substantial freedom to create their own organizational structures and select teachers, either from the entire local teacher union bargaining unit or from a broader market, sometimes including teachers with alternative certification. Regular public schools converting to charter status often start with complete teaching staffs. They can, however, gain the freedom to change their staff composition and pay scales as vacancies occur.

Most charter school laws give teachers the option of remaining in public retirement systems and health insurance schemes. New-start charter schools can, however, offer alternative benefits packages.

Student Assignment

Most charter school laws incorporate elements of student choice. Schools converting from regular public school status normally "grandfather in" the families and neighborhoods previously served. However, local school boards are usually willing to transfer small numbers of students whose parents object to changes in the school. If vacancies are not filled from within the school neighborhood, schools usually accept out-of-area applications and select students through a lottery.

New charters draw students from existing public schools. Because most offer a distinctive curriculum, approach to teaching, or method of involving adult volunteers, they do not appeal to all tastes. No parent is compelled to send a student to such a school; those who want to attend must apply. Student selection processes vary: in some states, all slots in new charter schools must be filled by lottery, while in other states a new school's charter might specify a favored catchment area or other identified group. Schools required to select all students by lottery can face the problem that school founders and donors, including some who may have spent years seeking the charter and organizing the school, cannot be guaranteed slots for their children.

Parents sending their children to charter schools have rights of immediate reentry into regular public schools. Most, however, are not guaranteed their pick of public schools.

Quality Control

A school's charter is supposed to specify its basic approach to instruction and other student services. School boards and other agencies authorized to approve charters are expected to exercise some judgment about applicants' qualifications and the soundness of their educational and business plans. Most charter-granting processes also include public hearings.

In theory, the agency that grants a charter will also take some interest in the school's performance. At least one higher-education institution, Central Michigan University, has actively promoted charter applications and built close ties between the new schools and professors in its School of Education. The school districts of Springfield, Massachusetts, and San Diego, California, have also maintained close ties with local charter schools. However, many local school boards consider charter schools unwelcome and improper competition; they are not likely to invest much effort in assisting those schools.

Whatever their day-to-day interest in the schools they have authorized, agencies retain some oversight responsibilities, plus the authority to revoke and renew charters. Few charters have been in effect long enough to need renewal. One Los Angeles school had its charter revoked in 1995, due to falling enrollment and financial mismanagement. It is not yet clear how state and local boards will hold charter schools accountable, or what they will do if a school gains strong parent support but cannot demonstrate strong academic performance. It is clear that many charter school operators reject standardized testing and other conventional assessment tools, and that few charters make explicit statements about what levels of achievement must be demonstrated and how.

Dean Millot and Robin Lake's interviews of charter applicants show that most are driven by excitement about instructional ideas and assume that success is assured. Few applicants anticipate convincing a skeptical public or a hostile renewal process. Few if any charters include specific language about performance measurement instruments or minimum performance standards. Most leave those issues to be negotiated at some future time, possibly creating a situation in which schools have no clear contractual rights to renewal and local boards have discretion limited only by local political processes.

Given these uncertainties about performance measurement and standards, quality control and accountability for charter schools might ultimately revert to a simpler process of parental choice, under which schools that attract students and maintain families' trust will be sustained and those with weaker bases of parental support will go out of business.

Problems with Charter School Laws

In practice, charter school statutes often deviate from the ideal of open competition. Educational interest-groups accustomed to dealing with a centralized public school system have opposed charter school legislation out of fear that it will threaten the job security of current school employees and eliminate programs that entitle some groups of students (e.g., the handicapped) to special services. This opposition often produces compromises that limit the numbers of charter schools that can be created and that restrict charter schools' autonomy and freedom to compete on an equal basis with regular public schools. Many legislators are willing to make important compromises on the principle of competition because they are more interested in a charters law as a way to head off a statewide voucher scheme rather than as a fundamental reform in its own right.

Moreover, advocates of charter schools often differ on important details of the concept and many are willing to compromise on the principle of competition. Many know what they want to do in their own schools and are satisfied with a law that lets them proceed, whether or not it rules out other possible charter plans.

Under charter school laws, local school boards cannot act affirmatively to invest in formation of possible charter school operators or to create a portfolio of charter schools that meets the needs of the whole community. It is up to individuals and groups to petition for charters, formulate educational plans, demonstrate to the satisfaction of public approving authorities that the school can be a going concern financially and educationally, and put the school into operation. These features of charter school laws create important barriers to entry. New charter schools face two major problems. First, only a small proportion of all the people who would like to run charter schools have the necessary combination of educational and business expertise; and second, new schools lack access to the financial capital necessary to support start-up and expansion.

Creating truly new schools can be a risky and failure-prone process. A relatively small group of people must reach at least a rudimentary agreement about the prospective school's instructional mission and approach. Staff members and students must then be recruited, preferably on the basis of affinity to the school mission and instructional approach. People who start new schools must find space and facilities, establish lines of credit and insurance, and find legal counsel to help them establish fair and workable contracts with public authorities. They must also accept major legal risks. Current school law defines the obligations of public school systems, not individual schools. Leaders of new schools must learn how to control their own budgets and keep a proper balance between instructional expenditures and investments such as staff training and building maintenance. Many people with promising school ideas have had to give up in the face of the cost and complexity of start-up. Some others have run into major financial difficulties as public authorities established to grant charters and contracts have become entangled in litigation or disputes with teacher unions.

Organizers of new-start charter schools are drawn mostly from the field of education, and few have experience running a business or dealing directly with government. The lack of balance between educational and business expertise in the pool of potential charter school operators restricts the number of applicants truly qualified to operate new charter schools. Currently, the number of possible suppliers of new schools is small. In California and Massachusetts, some charter school slots went unused during the first year, and there still have been no takers under the Georgia charter law. Limited business expertise also tends to limit the size of authorized schools to a level within the limited managerial and governmental capacity of the operators.[8]

Problems in obtaining access to capital may also inhibit the creation of charter schools. Because the charter school concept is motivated by a desire to make the public school system more efficient, not more expensive, state laws generally do not provide the schools with access to financing beyond their per capita student payments. Many start-up costs must be financed through the operators' "sweat equity" and pro bono professional support, but some require cash. For new charter schools, the largest such cost generally involves the lease, purchase, or renovation of a school building. In theory, the prospect of a stream of more or less guaranteed state payments should constitute an attractive form of financial security for a private loan, but charter schools are typically frozen out of private capital markets.

There are several reasons for this, but they all relate to doubts about repayment. Real estate loans are paid off over 25 or 30 years. Lenders are concerned that the charter school borrower might not survive for that period of time, and they fear that the local school board might unilaterally alter the rules under which the school operates. Existing public schools converting to charter status do not suffer the start-up problems of new schools, but they face their own obstacles. In most states, the chartering process does little to promote the autonomy of conversion schools. Conversion school applicants bear the burden of proof in justifying every waiver of rules or free use of resources. Thus, while in theory an existing school converting to charter status starts with many advantages (a functioning staff, a dedicated school building, access to central-office services), it may have difficulty breaking free of school board management.

Results of Millot and Lake's case studies in Massachusetts reveal that some small school districts (e.g., Marblehead) are resisting freeing up

---

8. In September 1995, a RAND-University of Washington conference on "The Business of Charter Schools," assembled charter school sponsors and business managers to identify the issues that new charters must resolve, lessons learned by successful sponsors, and sources of information and assistance for new sponsors.

money to pay on a per pupil basis for charter schools. In small districts the percentages of pupils who go into charters is large enough to force cutbacks in the remaining public schools. Some central offices are making those cuts as visibly and painfully as possible and stirring up real resentment against the charters on the part of parents in the remaining schools.

This is the dark side of Ted Kolderie's argument that charters will force a change in local school district operations. The local district might not, as Kolderie assumes, make changes that will allow other schools to become more charter-like. The district might instead hold onto all the existing central administrative staff and functions and bleed special resources and teachers out of the regular schools, thus polarizing the community.

Because of the uncertainties about charter school initiation and survival, no one knows whether to expect charter schools to remain marginal phenomena (fewer than 1/10 of 1 percent of the nation's schools) or to lead to a profound change in the way American public schools are governed.

Conclusion: Why Contracting Is a Superior Alternative

One can believe that site-based management will create school-level initiative, but only under the assumption that teachers and principals will respond to weak new incentives instead of the strong ones that have been in place for generations. One can believe that a pure demand-side reform like vouchers will reform public education, but only under the assumption that demand will spontaneously elicit a supply of high-quality schools for everyone, including the inner-city poor. One can believe that systemic reform will transform schools, but only under the assumption that a strong, centrally administered system of rewards and penalties will not accentuate the existing compliance mentality at the school level. One can believe that charter schools will inspire imitators and lead to pressures for more school-friendly governance of public education, but only under the assumption that large numbers of competent individuals will be willing to risk their time and money on ventures whose autonomy, accountability, and continued access to public funds are not clear.

Unlike three of the four alternatives described in this chapter, contracting works on both the demand side and the supply side. Unlike charter school laws, which also work on both the supply and demand sides, contracting creates clear, reliable, and legally enforceable relationships between school operators and public officials. Contracting imitates charter schools laws in encouraging creation of independent organizations to run schools, and in enabling school boards to sponsor schools that they do not run themselves. In many ways, contracting can be seen as an evolutionary development of the charter idea, focusing on the school as the main unit of performance in public education but creating clearer and more reliable relationships between schools and public authorities.

The importance of clarity in relationships between independent public schools and public authorities can be illustrated by the failure of one of the first private firms seeking to operate public schools, Education Alternatives, Inc. EAI lost its agreement to run twelve Baltimore public schools in 1995 and its contract to manage the entire Hartford public school system in early 1996. EAI's experience has revealed serious uncertainty about the meaning of the word "contract" as it has been loosely used in public education. EAI's arrangement with Baltimore anticipated performance evaluation based on student test scores, attendance, parental support, and other factors, but it did not specify how these were to be measured or judged. Opponents of the EAI contract, particularly the Baltimore Federation of Teachers, entered this vacuum and performed their own assessment, which, to no one's surprise, was strongly negative. Neither EAI nor the school system had the facts to make an effective rebuttal, and EAI's relationship with the Baltimore schools was ultimately terminated. Ironically, an evaluation done after EAI was fired showed that students in its schools during the 1994–95 school year learned at a higher rate than students in similar Baltimore schools. In its relationship with the Hartford school board EAI expected to gain control over basic district financing and to be able to reorganize and restaff failing schools (including contracting for their operation by additional independent organizations). In fact, EAI's contract was ambiguous about the residual powers of the school board, and the board effectively seized most of the powers back before ultimately withdrawing from the contract.

Both the company and the school boards with which it dealt have been so eager to enter arrangements that promised school improvement that they have been careless in establishing goals, responsibilities, and expectations. Provisions in EAI's contracts were so vague that neither the company nor the school board could confidently expect to define its rights in measurable terms or enforce them in court. The Hartford and Baltimore experiences illustrate the pitfalls of ambiguous contracts and Hollywood-style payment clauses that do not define such key factors as expected outcomes, gross and net costs, and how savings can be calculated.

Contracting imitates the voucher plan in providing parents with almost total freedom to choose a school that suits their children's needs and family preferences; it also ensures that schools that lose parental support will close and their funding will be reallocated to other schools. In many ways, contracting can be seen as a variant on the voucher proposal. It emphasizes parental choice and makes schools independent organizations that depend for their survival on parental satisfaction. Under contracting, many key functions are performed by markets: student applications and admissions, allocation of teachers and other staff members, and allocation of public funds all depend on decisions made by independent private actors.

Contracting also incorporates elements of the supply-side strategies. Like site-based management, it emphasizes control of key decisions at the level of the school. It goes far beyond site-based management, however, by treating schools as real organizations that control their own staff and resources, are responsible for their own performance, and make their own decisions about investments in new staff, training, and technology. Like systemic reform, contracting calls for statewide school performance standards that incorporate what is known about students' needs for skills and understanding. It goes far beyond systemic reform, however, by giving public authorities the ability to close schools that fail to provide the promised services or to meet state standards, and to replace failed schools by establishing new contracts.

As a reform strategy, however, contracting creates supply-side arrangements that all the others, including charter schools, lack. Contracting makes public officials responsible for ensuring that no neighborhood or group of students goes unserved and authorizes officials to find competent organizations willing to accept public funds to provide needed schools. Public officials can do so by offering contracts and guaranteeing public funding. Contracting also allows public officials to withdraw support from popular schools that fail to educate their students. If, as voucher critics assert, some parents will send their children to schools that offer inadequate educational programs, public officials will retain the power to intervene.

Contracting does not embrace the existing public school governance system, which allows board micro-management, control of funds at the central office, nonvolitional assignment of students, teachers, and administrators, and civil service and union protections for uncooperative or unproductive school employees. It provides an entirely new governance system, under which school board powers are limited to contracting-out, virtually all funds go directly to schools, and teachers and administrators adults must compete for jobs and pay. Contracting creates important new roles for public officials, especially school boards and superintendents, but it also strictly limits their power over schools. Boards can negotiate contracts with schools, but once contracts are let, they obligate and constrain all parties alike. As long as a school abides by its contract, no one, not even a Board majority, can unilaterally change requirements, payment schedules, staffing patterns, student assignment rules, or evaluation standards.

Just as voucher proposals have lent demand-side features to contracting, systemic reform has lent some supply-side features. States are required to establish student achievement goals and performance measurement systems that can permit clear and fair comparisons among schools. States also have the power to oversee the performance of local school boards and to contract directly for schools in areas that local boards have neglected.

In sum, contracting is a hybrid system that promises to do better than the current system and any competing strategy on support for initiative-taking in schools, creation of strong pressures for high performance in schools, stabilizing the funding schools receive and the rules under which they must work, and protecting children from failing schools. Subsequent chapters will discuss in detail how contracting will work.

PART II

IMPLEMENTING A CONTRACT SCHOOL SYSTEM

FIVE

How a Contract Strategy Would Work

Wilkinsburg's Turner School Initiative[*]

In March 1994, the Wilkinsburg School District launched an unusual attempt at public school change called the Turner School Initiative. Turner School is an elementary school serving fewer than 400 students, and Wilkinsburg has only four public schools. But for those interested in examining the possibility of using contracting as an engine for systemic educational change, the story of this effort is both compelling and thought provoking. The Turner School Initiative is the story of what happens when a community struggles to use new forms of power and leverage to remedy a set of problems that have become commonplace in U.S. public schools.

By 1994, economic decline had reduced Wilkinsburg from a strong middle-class community with a vibrant main street to a struggling town of 20,000 with urban problems more severe than those in Pittsburgh, which is just to its west. Over the previous two decades, Wilkinsburg's population had shrunk by more than 20 percent and become increasingly poor and transient. The 1990 census reported nearly a fifth of the population living in poverty, and Wilkinsburg had the largest share of subsidized housing in Allegheny county.

Wilkinsburg had seen its tradition of strong, quality public schools die as well. Once used by all segments of the community, public schools in Wilkinsburg had come to serve an overwhelmingly African-American student population even though the population of the borough was almost half white. Middle-class families of both races were moving away or sending their children to private schools.

[*] This section, except for the opening and closing paragraphs, was contributed by Jeremy Resnick.

The 1,900 children enrolled in Wilkinsburg's public schools were attending schools that were failing. The size of Wilkinsburg's graduating class had dwindled to fewer than fifty students, and even the best prepared of its graduates were finding themselves ill prepared for the world they were entering. The 1992 valedictorian had a C average, and even students at the top of the class were taking remedial coursework when they enrolled at area colleges and universities. This failure extended into the elementary schools as well. Scores on standardized tests were low in all subject areas with twice as many children scoring below the median in Wilkinsburg than elsewhere in Pennsylvania. Results from an earlier statewide assessment of low-level, grade school skills showed Wilkinsburg eighth graders performing worse than students in any of the other forty-two school districts in the county.

The 1993 elections had produced a Wilkinsburg school board determined to bring quality public schools back to the borough. It was also a board that understood that to achieve this end might require maverick action. Traditional kinds of restructuring that depend on trust and cooperation offered little hope for Wilkinsburg. Teacher strikes, tax increases to support strike settlements, and a teaching force that was no longer living in Wilkinsburg had all contributed to an atmosphere of mistrust. And efforts aimed at cultivating trust were not working. A joint effort at strategic planning underway during the elections and intended to bring together teachers and community members was aggravating bad feelings instead.

The Turner School Initiative, launched in March 1994, charted an entirely different kind of course that did not depend on mutual trust or good feelings. Rather than continuing to quietly cultivate the good will of its current professional staff, the board starkly outlined its frustration with public school failure and announced its determination to have an accountable school of excellence operating in Wilkinsburg within eighteen months. The board invited current teachers and administrators to be a part of the solution, but it also insisted that it would move ahead with or without their participation. Those who would not be part of the solution would be pushed aside.

The vehicle for announcing the Initiative and demonstrating this new, "whatever necessary" attitude was a request for proposals (RFP) inviting responses from groups interested in restructuring Turner School and then operating it on an outcome-based three- to five-year contract. The contract was to begin no later than September 1995. For Wilkinsburg school directors, the Initiative strategy was straightforward and sensible; for those inside the educational establishment, the Initiative strategy was anathema.

The proposed process challenged two of the underlying presumptions that had shaped a decade of efforts at public school restructuring: first, that every school district had an untapped reservoir of talent capable of designing and implementing a good restructuring plan; second, that a district's success in restructuring depended on the support and enthusiasm of its existing teaching force.

The Wilkinsburg school board was not sure whether the expertise for leading a fundamental restructuring of its schools did exist among its professional staff of 150 teachers and administrators. So even though its preference was to have its own teachers and administrators devise and implement a restructuring plan, the Initiative RFP invited groups from outside Wilkinsburg as well as those inside it to consider operating Turner School. The open, competitive process increased the chances that the district would end up with a viable plan and guaranteed that the board would have maximum information about all possible options when it finally decided how to proceed.

The school board was also unsure whether the NEA-affiliated union which represented its teachers would cooperate in implementing a restructuring plan that might require changes in the school calendar and staff structure. The Initiative RFP's most controversial feature was its explicit language in this regard. Those responding to the RFP were offered two options for teacher staffing at the new Turner School—to work with the existing teaching force or to hire a new one. If the board became convinced during the RFP process and subsequent negotiations that Turner School could not be turned around without its new operator being given the freedom to select its own teachers, the board was ready to dismiss part of the current Wilkinsburg teaching force to make that possible. The union would not have the power to veto the community's decision to radically remake its schools.

Wilkinsburg needed new energy and new kinds of behavior to get the changes it wanted. Rather than depend on goodwill to get them, the Turner School Initiative changed the set of rewards and penalties that shape people's behavior. Raising the issue of contracting, inviting outsiders to make a contribution in Wilkinsburg, and entertaining the possibility of laying off teachers were ways to change the rules of the game, to convince people in the establishment that schools, beginning with Turner, were really going to change, and to focus attention on how to make these revamped schools work well for children.

What happened in the months following the release of the Initiative RFP confirms the power of this strategy to mobilize new forces and change

behavior. Sixteen different groups expressed an interest in making a proposal to run Turner School. These groups ranged from local, community-
based, nonprofit agencies to public and private universities to national,
for-profit corporations. Eleven of them attended an all-day informational
conference whose highlight was an open discussion with parents about
problems at the school and parents' hopes for its future. A number of the
groups invested significant resources in assessing Wilkinsburg's problems
and exploring possible solutions.

While the Turner School Initiative has focused new resources on
Wilkinsburg's problems, it has also changed the quality and kind of activity seen among those who already had a role in Wilkinsburg's schools.
Even before any decision to contract or change the educational program
was made, parents, teachers, administrators, and school board members
were acting differently than they did before the announcement of the Initiative. The Turner parent organization grew from its pre-Initiative size of
just six members, and parents began to take on more than bake sales. Several RFP responders actively sought the advice of parents by going to their
homes, by convening focus groups, and by sponsoring public meetings.
And when the district received proposals and began deliberating on what
to do next, parents became vocal participants in separate meetings sponsored by the school board, the teachers' union, and community groups.
The Initiative empowered parents by putting them in a position to
strongly influence an important decision.

The Turner School Initiative had its most dramatic impact on Wilkinsburg's existing teaching force and their union, the Wilkinsburg Education Association (WEA). At first the WEA refused to acknowledge that the
board had the power to change the rules of the game. Legal action was
threatened, and the union indicated that it would not participate in any
process of change related to the Initiative; union leaders successfully discouraged individual teachers who expressed a desire to participate. But
even while continuing to challenge the right of the board to act as it had,
the behavior of the union seemed to change.

In June, just before the deadline for receipt of proposals, the WEA made
a joint presentation to the board with members of the University of Pittsburgh's School of Education faculty. At the meeting, they indicated they
had an alternative plan for revamping Turner School but provided few details. In August, after the board had received five proposals from outside
groups in response to the RFP, they returned and offered more details of
their plan for the school. While the plan was still sketchy, the fact that the
union had recognized a problem, had sought an outside partner, and was

ready to work to implement a restructuring plan represented a marked change from pre-Turner School Initiative behavior.

By the deadline for receipt of proposals on July 1, Wilkinsburg had five proposals for revamping Turner School in addition to the alternative plan presented by its teachers' union. An independent evaluation by the head of one of the nine New American Schools Development Corporation (NASDC) design teams identified the proposal of Alternative Public Schools (APS) as clearly superior to the others and as something superior in its own right. This group had assembled a design team of highly respected local African-American principals and presented a proposal with strong community support and many unusual features, including a longer school year, a longer school day, and a school-based social service hub. APS also insisted on the right to choose its own teaching force. In September 1994, just six months after announcing the Turner School Initiative and releasing the RFP, the school board found itself in the unusual position of having competing restructuring plans from which to choose. With the district still committed to a September 1995 opening of a revamped Turner School, the board would have to choose one path over the other. It would have to decide whether the outside APS proposal was something so much better than what its own staff could provide that it warranted assuming the legal risks and fighting the union battle that its choice might precipitate. It would not be an easy decision.

Negotiation with both APS and the WEA dragged on through the fall and winter. In January 1995, APS insisted on a Board decision. Unwilling to give up on the WEA, the district bought three more months of negotiating time with an option payment to APS. During that time, the district offered to forgo APS if the WEA would agree to implement what amounted to a scaled-down version of what APS was proposing for Turner School, including a slightly longer work school year and day. In March, with NEA president Keith Geiger leading a demonstration outside, and union negotiators showing no signs of movement, the board voted to sign a contract with APS on April 1, barring a last-minute accommodation with the WEA.

Between April and August, the focus shifted to Pennsylvania courts, where a series of rulings and appeals stopped and restarted plans at Turner. Finally, with only two weeks remaining before the start of school, a Supreme Court decision made it clear that APS would be able to open Turner with its own staff in September. With surprisingly little fanfare, the new Turner school opened the week after Labor Day in September 1995.

A final Supreme Court ruling in October questioned the constitutionality of a state school code that might prevent contracting while allowing conditions like those that prevailed at Turner School to continue. But the Court remanded the case to the trial court for a full hearing—dashing any hopes for a speedy, precedent-setting resolution. Wilkinsburg's contract with APS could continue, but other districts would have to wait.

Unable to overturn the contract in court, WEA activists focused their energies on the upcoming school board elections where five seats were up for election. A well-financed challenge from a slate of union-backed candidates provided Wilkinsburg residents with a clear choice. On election day, incumbent supporters of the APS contract were all reelected on a day of higher-than-anticipated voter turnout.

Since then, Turner School has been largely out of the news. A second year of school began in September 1996. The board, and everyone else, awaits indicators of academic success at the school that should begin to become evident after a second year at the school. In the meantime, parents seem by and large to be pleased.

Perhaps more importantly, the Turner School Initiative has engendered a sense of hope in Wilkinsburg. Parents have growing expectations, and all parties seem increasingly unaccepting of the status quo. The Turner School Initiative has led a community unfamiliar with excellent schools to begin anticipating them and has given a small-town school board the means to deliver what the community now wants.

The rest of this chapter describes many of the operational elements that a district like Wilkinsburg will have to consider when initiating a contract school system. The principal topics with which we grapple here are: the nature and content of a contract; the contracting process; characteristics of contractors and contractor responsibilities; and the revised roles to be played in a contract school system by state officials, local school boards, school administrators, instructional contractors and teachers, and auxiliary providers such as food service, transportation and maintenance firms, supply vendors, and various craft workers.

School Contracts

In a system of contract public schools, a contract is a legally binding written agreement in which a duly empowered school board willingly consents to the operation of a public school or schools by a responsible and qualified bidder in exchange for financial resources. The agreement must be consistent with state statutes authorizing a school board to contract for the operation of schools and must comply with court decisions, statutes, and legal opinions regarding contracts.

A successful contract would contain at least five major sections: (1) specification of the qualifications and expectations of the contractor, including operating domains over which the contractor would have decision discretion; (2) consideration, generally financing, for which the contractor would be entitled for providing specified services; (3) a description of the proposed program and program objectives; (4) agreed-upon evaluation criteria and procedures; and (5) terms under which the contract could be terminated, extended, or renewed.

A typical school contract might have the following components:

Contractor Qualifications. The school board specifies the expertise that it expects contractors to have or obtain, such as minimal levels of instructor experience and knowledge of subject matter. These are dimensions that a contract promises to bring to the school as contained, initially, in the contractor's bid to provide services.

Operating Procedures. Admission criteria for students; age or grade levels to be served; school calendar; grading mechanisms; academic-progress reporting; testing programs to be utilized; record keeping; maximum class sizes; length of school day, school year, and classes; school safety and emergency procedures; student disciplinary codes; parent grievance procedures; and dress and grooming codes—all are illustrative of the items to be agreed to in this category.

Here the contract specifies curriculum and service approaches such as the overall nature or theme, if any, of the school, academic content to be covered, learning outcomes to be sought by students, preschool and after-school activities, athletics, visual and performing arts offerings, food and transportation.

Facilities and Maintenance. Buildings, fields, storage, easements, etc. to be made available to the contractor or which the contractor is responsible to supply; levels of maintenance expected of the contractor and of the school district, types of spaces to be made available to students; and times of the day and year at which facilities will be open to students, parents, and others.

What public financing will be made available and on what schedule, contractor's financial responsibilities, insurance and liability, and any other obligations of the school district toward the contractor (e.g., ability to lease school district transportation vehicles).

Criteria by which the contractor's performance will be appraised, evaluation schedules, acceptable performance levels, role of parent opinion, specification of third-party evaluator, distribution of evaluation results.

Specification of the contract's intended length, terms under which it could be renewed, extended, or terminated.

Contractors

A contract school system assumes that literally thousands of local public schools will, in time, be managed by qualified instructional and, perhaps, auxiliary service vendors who have successfully bid to operate a school in keeping with a local school board's specifications. This is a heroic assumption, given that only a few dozen schools are now operated by contractors, and many of them are charter schools whose independence from local school boards is constrained and unreliable. There is, furthermore, only a handful of private organizations now seeking contracts to operate public schools. Our proposal requires the creation of a whole new supply of school operators. Who might such providers be, what qualifications should they possess, and what might motivate them to seek and accept contracts?

Who Might Bid?

Private-Sector Entrepreneurs. A few private vendors exist already. They are entrepreneurs who have contracted, or who are currently negotiating, with local school boards to operate specific individual local schools and, in some instances, school districts. Some of these entrepreneurs are relatively small consulting companies hoping to gain contracts and grow large. They include Alternative Public Schools, the Nashville firm currently under contract to operate Turner Elementary School in Wilkinsburg. Other firms, such as the Edison Schools, Education Alternatives Incorporated, Sabis International, and Jostens are already large and may hope to expand their services into the public school operations market. These companies are usually profit-oriented and hope to make money by operating public schools for local education authorities. They also promise specified improvements and agree to the means by which such gains are to be measured.

However, the few existing experiments with such entrepreneurs have proven controversial, exciting the opposition of entrenched interests. As we mentioned in chapter 4, many of the problems encountered with the EAI contracts in Hartford and Baltimore resulted from misunderstandings and ambiguous contracts. Also, the hands of a few entrepreneurial firms are themselves not entirely clean, the firms having admitted distorting student achievement results to gain a more positive public image. Experience in the 1960s, under the aegis of the federal government's Office of

Economic Opportunity, suggests that performance contracting in education is demanding of government as well as of contractors. Contractors cannot afford to promise outcomes that are extremely difficult to attain, and government cannot specify goals that can be met by selective admission of clients or by distorting curriculum to increase measured performance at the expense of other important aspects of schooling. Local school boards and potential contractors need to negotiate openly about appropriate performance standards. Contractors need to ensure that they are accountable for gains indexed on students' level of preparation, and government needs to ensure that key measures are collected and analyzed independently, not by contractors. School performance measurement presents new challenges both to educational measurement and to law. As was discussed in chapter 3, performance assessment for individual schools is necessary for any reform that tries to hold teachers and administrators accountable for student performance. A contracting system makes the need transparent but does not create it.

Teacher Unions. These organizations are a natural source of contractors. They embody unparalleled instructional expertise, intense knowledge of schools and children, financial stability, organizing acumen, experienced leadership, good relationships with parents, ideological commitment to education, and a vested interest in the success of public schooling. By bidding successfully to operate schools, teacher unions can practically express all of their aspirations for the improvement of education, unfettered by the conditions they have long claimed prevented them from doing their jobs correctly, i.e., oppressive bureaucratic regulation and rigid administration. They can also ensure employment for their members. American Federation of Teachers president Albert Shanker has already voiced his willingness to try such an idea.

Higher-Education Institutions. Contracting provides an opportunity for colleges and universities to assist in solving public education problems and to add to their usefulness and luster in the process. Many already have experience operating successful university laboratory schools. By designing creative programs and successfully operating schools, higher-education institutions could bring an enormous range of talents into play for improving education. Here would be a chance to weave together pedagogical theory and good practice, provide a ready-made practical setting for the professional training of new teachers, involve subject matter departments in the design and operation of public schools, and satisfy the needs of young faculty members for good schools for their own children.

However, colleges and universities should not easily assume they know how to operate public schools. They need to employ experienced, able, and politically sophisticated personnel. It may be too early to judge the success of Boston University in operating the Chelsea, Massachusetts, public schools, but what has happened so far suggests that the experience can be trying. Perhaps a way to approach the challenge, however, is to start with one or perhaps a few schools. Boston University contracted to operate an entire district.

Business Enterprises. Large businesses, those with many employees, might well want to bid for the operation of a school designed particularly around the needs and preferences of their employees. Such bidders might place the school in a location near their plant or office. They might offer before- and after-school child care, not to mention health services, cafeterias, and so on. Close proximity to their employment might enable parents to participate more productively in the schooling of their children. High-tech firms might use schools as a place to try out pilot products with instructional potential. A nationwide corporation, such as IBM, might want to bid to operate many schools in places where they had geographic concentrations of employees. Such employer-operated schools could be administered by a not-for-profit component of the business.

Not-for-Profit Organizations. Organizations such as the YMCA already have a great deal of successful experience in operating educational ventures. Contracting might provide such agencies with an expanded opportunity. If not-for profit organizations do not want to engage fully in operation, then they might at least want to bid on auxiliary service subcomponents such as child care, extra-curricular activities, and after-school recreation.

Parent Associations. A group of parents possessing the necessary experience and skills might choose to organize formally and bid to operate a school. If so, they would, of course, have to meet the requirements expected of any other equally situated group of bidders.

Child Advocacy Agencies. There exists a growing number of not-for-profit child advocacy groups. Many of them exhibit enormous stability and leadership. They might well wish to implement the practices they preach and to operate a school.

Religious Organizations. Religious organizations, such as a Catholic diocese or a Catholic religious order, Baptist or Lutheran churches or Hebrew congregations, and other denominational units, have long histories of operating effective schools. These organizations have the advantage of deep experience in education, networks of experienced teachers and administrators, and access to financing. They might choose to run nonsectarian schools just as some churches now sponsor public housing, as an exercise of social responsibility. In at least some states, they would be free to bid on a contract as long as they met the requirements for operating a contract school. Many religious organizations would not bid for contracts, however, because local public school boards would prohibit the teaching of religion and would require nondiscriminatory admissions processes.

School Administrators. Many currently serving central-office administrators and school principals are enormously capable individuals. However, they frequently chafe at the stifling restrictions piled upon them by regulations under which they must operate. They also can be frustrated by continued micro-management by some school boards and superintendents. Many have exciting ideas about the manner in which to organize and operate a school. Furthermore, many of these individuals are unusually dynamic and charismatic. If provided with an opening, they may well leap to organize and bid for the operation of a school, perhaps even the school in which they now are employed.

Assorted Other Individuals. There are many individuals who have always wanted to operate a school, have many good ideas, and with proper motivation and an opportunity might be able to do so quite successfully. These could include highly motivated teachers, retired private-sector or military executives, or experienced professionals eager for a change of careers. Such individuals, obviously, would have to raise sufficient capital to become bonded, recruit a cadre of talented colleagues, apprise themselves of the information necessary to bid for school contracts, acquire additional training if such was in order, and give careful consideration to the manner in which they would propose to operate a school.

Contractors' Minimum Qualifications

School boards will need assurances about bidders. Even if they proved to be only a slender minority, incompetent vendors could spoil schools and, even if only for a short time, disrupt the lives of the families and children involved. In order to minimize such risks, states would establish a minimum set of bidder qualifications. In effect, bidders would be asked to acquire a state-issued "Instructional Contractor's License." (At this point, critics of the overall idea of contract schools are probably saying: "Here comes the bureaucratic regulatory overlay." There is no absolute guarantee that someone somewhere will not use the licensing function as an excuse to discourage proposals or impose crippling regulations on contractors. Contracting is an arrangement in human affairs and is not proof against abuse either by private organizations or by government. The best that designers of a contracting system can do is to create a system where the incentives against abuse are strong. In the case of state licenses for contractors, the state's need to qualify enough contractors to ensure a provider for every school is an incentive against over-regulation. But an incentive is not a guarantee. A perverse state licensing authority could try to wreck contracting by driving qualified providers away—just as a corrupt official could demand financial kickbacks from contractors. These things probably will happen in some instances, but they would constitute malfeasance in office and should be treated as such.)

Contractor licensing procedures would require evidence of liability insurance and financial probity. Contractors would understand that failure to comply with operational specifications could result in immediate suspension of the contract and forfeiture of the bond.

Contractors would have to display knowledge of existing state and federal education regulations pertinent to the type of school they proposed to operate. They also would have to be free of any pending criminal charges or felony convictions.

Licensing of providers can give families more protection than now exists in either private or public schools. No parent can currently enter a public or private school and be assured that the overall organization, responsible for all components of the school's day-to day operation, has been certified as knowledgeable and responsible. School superintendents, principals, and teachers are currently credentialed only by the state. This is testimony that they have sat through a specified set of education courses and received a minimum grade-point average and score on the National Teachers Examination or equivalent state examination. Some states require an internship before receiving a final teaching credential. There is virtually no performance assessment or instructional knowledge guarantee involved in such credentialing.

Under the proposed contract system, parents will have substantially more and better information regarding the operation of a school and of the intended offerings and expected outcomes than exist now. Before choosing a school, parents will have a far better opportunity to know what they are selecting. In effect, they can protect themselves in advance, something seldom possible in today's system of public schooling.

Reasons for Bidding on School Contracts

Why would you go to the trouble of becoming a licensed contractor, organizing a team of professional participants, writing an involved proposal, negotiating a complicated contract, and putting up with the day-to-day frustrations of operating a school if you could do something else and still earn a living?

There are two principal answers. First, because you can make a good living. Because a contractor would be free to pay more for effective teachers, there is also the prospect of making more than under current salary schedules or union contracts. There are reasonable salaries to be made, and if a school is operated efficiently there is the possibility of end-of-year bonuses.

Moreover, and this is the second point, you can live well doing something that is rewarding and fulfilling. Education need not be boring or intellectually stultifying. A contractor and all the teachers and others who work in a contract school may see themselves as part of an exciting enterprise, one that is theirs to operate and to make succeed. This feeling of excitement is rare in today's public schools: there is little chance for excitement because there is no sense of ownership. The school and its rules are all controlled by someone else. Principals and teachers are constrained by rules instituted by individuals they do not know and who do not know their schools. There are few rewards or negative consequences for either succeeding or failing. Contract schools would liberate administrators and teachers from such stifling circumstances, and, we believe, they will be quick to see the advantages.

School Boards: At the Policy Center of a Contract School System

School boards are a crucial component in a system of contract schools. They constitute the principal mechanism for ensuring that public schools belong to the public. They are means through which the offerings of schools meet public needs, ensuring that education not only serves individual students and their families but also acts in the interest of the broader community. In the absence of thoughtful school boards, reformers might simply call for a full-blown voucher system whereby the principal decision-making unit would become the individual household.

The most dramatic difference between the public schools as they now operate and contract schools is not what school boards would do, but, rather, what they would no longer do. They would no longer have responsibility for directly hiring, evaluating, paying, or dismissing teachers, administrators, or other employees for individual schools. In essence, neither school boards nor central-office administrative staff would be responsible for managing day-to-day practical operations of the schools within their jurisdiction. What then would school boards be expected to do, and why is it important?

Under a contract school system, school boards will have an opportunity to assume a true policy-making role. Specifically, school boards should be authorized (1) to employ a chief executive officer for the district and a restricted number of central-office subordinates; (2) hold public hearings regarding the qualifications of contractors and the nature of the school characteristics to embed in requests for proposals (RFPs); (3) select among competitively submitted contract bids; (4) arrange for evaluations of schools by objective, third-party, qualified evaluators; (5) compile and effectively distribute information regarding individual local schools; and (6) establish a grievance or complaint-review process and sit as a panel of near last resort in this local undertaking.

In addition, school boards would also engage in long-range strategic planning for the district, tracking demographic changes and economic developments that imply the need for new kinds of schools. School boards would also broker contracts for auxiliary services (such as transportation, printing and graphics, or food service) where schools within their district requested such assistance, oversee a capital improvement and school emergency loan fund, and in extreme cases sit as a tribunal to adjudicate grievances between parents and contractors for individual schools.

In all of these activities school boards would be assisted by their chief executive officer and central-office staff. However, because the school board role would be substantially altered, compared with vast operating organizations which now characterize most large American school districts, the need for central-office managers would be substantially reduced.

What would the contracting process be like? Through what stages would a local school board move in arriving at specifications for bids, deciding among prospective contractors, monitoring the performance of contractors, and making decisions about contract renewal or termination? These steps are described below.

Defining Objectives and Issuing Requests for Proposals (RFPs)

Under a contract school system, determining the general standards for student performance and educational offerings would become the principal function of a school board. Once these expectations had been determined, and transformed into measurable means, the superintendent's staff would be responsible for embedding them in Requests for Proposals (RFPs).

Providers possessing specified professional qualifications would then bid to operate individual schools.

General Structure of the RFP. A request for proposals to operate contract schools in a district should try to encourage the broadest possible range of proposals. A general-purpose RFP would outline the requirements and conditions under which a contractor could bid to operate a school in the district. It might, based upon public hearings and board discussions, list the kinds of schools and programs that would be given priority by the board. The RFP should not, however, preclude any specific program or contractor from submitting a bid. If, for example, a group of teachers wanted to start a special-purpose school that was not a listed priority, say for African-American students, it could submit a proposal. In this case the burden would be on the group to convince the school board that it could operate an effective school and attract students. The district's general-purpose RFP should also include a mechanism by which the board could solicit proposals on a sole procurement basis. For example, the board might want to approach the college of engineering at a local university to submit a proposal for an engineering and technology academy within the district.

RFP Specifications. Requests for proposals should address four concerns: (1) general contract conditions and requirements, (2) preferred school offerings, (3) student performance outcomes, and (4) overall school environment.

A statement of general contract conditions and requirements would be the framework for operating a contract school in the district.

The state-specified core curriculum, plus whatever additional course offerings, extracurricular activities, and services (e.g., child care) are desired, should be placed in a minimum "expected offering" section. In addition, this section would include a list of the specific school programs that the board would like to have offered in the district.

Student achievement expectations and performance standards, including discipline expectations, would be placed in an outcome section of an RFP.

A fourth RFP section should describe the overall purpose, tone, and general organizational culture or sense of community that the school board and parents prefer. This section will be difficult to render specific. Nevertheless, it should be included to provide bidders with a better sense of what is expected.

RFP documents should also include sociodemographic information about the school, such as the approximate number of anticipated enrollees; their socioeconomic characteristics and past school performance; school eligibility for federal and state categorical-aid funding; state and federal regulations that apply to the school; and whether or not contractors are also expected to operate auxiliary services such as food service and transportation.

RFPs should not specify the "how" of instruction and school operation. This is an area which deliberately should be left to the discretion and professional judgment of bidders. For example, an RFP should not specify class size or professional-to-pupil ratios. These should be left to provider discretion to propose. Teacher and administrator qualifications, other than some threshold minima, should not be part of an RFP. A school board can always reject all RFPs and begin the bidding again if dissatisfied. Also, instructional strategies and techniques should not be specified. This should be another dimension left to the creativity and professional judgment of bidders, and a dimension on which contractors should compete.

Parent Involvement. Prior to issuing the general-purpose RFP, a school board should hold a public hearing or otherwise receive the preferences of parents and, at the secondary school level, perhaps students. Here, whatever is to be added to the state-mandated curriculum core should be discussed. School discipline and grading policies should be addressed. The school board would then take these preferences into account, deliberate, and find the appropriate mix of specifications for the RFP.

Auxiliary Services. Schools currently engage in many activities which are not strictly related to instruction. Nevertheless, many of these activities enhance instruction or, at least, certainly make it easier for parents and others. Transportation and food service are two large examples. There are others, such as before- and after-school child care, athletics, after-school arts and crafts, club activities, and a wide variety of recreational endeavors. School boards should leave these matters for individual contractors to include or not include in their proposals. A school might want to forgo interschool athletics to provide resources to run an arts or special science program.

Price. The request for proposal should clearly specify the per pupil allocation available to successful bidders. A school's budget is then the product of the per pupil allocation times the number of enrolled. Because a school will not know the exact number of students who will choose to attend, a bidder must estimate enrollment, recognizing that adjustments eventually will be made to the budget on the basis of actual enrollment figures. The school budget should include all the costs of operating the school, including an appropriate market rent for the facilities, transportation, food service, and employee benefits. Specifying the amount available for contractors will eliminate price competition among potential vendors. In other words, contractors will have to compete in terms of program characteristics and quality rather than price. While a district may lose the potential of some efficiencies from price competition, it will benefit from the assurance that all students are starting with an equal funding base.

Evaluating Bids and Negotiating Contracts

Advertising and soliciting bids, convening bidder conferences, responding to prospective bidder inquiries, and contracting preliminary proposal reviewers are all activities to which a school board reasonably should delegate to its central-office administrative staff. Once competitive bids have been received, a preliminary assessment of them should also be undertaken administratively. The superintendent should bring two or three front-running proposals to the board for discussion. The pros and cons of proposals should be weighted by the school board. If there are personnel components in need of discussion, then the board could retire to executive session. However, the final vote on a contract should always be made public. Moreover, the winning bid should be made public, as well as the eventually negotiated price of the contract. Vendors whose proposals were found to be unacceptable or who were not awarded the final contract should be informed in writing and provided with as much objective information as possible regarding the reason for their failure.

Contract Award Criteria. Fundamental criteria for judging bids and arriving at final decisions regarding contracts should include objective dimensions such as a vendor's professional qualifications, quality of proposed instructional personnel, successful prior experience, creativity of instructional designs, means for attracting parents and inducing their participation in school activities, quality of extracurricular activities, potential integration with other social-sector services, compatibility with auxiliary services, and overall plan for enhancing student performance.

Negotiating with Finalists. No contract should be considered final until all negotiations have been concluded, important details and references have been checked, and documents have been signed. Because of the complexity of such an undertaking, school boards might well be advertising for bids at least twelve months in advance of the need for an operator at a particular school. Also, in addition to important matters such as negotiating the overall price of the contract and the time period involved (three years would seem to be the minimum, with five years probably being most sensible), attention should be given in the contract to the criteria by which the vendor's performance will be assessed.

Grievance Procedures. It is difficult to draft a contract which anticipates every detail. Indeed, if such were done, there probably would be no need for outside contractors. Under such rigidly imposed contractual conditions, a school would likely be as stifling as the public school it was intended to replace. Nevertheless, legitimate differences of opinion and disagreements will arise, and a procedure will be needed to adjudicate them. The school board particularly will need some kind of grievance procedure for a parent who believes his or her child has been ill-served or wronged by a contractor. This need be no more complicated than the current appeals procedures already existing in most public school districts.

Contractors are likely to be reluctant to provoke controversy with parents or unnecessarily or unduly to discipline students. Contractors will be eager to have their contracts renewed and, thus, will want to establish a good reputation among families. Under contracting, parents can choose the public school they like, constrained only by the transactions cost of a change and availability of a seat in another school. Inevitably, parents who live near many schools or a good public transportation system will find it easier to exercise choices than those who face high transportation costs or have few resources. This is true under the current governance arrangements for public schools, as it would be under any other system that was not willing to provide an absolute guarantee of free pupil transportation. However, all parents would be free to withdraw a child from an unacceptable school, and families would make their own assessments of the costs and benefits of a school transfer. School managers could never be sure whether a family would carry out a threat to move.

Contract Monitoring and Performance Evaluation

The overall appraisal of a contractor's performance should be undertaken by an outside evaluation expert, whose services should be arranged and mutually agreed upon at the time a contract is negotiated. This third-party evaluation should be conducted in keeping with performance arranged and mutually agreed upon at the time a contract is negotiated. This third-party evaluation should be based on performance criteria specified in the contract itself. A formative evaluation can be undertaken at the midpoint of the contract, and a summative evaluation submitted prior to the contract conclusion period. This summative appraisal can be used as a basis for renewing or extending the contract. Conversely, if the contractor's performance is judged wanting, then the school can be re-bid. If the central-administration contract monitor is fearful that the summative evaluation may be overwhelmingly negative, then an earlier date should be arranged for its completion. This would be done in the event it were found necessary to replace the contractor. Sufficient lead time would be available to re-bid and still open the school on time for the subsequent school year.

The choice of school performance measures and standards is critical to the success of a contract system. Performance measures and standards must be of two kinds: those that reflect the school's own particular instructional objectives and strategies, and those that permit valid comparison between schools and over time. The former measures should be part of a school's overall educational strategy, and thus be established in its contract. A career-oriented school, for example, aspires to outcomes that a more academic school does not seek, i.e., job placement in specific fields, or admission to advanced skills training programs. Other schools might frankly aspire to high scores on college placement tests and admission to competitive four-year colleges. Measures that permit valid comparisons among schools and over time must include student achievement tests—these can be mandated statewide or locally by public education authorities.

Educators have little experience with school-specific performance measures. Public schools are not in the habit of assessing themselves or initiating public discussions of their performance. Public education agencies have developed testing programs that allow comparisons among schools, but these are insensitive to differences in schools' educational approaches, or to differences in the prior educational attainment of students who attend particular schools.

For real school-level accountability, school staffs must devise performance measures that are logically related to school-specific goals and methods. Schools will need to say what a student is expected to know and do at particular grade levels, and produce credible evidence. Student portfolios and live performances might be important elements of some schools' self-assessment. Schools that intend to affect students' attitudes or their capacity to contribute to the broader community will need to find ways of measuring and demonstrating results. Schools that send students on to other schools (e.g., from elementary to middle school, middle to high school, or high school to college) will need to find ways of tracking their own graduates' performance. Schools that intend to keep pace with similar schools elsewhere (e.g., schools specializing in science, mathematics, or classical education) can submit themselves to judgment by inspectors or accreditors who draw comparisons among schools with similar announced goals.

Few, very few, public schools now do these things. Though a small number of public school principals are willing to be evaluated and take the consequences, most are convinced that evaluation is insensitive to school-specific needs and accomplishments. Feelings against evaluation are so high that few school staffs can sustain a discussion about how they would like to be evaluated. Most conclude only that they should be trusted to serve their students. In a contract system, however, school-specific evaluation is inevitable. If schools cannot say what they expect to accomplish, local education officials have no basis on which to establish contracts and perform their responsibility to protect students. Schools that lack clear performance expectations are also defenseless if they become controversial, or if small groups of parents or interest-group leaders complain about them.

Real school-level accountability also requires cross-school comparisons. Student performances, portfolios, postgraduation experience, and accreditation can all serve this purpose if they are rigorously and fairly scored. But doing so requires benchmarks for portfolios and performances, and equivalency of methods in tracking of graduates and in accreditation. Even if all these things are done, however, parents and public authorities will still want student test scores. There is no way a contract system can operate in the absence of student achievement test scores, including averages and ranges for all students, and for minority or low-income students, in every school.

Most states and many localities run student testing programs that can readily produce such information. No state or locality, however, now analyzes student test scores in ways that meet all the needs of contract schools. Contracting requires a method of establishing specific reasonable expectations for every school. Under contracting, individual schools will be responsible for saying exactly what the students will achieve. Staff must take account of the effectiveness of their instructional approach and their students' degree of academic preparation. A potential school provider that promises very little will have a hard time winning a contract; however, a school that promises too much will quickly get into trouble.

If contracting is to work, local education authorities must be capable of frank discussion with school contractors. What is realistic to expect in a school that serves a shifting population of new immigrants? If a contractor provides a school in a neighborhood where many resident students have for years failed to learn to read and drop out in the ninth grade, what is a reasonable performance expectation? How much improvement can be expected in a school that already has the best outcomes in the district? It may be good politics to say that all schools are expected to get steadily better, and that every student is expected to meet statewide standards, but a contracting system that did not take account of student body and neighborhood needs would fail. Public authorities that imposed unattainable performance standards would either get no offers or be forced to deal with people who would promise anything to get a contract. Potential school providers who promised steady but gradual improvement would always lose the competition of promises.

The only solution is for school performance goals to be negotiated openly, in light of information about the range of real performance in schools of different types. In a given state or locality there is usually a small number of schools doing an especially good job with disadvantaged students, and others serving their own particular populations especially well. Such schools, or national benchmark schools, could be used as standards, and contractors could cast their proposals in terms of how quickly their students' performance would rise relative to high levels of performance observed elsewhere.

Today's public education system evades such frank discussions with rhetoric suggesting that it is unfair to expect less of some students than others. Many schools are evaluated on standards they cannot meet and then condemned for failure, but nothing changes. In the long run, all students can indeed learn to have high standards. But in the short run it is better to have well thought-out plans and demanding but realistic expectations than to hope for magical solutions. A system of contract schools makes it possible for local education authorities to choose realistic progress over extravagant rhetoric.

Parent Opinion. A component of any evaluation agreement should be a provision for determining the views of families about their schools. The third-party evaluator should include steps to sample or survey parent opinion. The results of such efforts should be included as a special section in the evaluation report made available to the school board.

Contract Monitoring. In addition to the above-mentioned formal school evaluations by an outside party, the superintendent should assign a central-office staff member who acts as a contract monitor for a group of schools, perhaps one monitor for every five or six schools in the district. Each school should be visited at least once a week, and conversations held with the principal (contract leader) about the operation of the school. In addition, central-office contract monitors should have weekly conversations with the parent-advisory council chair. Both the contractor and the district's contract monitor should submit monthly or quarterly progress reports to the school board.

Contractor Default and Insolvency

The initial, and best, guarantee against contractor misfeasance is in the initial selection and negotiation process. However, regardless of the care initially taken, mistakes will occur and some contractors will not be able to perform. They may budget improperly, entrust a school to a poor principal, or simply use bad judgment. The role of central-office monitors is to ensure that contractors are not approaching some abyss, either operationally or financially. To protect the district's interests, however, contractors should be required to carry substantial liability insurance. Also, a district should have a contingency plan—much in the manner that fire and police departments now have cooperative assistance arrangements—in the rare instance where a school contractor cannot or will not perform appropriately and an emergency replacement must be made. We suspect that vendors will actually arise who will specialize in such a service. This might also be a service provided by a MAP (Management and Assistance Providers) as described in chapter 3.

Won't School Boards Just "Talk" All the Time and Still Micro-manage?

We think school boards will talk all the time, but that is what they ought to do. The difference now is that they will talk about what individual schools are expected to accomplish, and whether or not each is doing so under its present contractor.

Under a contracting system school boards will not be talking about whether or not so-and-so should be principal at a school, or where Ms. Jones will be assigned as a teacher. They will also not be making detailed budget decisions. Most of the district's revenues must be spent at schools, and most will be spent in large sums through the conveyance of operating contracts with providers. Also, school boards will not be talking about teachers' and other school-level employees' wages and salaries. Those issues will be resolved at the school level. (The exceptions will be the superintendent and a few central-office staff who will continue to report to the school board.)

If a school board, or an individual school board member, attempts to interfere in the day-to-day operation of a school, a contractor has a different kind of protection than principals and teachers now have. They are or should be protected by the terms of their contract. School board members have only the authority to enter into or, on the basis of contractor nonperformance, to discontinue school contracts. Otherwise, the authority of the school board is limited to the supervision of the superintendent and oversight of central-office functions such as check-writing, public information, hiring independent evaluators, and student assignment to schools of choice.

Contractor Responsibilities

Contractor responsibilities toward the school district and for the school they propose to operate will be specified in the contract. All school providers will prepare proposals, organize a school program, hire and supervise staff, and recruit students.

Preparing a Proposal

A proposal should specify all important components of the school the contractor proposes to operate. Of course, such a proposal should be responsive to the Request for Proposal issued by the school board. In addition, however, it should be far more than a mechanical or formulaic response. It should be a lively, albeit accurate, portrayal of the kind of school the vendor hopes to achieve. It should specify a vision for the school, describe the qualifications of those in important positions, explain means for engaging parents and the community, describe the curriculum, and emphasize whatever the school's special features are intended to be.

Organizing a School Program

If the bidder is selected, then, as usual, the hard work of actually organizing a school must be undertaken. A great deal of this planning should be a result of the proposal writing process. This is when arrangements would be made for key staff persons and thought given to the curriculum, instructional modes, and instructional materials. Nevertheless, no matter how much planning has taken place, the actual reality of an efficiently functioning school will take a great deal of effort.

Obtaining a Facility

If the school district has facilities it is willing to lease, finding a school facility may be a relatively simple task. Otherwise, finding a suitable building for a school is seldom easy. Churches, storefronts, private homes, former private school buildings, commercial offices, even former warehouses and factories have proven to be successful as schools, given sufficient creativity and ingenuity. This topic is covered in more detail in the next chapter.

Recruiting Students

This may require a marketing effort. Identifying prospective students, providing households with accurate information, responding to inquiries, ensuring eligibility will all occupy time, but are, nevertheless, crucial elements to success.

Role of the State

Under a contract school system, the role of the state becomes both more important and more streamlined. The principal role of state officials in a contract system is to stimulate the supply of responsible providers, license contractors, protect the rights of children and parents, specify a mandatory minimum core curriculum, provide technical assistance to local school districts in constructing RFPs and monitoring contracts, oversee a statewide testing system which appraises student performance on core-curriculum subject-matter areas, arrange for data collection regarding schools and school districts, undertake disbursement of funds to schools and school districts, and ensure local-district compliance with regulations regarding special-needs categories such as the handicapped. Some of these activities, such as testing and data collection, can themselves be contracted out to vendors. Several other conventional state activities such as adopting textbooks can be dropped entirely.

Stimulating Supply of Contract Providers

The state role in stimulating a good supply of contract providers is critical. In the absence of a continuous effort to increase the supply of qualified contractors, many localities might have no more options after contracting than before. Though many school systems might choose to enter contracts with some existing school staffs, a local district without alternative providers might be forced to re-create, through contracts, school plans and labor relations arrangements that closely resemble the ones that existed under the old bureaucratic system. Local authorities with real choices can demand performance and fair prices. Scarcity of contractors will inevitably limit local authorities' options and reduce their leverage on contractors who are not performing well.

A serious state investment in contractor development, through small subsidies for new providers' start-up costs, and efforts to identify and attract good contractors working in other states are needed to ensure that local education authorities have options. A state investment program, such as was attempted on the national level by the New American Schools Development Corporation (NAS), should further enhance the supply. Ohio has a small venture-capital fund that could, if expanded, be used for a similar purpose. State colleges and universities might also become incubators for new contract school providers.

State education agencies themselves might invest in creating contract providers, and then spin them off as independent organizations. If states agreed to specialize in developing different types of schools—one state specializing in career-focused schools, another in schools focused on arts and the classics—they could enhance the supply of providers for their own localities and others.

Standard Setting and Quality Control

The state would also have a continuing role to play in standard setting and quality control. States should continue establishing requirements for high school graduation and for performance of key measurable academic skills. Few localities have the research and development capabilities for such efforts, and many may be pressed by parent groups and contractors to lower their standards over time. The state government could countervail these forces by continuing to set graduation requirements. The state can also ensure that local education authorities and parents have good and unbiased information when they choose among contractors. Publication of performance data for every school and for every contractor (especially for contractors that operate in multiple districts) could ensure that local education authorities' decisions are well informed.

The state's role in setting standards and providing information should be modest. A system designed around diversity does not need and cannot use exhaustive standard measures of all aspects of school service, delivery, and performance. But it does need simple measures of school performance that are appropriate to all schools whatever their instructional method. In addition to testing, school performance could be measured and reported in terms of student attendance rates, rates of credit accumulation, minority students' access to college preparatory courses, promotion and graduation rates, and graduates' rates of progress at higher levels of education and in employment.

Collecting and publishing school performance data would give the state the information to identify local education agencies that were not replacing contractors despite poor performance, or that had, for an extended period of time, failed to find a contractor able to get good results in a particular school site. In such cases the state education agency could take a number of alternative actions: it could ensure that the local district knew about potentially more effective contractors, and it could determine whether the district was unable to attract better contractors because of local board conduct or unrealistic spending limitations. If the local district were able to find better contractors and spend more but refused to do so (e.g. because it refused to increase the share of per pupil expenditure allocated directly to schools), the state education agency could requisition local funds and hire new contractors itself. If the district had too weak an economic base to provide adequate contractor payments, the state would have to face the necessity of increasing its funding for the affected schools, or for the district as a whole.

Defining a Common School Core-Curriculum

This is perhaps the state's most important function. It is worthy of substantial deliberation. It hinges upon the question: "What knowledge is of most worth?" No two states are likely to reach the precise same conclusion, and any particular state almost assuredly will change its answer over time. Indeed, the answer should change from time to time because the state of knowledge has probably never changed faster than it is changing currently. Thus, deliberations about a core curriculum should be continual. Moreover, the debate about what should be taught is valuable in itself. It informs the public and provides an avenue for the polity continually to define itself.

All schools operating under contract with local public school boards should be required to offer courses in the state-specified minimum core curriculum. Local officials will be free to add to the minimum core, in keeping with their preferences and the desires of parents at particular schools. Presumably, schools will also add to their curriculum depending upon the grade levels they encompass, parents' aspirations, college and university entrance requirements, and qualifications sought by prospective employers such as the military and private-sector firms.

Evaluating School Performance

The principal means available to the state to enforce local district and school compliance with core curricula objectives is through the state's annual evaluation of student performance. The state should contract, through competitively sought bids, for the construction and administration of statewide tests. These tests would appraise student knowledge in specified core curriculum areas. Obviously, tests would be constructed to be consistent with the age or grade level of students involved.

Such examinations need not be given to every child at every grade level. The purpose of state testing, in this instance, is to appraise the quality of the state's overall school system, protect the state against malfeasance by a local school board or particular contractors, and inform parents about the performance of particular schools and school districts. Given these purposes, a sample of students sufficient to represent individual schools can be selected and tested at significant grade levels, such as one, three, five, six, eight, and eleven.

Of course, local districts and individual schools are perfectly free to test with greater frequency, if they decide they want to. Through the use of scientific procedures such as matrix sampling and spiraling, test results can be generalized to a school without testing every enrolled youngster. However, in the long run, when testing technology has been further developed, contracting implies the use of "value added" testing, which permits a calibration not only of how much a child has learned over the period since last examined but of how much of the increment can reasonably be attributed to the influence of the school.

Results on statewide tests should be released publicly with each school district and each school identified. Such test results should be a factor taken into consideration by local school boards in determining whether or not to renew a provider's contract. Also, the availability of school-by-school test results will be a major asset to parents considering where to enroll their children.

By testing in each of the specified core curricular areas, state officials will be able to determine the extent to which state interests are being served. Finally, should the present level of opposition to national testing ever be overcome, state tests could be coordinated with national examination systems. In this way, not only could a state determine the performance of students school-by-school and district-by-district, it also could measure the state's overall performance relative to other states and foreign countries.

Providing Other Specialized Services

State education departments or county offices of education might consider developing an array of specialized services that they could offer to school contractors. For example, providing instruction to handicapped students is an expensive undertaking, especially if there are no scale economies involved and a school or school district must offer expensive services in a specialized few instances. Often the expense of these unusual services can be reduced if sufficient numbers of similarly situated students can be grouped together. State education departments and county offices frequently have the personnel who are most experienced in these matters and who are thoroughly familiar with federal and state regulations. Individual school contractors might be eager to enter into subcontracts with such specialists. Probably students and the public budget would all benefit.

Other potential specialized services include technical assistance on programs for gifted students, foreign language instruction, before- and after-school child care, food service provision, facility maintenance and gardening, transportation, in-school testing and guidance counseling, and fringe benefit provision and management.

Bulk buying of goods for schools has generally been less efficient than proponents have hoped. The usual argument is that large school districts or consortia of school districts banded together for purchasing purposes could derive significant cost savings through cooperative buying. In the past, whatever financial advantage has been gained through such large-scale buying has been lost through inefficient, central-office supervised, district-operated warehousing and district distribution arrangements. Also, such central purchasing arrangements have proven inflexible regarding products and unresponsive regarding the time of teachers and administrators at individual schools.

However, new communication and inventory-control techniques may be able to remedy these past problems. Big-discount retail organizations have pioneered inventory-control procedures and vendor communications which permit just-on-time deliveries directly to a user's site. States or counties could assist local school districts and individual schools by brokering or managing such supply arrangements. Local schools and the contractors operating them would be under no compulsion to utilize such state-organized purchasing assistance, but if they thought they would save money and suffer no inconvenience, they almost assuredly would be eager participants.

Pooled purchasing of large capital items such as school buses would almost certainly be of interest to some school districts. Many states already provide cooperative purchasing for such items. However, in a contract school system, state education departments would have to prove that they were at least as efficient as private-sector providers. One can imagine an entrepreneurial private-sector broker who would organize local schools, particularly in rural areas, and offer transportation services, perhaps at lower per passenger rates than now prevail. We do not advocate either private or public brokering in matters such as this. We only mention the idea as a service that state education departments might fulfill, if they could do so in fair competition with private-sector agents.

Licensing Contractors

As was mentioned in a previous section, another new role for a state will be licensing contractors and approving their qualifications. Contractors will have to apply to the state, meet minimum qualifications such as level of organizational experience, be cleared for criminal record purposes, and be capable of obtaining insurance.

Educator Retirement and Health Plans

State teacher retirement systems will need to be adjusted in order to accommodate contract teachers. This could be done, for example, by dividing the year into quarters. For every quarter a teacher was employed on contract, he or she would receive a three-month retirement credit, and the contractor would be required to make whatever payments to the state were necessary. Alternatively, teacher unions could provide retirement programs to which their members subscribed. Finally, an organization for public school teachers could form, which would parallel what now exists for many college faculty. Here the Teachers Income Annuity Association, initiated by the Carnegie Foundation, provides retirement plans for faculty which move with them from one institution to the next. Each faculty member contributes, as do employers. No matter where a faculty member teaches, he or she continues the personalized retirement plan.

A national health insurance plan would resolve most of the issues about health insurance for contract school employees. In its absence, state reform statutes establishing a school contracting system should require school contractors to offer health insurance to all their employees. In the absence of a national or state mandatory program, there would be a risk that contractors in labor surplus markets would force teachers to bid for employment by giving up important health insurance benefits. This would benefit neither teachers nor the nation in the long run.

Professional Educators and Other School Providers

This category principally includes school administrators, teacher unions, and teachers. We believe their roles will be continued, often in more important ways than is now the case. It should be acknowledged from the outset, however, that these roles involve greater risk and responsibility than now exists in public schools. Correspondingly, we propose to compensate such professionals with an opportunity for greater rewards, both financial and professional.

Superintendents and Central-Office Managers

Local boards of education will continue to need the services of a chief executive officer. However, under a contract school arrangement, this role will now change to one principally engaged in long-range planning, the distillation of community and parent preferences into Requests for Proposals, liaison with state and other government agencies, and oversight of the third-party school evaluation processes. School boards will also rely heavily upon their chief executives for appraisals and recommendations from among the competitive bids they receive from potential school operators. However, superintendents will no longer have direct responsibility for operating schools or supervising their staffs, or providing other auxiliary services (except through pay-for-service agreements with providers at individual schools). In addition, a superintendent will have to supervise a few central-office staff members responsible for contract monitoring, arrange for third-party, independent evaluations of schools, and assist the school board and others in interpreting results of school evaluations.

Central-office units built to assist the superintendent will not wither away entirely although their roles will shift. Central offices will not employ large numbers of staff development, curriculum, or compliance specialists. They could, however, employ people capable of helping schools gain access to independent sources of help in such areas. Such services should be funded by fees paid by schools, not by mandatory reductions in cash made available to the schools. The central office could also offer some services, such as building maintenance, food service, payroll, and negotiation with insurance and annuity providers, on a fee basis and at the discretion of individual schools.

The main instructionally related functions of the central office would be to maintain a school-based information system to support the superintendent's long-range planning activities, allocate funds (real dollars) to schools on a strict per pupil basis, and hire and supervise contractors who would collect and disseminate information on schools and school performance. In most cases, independent organizations, not permanent central-office staff, would design school evaluations and collect data. This would ensure that evaluation methods were not limited by the capabilities of a fixed staff and could be continuously tailored to the instructional methods and objectives of individual schools. Central offices might staff or sponsor parent information centers, intended to help parents understand what is going on in schools and inform the school-choice process.

The superintendent and school board would continue to be legally responsible for the school district's compliance with laws affecting public-sector entities, as well as with laws, regulations, and court orders specifically pertaining to public school districts. School boards might also offer free or fee-based legal assistance to schools. To perform all these functions, some central offices might employ legal staffs, but most would probably retain independent legal counsel. The volume of legal work to be done would depend on whether state and federal laws affecting school districts could be simplified, as described in chapter 7.

Central offices might also employ professional property managers who would maintain buildings, subdivide large buildings so that multiple small schools could use them, and find space for new schools. These managers should also have the power to lease or sell unused school buildings on the open market, and to help schools that cannot be housed in district-owned buildings find and lease privately owned facilities.

To limit the number of central-office employees, the superintendent should have to propose a central-office budget and have some discretion in deciding how many people would work in the central office. To ensure that future superintendents are not hamstrung by past staff choices, most central-office employees would serve at the pleasure of the superintendent, not as tenured civil servants. The money saved by trimming district administration would go directly to the schools. Some cost savings created by reducing the permanent central-office staff would, however, be offset by hiring additional legal and management specialists and by increased levels of contracting-out for data systems, evaluations, and legal services.

Principals

Individual schools will continue to need chief executives. In small schools, this position may well be filled by a head teacher, an individual who continues to have responsibility both for management and instruction. As in private schools, most administrators would also do some teaching. When administrators are full-time managers, they risk losing touch with the difficult task of teaching and, as a result, they dilute their legitimacy in the eyes of their teachers.

The task of the principal is to oversee every facet of the day-to-day operation of a school. Even if the school relies upon subcontractors for the provision of auxiliary services, one person has to be in a position to coordinate and evaluate every facet. Also, the principal should serve as either the contractor or the contractor's chief representative at the school. Principals who are prime contractors might be individual entrepreneurs, but most would be the leading member of a teacher cooperative or as the head of a professional partnership.

Teacher Unions

The roles of teacher unions would change, but unions would not disappear. They might still bargain with the school district over benefits, but pay and working conditions would be set by schools, constrained only by the terms of their individual agreements with the school board. Teachers in different schools could have different employment contracts; unions could represent teachers in their relationships with schools.

Teachers would still need a professional association. Teacher unions could continue to engage in activities such as arranging insurance and other fringe benefits for teachers. They might also offer training for current and prospective teachers, and act as hiring halls or guilds from which schools could find teaching talent. Unions might even enter agreements to manage certain schools. If they ran some schools, teacher unions would no longer simply be "labor"; they would also become entrepreneurs or providers, like professionals in other fields such as law, medicine, and accounting.

Removing the school board and central office from the process of delivering instruction and defining school operations makes schools the primary managers of education. Schools would choose their own teachers. They might seek assistance in the hiring process from the central office or the teacher's union; they might also simply consult a registry of certified teachers or advertise job vacancies on the open market.

These changes would create a true labor market for instructional and administrative staff. Schools would make decisions about hiring, evaluating, and terminating their own staff members. School board RFPs should specify that contractors must be equal opportunity employers. Teachers and administrators would enjoy the same protections against arbitrary treatment that state and federal laws extend to other salaried employees, but they would no longer hold lifetime civil service posts. On the other hand, teachers and administrators would be free to assess and select their workplaces and to make wage demands consistent with their training and personal reputations. Some schools might accept a district-wide salary schedule, or some might join with other schools in a hiring pool that contracted with a professional teachers' association that trained, assessed, certified, and supplied teachers. Teachers from groups of schools might also create their own multischool unions, but such unions would have to be built up school by school, not imposed from above.

Individual Teachers

Some number of teachers will initially be threatened by these proposals. Many people entered teaching expecting the protection of civil service tenure and work-restrictive contract provisions, and they will find the change worrisome. However, for many other teachers, being involved in operating a contract school will be exciting. For them the opportunity to cooperate with professional peers in an environment in which their participation is valued and their efforts appropriately rewarded is long overdue.

Some schools run by teacher cooperatives might agree to highly structured salary schedules, possibly including identical salaries for all teachers. Other schools might prefer to let individual teacher salaries be set by the market. In any case, schools could compete for teachers by providing incentives such as a good benefits package or training programs. Teachers could demand higher pay for difficult situations or heavy responsibilities. Contractors bidding to operate schools in remote rural or in highly stressed inner-city areas may have to offer higher salaries to obtain quality teachers. Most schools would have to offer pay premiums for teachers in shortage categories (e.g., mathematics, science, and bilingual education).

A school's hiring, training, pay, and firing policies would be driven by its instructional strategy and student needs, not by a standard staffing table. Staffing would be a key element in each school's own effort to maintain quality and to survive in a competitive market for students. Schools that prove to be poor judges of teachers, or whose managers cannot maintain a stable and high-quality teaching force, will almost certainly turn in poor performance figures and fail to attract students. For-profit firms, subject to the same competitive pressures, will not be able to offer lower salaries or worse working conditions than schools run by neighborhood groups or nonprofits. Local school boards can monitor teacher turnover and qualifications as a leading indicator of possible problems in a school.

School contractors will be under pressure to obtain the services of good teachers, in order to provide the most convincing proposals to local school boards and impress parents.

A teacher labor market can contribute toward school quality and accountability. As long is there is competition among schools and parental choice, there is no need for state regulation of staff salaries. If, however, local boards cannot or will not enforce the performance terms of their contracts with schools, the state might need to limit profit-taking by establishing floors for teacher salaries.

No one can say in advance whether these arrangements will increase or decrease average teacher pay. Some are concerned that for-profit firms might try to maximize profits by holding down teacher salaries; but the performance and reputations of such schools would almost certainly suffer. Teacher cooperatives might, as do current teacher unions, try to maximize teachers' share of school income by offering generous pay, benefits, time off, etc. But they, unlike contemporary teacher unions, would be constrained by competition. As under the present system, the adults who run schools will try to control as much money as they can. Neither competition nor regulation can eliminate this tendency, but competition is a more effective constraint than is regulation.

Evaluators

The performance of individual schools would need to be appraised systematically by an objective, highly qualified, independent third party. The criteria against which a school's and its students' performance would be judged would be specified initially in the contract with the school district. The evaluation strategies and techniques of the third-party appraiser would be specified in its proposals to school boards. Presumably, a wide number of formats would be employed in such assessments. Evaluation results should be provided to the local school board, to the contractor, to parents at an individual school, and, perhaps, to the public at large.

Such evaluation should be done on contract to the local school board. Professional and qualified firms and individuals would bid to undertake evaluations for a school board. They could evaluate one or more schools, depending upon the school board preference. (We would counsel using multiple contractors, because in this way the school board would continually be engaging in a natural experiment to see which evaluation techniques and formats served their purposes best.)

Third-party evaluators would also incorporate the results of statewide testing programs into their report for an individual school. It would be the responsibility of the evaluator to interpret the scores accurately and understandably to the audiences to which the report would be made available.

Many qualified evaluators and evaluation firms already exist. Such a third-party assessment mandate would probably enhance the field. Even larger numbers of capable professionals would enter this line of work.

Private Fee-Charging Providers

Schools would have broad discretion about what goods and services to buy and from whom. Private organizations could sell goods and services ranging from books and pencils to tutoring services. As Ted Kolderie suggests, groups of teachers could offer and schools could buy specialized services (e.g., tutoring for slow-learning students; whole courses in foreign languages, science, and mathematics). Schools might contract with building maintenance organizations, accounting firms, and even law firms that could advise, e.g., on drafting an agreement with the central office or complying with labor or civil rights laws.

A whole industry of providers is likely to grow up around a truly decentralized school system. There is no way to guarantee that all such providers will be of high quality—just as there is no way to ensure that all central-office services are needed, effective, and efficiently provided. School system central offices might help individual schools by rating the performance of service providers and providing a brokerage service for schools seeking particular kinds of help. Central offices and state-funded regional service districts might also compete for schools' business, but they should not be able to anoint themselves sole providers. A system in which schools control funds and can choose among independent vendors has a great advantage over a service monopoly by the central-office bureaucracy: a school can fire and replace an ineffective provider.

Independent Organizations Funded by Business and Foundations

Under the current public education arrangements, few school districts have the money required to offer extensive assistance to all the schools that need it, or to conduct the research, development, or evaluation that can lead to well-grounded changes in practice. This is probably a permanent condition: the pressure to add new programs at the school level or to reduce class size virtually guarantees that increments of money go to staff salaries rather than to investment. Contracting will increase the amount of money that is spent at the school level, but it is unlikely to change the imperative for schools to spend every penny they can get their hands on for direct services to students. Under contracting, the shortage of funding for program development, evaluation, dissemination, staff training, and assistance to whole schools will continue.

If neither schools nor school districts can fully finance needed investments in quality improvement, where can the new intellectual resources come from? Some forms of high-quality assistance may ultimately be available only from the state education agency, colleges and universities, Management and Assistance Providers, and independent organizations funded by businesses and foundations. Schools will be able to pay some fees, but most high-quality assistance organizations will continue to rely on business or foundation grants to pay for their basic research, development, and self-evaluation, as well as for many of the services they provide schools. Under the decentralized public education system sketched here, the need for such organizations funded by charitable contributions is likely to grow.

In addition to assistance with instructional improvement, schools will need help with business management. When contract schools gain control of their funds, staffs, and facilities, they will be, in effect, fiscally accountable small businesses. Contract school leaders will definitely need training, but there will probably also be a permanent requirement for purchased or contributed business services that will let teachers and administrators focus on instructional leadership. Local businesses interested in helping individual schools can commit, on a long-term basis, to providing such services as accounting, funds management, insurance brokerage, formation of purchasing pools, warehousing, and building maintenance.

Contract schools will also need legal advice and representation on contracts, labor law, and liability. As Dean Millot has found, the law pertaining to individual schools is evolving rapidly. For the foreseeable future, contract schools will face real uncertainties about their legal rights and obligations. Foundation-funded school law centers, offering legal advice and occasional representation, may be necessary complements to a decentralized public school system.

Some public school districts may offer these forms of support from public funds, and all should help schools find and assess the relevance of privately provided services. But a mixture of private and public assistance to schools is more compatible with decentralization than is a public monopoly. If school districts can fund their own operations by taxing school budgets or skimming dollars off the top, they can quickly upset the fine balance of school autonomy and accountability that contracting is intended to create. In education, as in all other areas, the power to tax is the power to destroy. A rich variety of providers of instructional improvement and business services is necessary for a successful and stable contract system.

Parents

Parents have two formal places for expressing preferences for schooling. In hearings and deliberations where local school boards determine individual school contract specifications, parents should be represented intensely. Additionally, each contractor should be expected to establish a parent-site council at the school itself. The role of the site council is simultaneously to advise the contractor and to provide a setting for communicating parent preferences, within the contract, to the contract director (principal).

The parent advisory council can also serve as an early level in a grievance hearing process, should a disagreement arise between a school contractor and an individual parent.

In addition to providing advice and expressing preferences through formal decision-making channels, parents have a role to play as individual households. Each local school district, in implementing a parent-choice plan, should require each household with a child of school age to choose a school. Every reasonable effort should be made to fulfill first choices. However, if a school has more applicants than places, then some households will have to settle for their second choice. Once a contract system is established, a school board would have an obligation to reproduce schools that have many more applicants than spaces. Experience with public school choice plans in communities such as Cambridge, Massachusetts, suggest that virtually all households (85 percent) can have either their first or second choice satisfied. Parents would select the public school of their choice at the beginning of each school year. In the instance of a dissatisfied parent, a change of schools, assuming sufficient space at the receiving school, can be made at the end of each quarter or semester.

Citizens

Citizens will participate in a contract school system by running or voting for local school- and state-elected positions. Also, of course, citizens will continue to have opportunities to express their views on education matters by attending and participating in local school board meetings and various state-level policy deliberations about education matters. Citizens will not have an opportunity to participate in discussions regarding fund raising at a particular school, in that funding beyond the contract amount would be raised at the initiative of parents and staff. Hence, this is not an appropriate setting for citizen participation.

Any individual eligible voter may participate in a local school board election. However, any prospective contract provider who contributes materially to, or who actively participates in a local school board electoral campaign, will forfeit his or her opportunity to bid on any contract during the time period that the school board member in question serves in office.

Conclusion

The foregoing is a radical vision of public school governance and management, but it is perfectly straightforward and commonplace in most other regards. It assumes, as do the systems of contracts that define productive collaborations in the private sector, that clear goals and flexible resources lead to efficient arrangements. It rejects the "governmentalist" assumption that an enterprise seeking a public good must be overseen in detail by large numbers of civil servants. It embraces the idea that schools should be controlled to the greatest degree possible by professionals and the families they serve; yet it provides for a residual public authority that can adjust its portfolio of schools in response to new needs and that can take action to replace unproductive schools with better ones. It establishes clear and permanent assistance and quality-control functions for local business and charitable organizations.

In addition to these managerial requirements, it is clear that a contract school system must value ideas and embody them in schools. Better instruction is not just a question of teacher morale and technique. It requires each school to be built on a definite philosophy of instruction. A school that is able to develop its own distinctive mission and instructional philosophy should be free to do so. But groups of parents, teachers, and administrators who have worked together for years in a regulated public school system may not be able to define or agree on a single educational mission or approach to instruction. If contracting is to produce effective instruction, most schools must accept outside help, in the form of a mission and philosophy based on the experience of others.

In summary, creation of a system of effective schools requires many things in addition to increasing initiative at the school-site level. It requires new public management capacities that let public officials, particularly school superintendents, oversee portfolios of distinctive schools, take aggressive action to close and recommission schools that fail, and to recommission new ones. It takes acceptance among educators and the public that good public schools can and should be different from one another. And it requires well-developed educational philosophies and arrangements for helping school communities to learn about and implement these philosophies.

Of all these prerequisites, the last will be the hardest to obtain on a large scale. Aside from existing philosophy-driven school networks, such as Montessori, Waldorf, and those created by religious organizations, there are only a few organizations able to lead and train the staffs of independent public schools. These might include Ted Sizer's Coalition of Essential Schools, school reform organizations headed by Deborah Meier, James Comer, and Henry Levin, and some of the "break the mold" school design teams sponsored by the New American Schools Development Corporation. Other philosophy-based assistance providers might emerge as schools form voluntary networks and work with universities to develop, test, and document new instructional approaches.

SIX

Paying for Contract Schools

P revious chapters described the concept of contracting for educational services and the operations of contract schools. A new system of school finance is also required, one that supports independent, self-operating schools.

A School Finance Proposal

Most school districts are technically or legally units of state government, not local government. Every state except Hawaii has established local school districts and requires them (and in some cases municipal governments) to raise a significant proportion of school revenues. Because the abilities of school districts to raise revenues vary a great deal, the shared state and local responsibility for financing public education creates inequities in educational opportunity within most states. Our proposal is to turn responsibility for financing primary and secondary education over to the states. A system of full-state funding would eliminate the persistent patterns of expenditure that have ensnared over half of the states in costly and divisive litigation. By eliminating local property tax support for schools, localities may be able to reduce property taxes or use them to support other important community services for roads, public safety, and social services. Instead of being a competitor for scarce local resources, schools would be able to collaborate with local social service agencies to improve education. Finally, it would make the education system and its means of financing understandable.

A reformed finance system should ensure that state dollars follow students, so that each student has an equal opportunity of receiving a high-quality education. School districts should be required to pass a minimum of 95 percent of revenues they receive to local schools on a per pupil basis. Students should be able to choose any school within or outside their district provided there is space. When students move from one district to another, state dollars should follow them.

Shifting responsibility for the financing of public schools to the state will require additional state-generated dollars. States will vary on how to generate new revenues depending on their existing tax structure. In general, states should finance public education from the state's general fund, with revenues raised from some combination of income taxes, sales and other excise taxes, statewide property taxes on utilities and natural resources, and other sources such as lotteries and casinos. Because localities will be relieved of the burden of paying for schools, states will be able to reduce revenue-sharing programs and use the money saved for financing public schools.

Local control and local flexibility are part of the education tradition in this nation and should be preserved. The ability to choose a school and to register satisfaction or dissatisfaction with a school by enrolling or withdrawing a child will strengthen local control.

In addition a new school finance system should permit parents of students at a school to raise additional amounts through fund raising or, in some cases, by accepting voluntary payments. Additional fund raising must be entirely voluntary and must not be treated as any sort of precondition for admission. Parents should be encouraged to contribute time and effort, both to reduce the school's operating costs and to help the school raise money from businesses, foundations, and other sources. Schools seeking to serve especially needy populations may want to raise money in order to attract and serve disadvantaged children. As in some private schools, richer parents may want to subsidize the school's outreach to low-income and diverse populations by contributing funds for preschool education, extra programs, or academic support. Parents may also want to pay for computers or an extended school year.

State per pupil support for schools should also include enough money to cover the cost of facilities. Existing school facilities should be rented to the school operators at a fair market value. If the schools were built with state funds, the rent would be paid to the state to retire bonds or go to the state general fund. If districts built the schools, the rent would be used to retire local bonds or be put into a reserve for future building or renovation of facilities. Schools should also have the option of renting space from private parties or nonprofit organizations. Because the state's per pupil allocation covers all the costs of providing education, including capital costs, a new school provider should be able to borrow money to build a new school to be paid off with a portion of the projected per pupil revenues.

The goal of the new finance system is a fairer, more efficient, more democratic, more flexible, and more understandable way of paying for public education.[1]

Principles for Funding a New School Finance System

Five principles should underlie any system of school finance. They can be summarized in five words: equity, efficiency, democracy, flexibility, and simplicity.

Equity

Equity is one of the foundation values of American public education and one of the hardest to achieve. The concept is imbedded in most state constitutions, in such phrases as the state must provide a "uniform and general" or a "thorough and efficient" free and basic education. State statutes almost always say something about providing an equal educational opportunity through the state finance formula. There are of course many complex issues in deciding what is fair or equal education, or what provides a "level playing field," when it comes to financing schools. Whether to finance equal educational inputs or try to achieve equal results has been the topic of intense legislative debates and numerous professional books and articles (Guthrie, Garms, and Pierce 1988).

Although this debate will continue, there are practical steps which can improve the equity of most school finance systems. In most states the dollars available at the school for education vary widely, depending largely on the property wealth of the district in which the school is located. Furthermore, attempts to compensate urban districts for the high costs of urban inner-city schools or to redress past inequities have done little to change the persistent pattern of failure in many inner-city schools.

More equitable funding will not solve all the problems of our current school systems. It is a necessary component, however, of an effective finance system. In establishing a system of contract schools, states should be guided by the following principles:

1.1 Each state should ensure that educational dollars are distributed more or less equally on a per pupil basis.

1.2 The state distribution formula should include all of the costs of ed-

---

1. Existing school finance arrangements are extremely complex, and their complexity is in itself a strong warrant for a reform proposal like the one we present here. For a primer on current school finance arrangements, see Appendix B.

ucation, including operating costs, capital costs, and the costs of providing social services needed for children to be ready to learn.

1.3   Equal or equitable per pupil allocations may be adjusted to recognize real extra costs of operating certain kinds of schools, such as small schools in sparsely populated communities, urban schools, and the extra costs of educating disabled and disadvantaged children.

Efficiency

Efficiency, like equity, is hard to define in education. Many educators equate efficiency with cutting costs and reducing taxes. Efficiency for them, therefore, has a distinctly pejorative ring to it. Most will agree that schools should be more efficient, but they get enthusiastic about the idea only when it means cutting someone else's program.

In its simplest terms, efficiency increases when outcomes increase with the same level of resources (sometimes called greater effectiveness) or when outcomes remain the same with a lower level of resources (sometimes called increased productivity) (Guthrie, Garms, and Pierce 1988).

The major concern in American education is the low level of academic achievement of too many school graduates. Our top graduates do well in international comparisons. But the average test scores for American students on science and mathematics examinations are below the average scores on comparable examinations for students in many industrialized nations, especially those in Asia. And most alarming, the bottom quarter of American high school students either do not graduate or have difficulty passing basic literacy examinations.

The concern with the achievement of the bottom third of public school students is relatively new. Until the 1960s, we expected a third of the students to fail or drop out of school. They could find jobs in agriculture and the factories. Today low-skill jobs are disappearing or are incapable of supporting a family. The price for dropping out of school or failing to learn high school subjects is a life of poverty on the margins of American society. The 1990s has seen a growing acceptance of the idea that all children must be given the opportunity and a reasonable chance of obtaining a quality education.

Increasing efficiency in schools, therefore, has a lot to do with how resources are deployed in ways that result in substantially improved learning for all children. There is little evidence that the public thinks too much is being spent on public education. Some polls even suggest people would be willing to spend more if it would produce better results. Consequently, efficiency should be pursued in ways that improve the outcomes of schooling, which include such indicators as the high school graduation rate, test scores, the readiness of students to enter the work force, and ability to effectively participate in democratic institutions.

Increasing efficiency in terms of improving outcomes with available resources must be the most important and central feature of a new school finance system to support contract schools. Such a system should focus on the following principles:

2.1 Most state education dollars should be allocated to decision-makers at the school site who have the greatest ability to improve student outcomes.

2.2 Schools should be given the maximum flexibility in how resources are utilized to encourage efforts to improve student performance.

2.3 The state finance system should provide incentives that reward high-achieving schools.

Democracy

Public education remains the most important institution for bringing Americans together. It not only creates a common core of information required for effective participation in our civic culture but also encourages children from a broad range of backgrounds to address common problems. This socializing and integrating function of public education is worth preserving and strengthening. A good way of doing that is to make schools as democratic as possible. Students should see that schools are operated democratically and learn through their own participation in school activities how effectively to share in the decisions that most affect their lives. It is a truism that children learn as much from how they are taught as from what they are taught. To fulfill their mission of preparing students for participation in a democracy, schools themselves should be more democratic.

The implications of this principle for school finance are as follows:

3.1 The new school finance system should encourage the broadest possible participation of teachers, parents, and students in school decisions.

3.2 Parents and students should have the right to choose which schools they want to attend, with funds following students on a per pupil basis.

Flexibility

There is no one best way to ensure that all students get a good education. Children learn in different ways and respond to different kinds of instructional strategies. The experiences and understandings that students from rural communities bring to school are likely to be much different from those that their contemporaries in inner cities bring to schools. Effective educational strategies are tailored to accommodate these differences.[2]

Hierarchical forms of organization, which dominate in public education, purport to increase efficiency by reducing variation to the lowest common denominator. Curriculum guidelines and rules try to construct a single best way to teach all students. State textbook selection reinforces such regulation. The result of the regulation is schools designed for everyone which serve few students well. In order to serve all students, schools need to be encouraged to adjust their programs to the needs of students in the school. This requires both organizational and financial flexibility.

To increase flexibility, the finance system should adhere to the following principles:

4.1 Once a school receives its budget, there should be very few rules on how the dollars actually are spent.

4.2 Schools should be allowed to utilize savings from efficient practices and should be allowed to carry forward savings from one year to another.

4.3 Schools should be encouraged to cut costs or secure additional revenues by seeking outside funds and participating in entrepreneurial activities.

Simplicity

State school-finance formulas, school budgets, and schools in general have become so complicated that few individuals can understand them. Effective parent participation and community support are only possible if people understand the mission of schools, the programs being offered, and how the budget of a school is developed and implemented. One of the advantages of contract schools is their simplicity. By focusing the manage-

---

2. Two of the authors were the principal writers of an Educational Commission of the States report on flexibility entitled *Bending without Breaking: Improving Education Through Flexibility and Choice* (Denver: Education Commission of the States, June 1996).

ment and financing of schools at the school level, the public will have a better understanding of schools and be willing to support them.

The new school finance system should also aim at being understandable to the citizens of the state. This is possible if the following principles are followed:

5.1   To the extent possible, dollars should be allocated to schools on a per student basis with no or few strings attached. All students in a state who are similarly situated (e.g., in the third grade without special needs) should receive the same dollar level of resources.

5.2   Schools should publish and make available to the public a simple program budget explaining the manner in which school revenues will be spent to achieve the school's program objectives.

The State Role in Financing Public Education

Full State Support for Public Education

Expenditure inequities that plague most state school finance systems result primarily from states sharing the responsibility for financing of schools with local school districts. Because local districts vary in their ability to raise money for schools, school spending varies unless the state equalizes local revenue-raising capacity. With unlimited resources, states could do this. However, in the real world of limited revenues, funds for equalization are difficult to find. The mixed nature of school finance also encourages legislators to wheel and deal as they seek advantages for their constituents, in the form of either larger state appropriations for their school districts or a smaller local share of the total costs. The best way to provide equitable funding for schools and to reduce legislative manipulation of the finance formula is to place the responsibility for funding public education solely on the shoulders of state government. In states that have followed this path, such as California, Washington, Oregon, and Hawaii (which has only one school district), expenditure differentials among school districts are much smaller.[3]

---

3. There is a possible downside to full state financing of public schools. States that rely most heavily upon locally levied property taxes are, on balance, the states that have the higher per pupil spending. The tradeoff is that these are also the states with the highest degree of per pupil spending inequalities. Our proposal for full state funding is different on a crucial dimension, however. It proposes full state funding, but places the resources at school sites. This closer connection with individual schools and the resulting transparency by which parents can see how resources are being spent will result in a greater willingness to support schools by the public.

Most states rely on some local funding, for several reasons. Policymakers are reluctant to raise state taxes. Some legislators and education lobbyists also argue that it is easier to get voters to approve local taxes for schools than statewide taxes. Proponents of local control argue that requiring local voters to approve school operating and capital improvement levies helps let people know what they are buying with their tax dollars.

Efforts to construct equitable school finance formulas that combine state and local revenues have not been successful in eliminating or substantially reducing the inequities in our current school finance system, however. The best way to do this is to shift the responsibility for funding schools to the states, where constitutionally it belongs.

New Revenue Sources

Because states currently, on average, pay only about half the cost of public schools, they will need to raise additional revenues or allocate a larger share of existing state revenues to schools in order to fully fund public education. States should consider both strategies. In general, states fund public education from the state's general fund. Most states rely heavily on the individual income tax, corporate income tax, excise taxes on alcohol and tobacco, and a state sales tax to pay for general fund programs. If new revenues are needed, consideration might be given to a statewide property tax on utilities and natural resources. In many areas of the nation, natural gas lines, hydroelectric dams, and electrical transmission lines are located in sparsely populated areas and are taxed at relatively low rates. The same is true of extractable natural resources such as natural gas and oil, minerals, and private timber. When these utilities and natural resources are taxed by local school districts, they tend to benefit a very few students who live in remote areas. These resources and services can serve all the citizens of the state by having the state collect the property tax and use the revenues to support education across the state.

The taxation of real property should remain substantially at the local level and be used to support local services other than public education. It is possible that with the relief from supporting schools, local property taxes could be used to pay some of the state's contribution to local road building and repair and community services for the unemployed and elderly. This would release state revenues for school support and reduce the amount of new tax dollars needed to fully fund the state school finance formula.

Many states dedicate revenues from lotteries and casinos to support education. In general, this is fine. The problem in relying on lottery and gaming revenues, however, is that they tend to be unreliable and may have to be replaced when and if the public gets wise to or tires of the unfavorable odds they face when buying a lottery ticket or rolling the dice. The introduction of lotteries, casinos, and video poker also increases social service costs as states are forced to spend more for law enforcement, public assistance, and compulsive gambling assistance programs. It is best to rely on progressive taxes, those that raise money for government in proportion to a citizen's ability to pay. This is particularly important in the area of education that has historically served upper-income families better than poor ones. Because lotteries and gambling attract a disproportionate number of people who cannot afford to lose money on these games, it seems doubly cruel to finance education on the backs of those least able to pay.

Distributing State Education Dollars

Most formulas for distributing state education dollars are unbelievably complex. They attempt to share the costs of public education with local school districts that differ widely in educational values and abilities to support schools. States try to assure that funding is fair, efficient, and faithful to the tradition of local control. In attempting to accomplish all of these purposes, state formulas serve few of these purposes well, if at all.

Full state funding can accomplish the goals of equity, efficiency, and local flexibility, and still be understandable to both policy makers and the public. The state legislature should establish the per pupil cost of providing an adequate education. A determination of adequacy will have to consider dimensions such as typical staffing ratios, salary levels required to attract high-quality teachers, and the length of the school day and school year. An adequate level of support should also include the costs of providing adequate facilities, equipment, and teaching materials. There will be many factors to consider, and there will be opposing views on what an adequate education should cost. However, once an education appropriation is enacted, the formula for distributing state education dollars should be straightforward. The state should award to each school district an amount equal to the product of the per pupil allocation times the number of students enrolled in the district.

There will probably need to be a few adjustments to the formula. The costs of providing adequate elementary and secondary education, for instance, may differ sufficiently to be recognized in the formula. For example, the state may allocate $4,500 for each student in grades K through 8, and $5,000 for each student in grades 9 through 12.

Personnel costs often constitute 70 to 80 percent of a school's budget.

Consequently, differences in the cost of living or cost of attracting teachers to certain rural areas or urban schools that are perceived by some to be unattractive may have to be adjusted in the formula to assure that each school has approximately the same effective level of resources per student.

There may be a few other adjustments required to ensure that students have access to roughly equal resources. But these adjustments should be kept to a minimum to avoid adding complexity to the formula. It is important that average citizens understand the formula so that they trust their children are being treated fairly.

The purpose of the state formula is to deliver to each school an amount of money that places it at the same starting point as any other school in the state with the same number and kinds of students. While the formula will provide funds to school districts, districts should be required to pass 95 percent or more of the money directly to schools in proportion to their enrollments.

Local Adjustments to State Finance

The District's Role in Financing Schools

The district's role in school finance should be minimized and possibly eliminated. In a system of contract schools, the school board and the central-office staff serve as policy makers and facilitators. Once they select contractors to operate schools, the district should stay out of the day-to-day operations of schools. Some state money will be needed to hold school board meetings, for the staff to prepare RFPs and award contracts, and to evaluate and disseminate information on school performance. For the most part, districts should pass most of the money received from the state to schools. The central district office will also be responsible for transferring and receiving funds from other districts resulting from net transfers of students from one district to another.

Providing Financial Flexibility at the School Level

As indicated in the previous chapter, schools should be able to raise funds and accept donations. This might be crucial for schools that try to serve a diverse population by providing strong instructional support for disadvantaged students. Some states may want to try out the idea of permitting schools to ask the parents of children in the school to collect fees that could increase a school's expenditures per pupil by no more than 25 percent of the state per pupil allocation. Local school operators would have to receive the support of, say, two-thirds of the parents to charge the extra fees. In most cases, added fees would be deployed for specific purposes, perhaps to extend the school year, to buy computers, to provide field trips, to renovate facilities, and so on.

To ensure that each school has an equal chance of obtaining parent approval for the local add-on, school revenues raised for enrichment could be means-adjusted. This could be done by providing an income tax credit or state rebate to parents paying local school charges. Eligibility for the income tax credit or rebate would depend on a family's adjusted gross income. The lower the family income, the greater the tax credit or rebate. However constructed, the law should attempt to make the choice of a local add-on as income-neutral as possible. Local fees should place approximately the same fiscal burden on all families, regardless of their income level.

In schools with large numbers of low-income families, parents may be unable to contribute extra fees at the beginning of the school year, even if they support the enrichment activities. Schools should be allowed to borrow the money in anticipation of the tax refunds or rebates.

Placing the responsibility and burden for raising enrichment funds at the school level is sensible. Local moneys are for enrichment programs above what the state decides is required for an adequate education, and it will be the families of the students that are most likely to benefit from the additional services. Consequently, they should be the ones to decide on the enrichment program and also bear its costs via various forms of fund raising. Despite the higher personal cost, parents of schoolchildren are also more likely to support a local-option fee than the public at large, again because their children will benefit and they will have participated in the decision to adopt the fee. If a family opposes the fund raising, it has the option of transferring a student to a school with lower aspirations.

Schools should also be encouraged and assisted by the district office to submit funding proposals to public and private foundations and agencies. The central office might have a grants coordinator who would provide school personnel with information on funding opportunities. The grants coordinator can offer seminars and provide personal assistance to teachers preparing grant proposals. When appropriate, the district office should also assist schools in identifying collaborators to submit grants. Numerous funding opportunities exist for schools in partnership with local universities, nonprofit organizations, community social-service providers, and businesses to submit grants applications. Central-office auxiliary services such as these should be charged back, as a service fee, to local schools.

There are many other ways for schools to raise funds or expand opportunities that improve education for their children. Teachers can offer professional development workshops for teachers in other schools. Multimedia courseware developed by teachers and parents might be sold to other teachers and the profits plowed back into the school's budget. Schools might develop partnerships with businesses that will provide equipment for laboratories, technical assistance in operating computer or science laboratories, research or vocational education experiences for students, or even summer employment for teachers in the school. School providers should be encouraged to contract out services when doing so reduces costs and frees funds for other educational purposes.

The idea is to remove the constraints on a school's ability to raise funds locally and to provide incentives for them to do so. Let's say that a school decided to build a local area network for computers in every classroom. It could request parents to pay fees to cover the costs. It could seek foundation support for the project or ask local businesses to contribute the computers and assistance in networking the building. Because schools will be competing for students, decision-makers at a school will want to find the least expensive way of enhancing its program. Extra fees, if allowable, would be the last option considered because they will increase a family's cost to attend the school. On the other hand, they may greatly contribute to the school's success in serving students.

Turning school administrators and teachers into educational entrepreneurs will not be easy. But this step may be necessary to develop the kind of creative management that is needed to improve school performance.

Managing the Fiscal Resources of Schools

This is a chapter on the financing of a decentralized system of contract schools. In most cases, finance refers to the processes by which money for the support of schools is raised and distributed. Once the money is in the hands of individual schools, administration more accurately describes the mechanisms for deciding how the money is spent. There is a certain amount of overlap, however, between finance and administration, and this section deals with several of those areas.

Acquiring Facilities

One of the problems in shifting from large, centralized, and bureaucratic school districts to a system of decentralized, contract schools involves the use of existing facilities. School districts have a large investment in existing schools. Many of the buildings are relatively modern and should be used in the future. Some schools in poor rural areas and in the inner cities are so dilapidated and unattractive that they should be torn down. Many schools are too big to be effective and should be remodeled to a smaller scale or used to house several schools in the same building.

As we mentioned earlier, facilities' costs should be a part of the operating budgets funded by the state finance formula. School administrators, in making decisions about how best to run the school, should be able to consider the costs of facilities along with all the other costs entailed in operating a school. Some providers may choose to rent less attractive space in a church or local shopping mall in order to be able to employ additional technical or paraprofessional staff, while another provider might decide to build a new high-technology facility, pledging a portion of its state operating budget to pay off a privately negotiated construction loan or mortgage on the facility.

Some providers will want to use existing school facilities. As part of the proposal process, these providers would negotiate a market rent for the use of these facilities. If the facilities were built with revenues from locally issued bonds, then the rents should be deployed to pay the principal and interest on the bonds. If the facilities were built with state funds, the rent would be distributed to the appropriate state agency to retire the bonds.

The important point is that providing adequate and attractive facilities should become the responsibility of school providers. They should not be required to use existing facilities if the facilities are inadequate or if less expensive space of equal quality can be purchased, leased, rented, or used for free in either the private or notprofit sectors. Existing buildings may be rented or sold to school providers by school districts. If no one wants an existing school building, then the school should be torn down or converted for use by another community user. The city, county, or state may need extra office space. Some states require school districts to offer their surplus property to other governmental agencies before they may market it publicly, and laws often permit school districts to sell the property to other agencies at lower than market value. Unfortunately, nonschool uses of school facilities are limited, thus reducing the price that can be obtained for them. In some cities, surplus schools have been bought by businesses for warehouses. In some other cities, old schools have been converted into attractive condominiums and apartments.

One advantage of renting facilities from either the local school district or any other landlord is that it creates an incentive for the landlord to maintain the facility. If the facility is not adequately maintained, the provider would have the choice of finding a landlord who will provide adequate maintenance. If the provider owned the school facility, it would have sufficient incentive to ensure that regular maintenance is performed and that the buildings meet state health and safety standards.

Liability Insurance

Each school would have to have casualty and liability insurance in case of fire or injuries to students in the school or on field trips. Schools could band together to purchase pooled insurance, or the local school board could arrange pooled insurance programs for its contract schools.

Transportation

Transportation has become a costly and controversial part of public school budgets. Many districts are under court order to provide transportation for the purpose of ensuring racial balance in the district's schools. Rural areas face increasing transportation expenditures as the costs of buses, insurance, and fuels increase. And as in the case of other parts of the school bureaucracy, bus drivers constitute a potent political lobby that in some states has been able to secure for its members above-market salaries and considerable job security. In Louisiana, for example, school-bus drivers have tenure and cannot be fired. Others have the right to own their buses and charge school districts fees, like a public utility.

We would delegate responsibility for transportation, just as for all other facets for running a school, to the contract schools. Transportation costs should be included in the state allocation to schools, and additional amounts should be provided for rural schools that are likely to have higher-than-average transportation costs. But once the funds are provided, each school should decide how best to move students to and from schools. Many options are available. Some parents may choose to transport their own children or to organize car pools to transport their children to and from schools. A single school or group of schools could contract with a private bus company to provide transportation for children to the schools. School providers might negotiate with the local public transportation agency to use public transportation to the schools. School hours might be adjusted to avoid the peak loading times of other public users. In rare cases, a school might buy its own buses, which could be used for basic transportation and other educational activities off the school campus. The decision about how best to provide transportation should be made by administrators, teachers, and parents at the school level, who have first-hand knowledge of the transportation needs of families in the school and how those needs mesh with the academic program of the school. Many religious and independent schools solve these problems locally, so it should not be difficult for contract schools to do the same.

Operating and Maintenance Costs

The cost of operating and maintaining schools constitutes a substantial part of current school budgets, often between 10 and 15 percent, depending on the items included in these categories. Many people complain about the low quality of administrative services and the disrepair of schools. There are several reasons for these problems. In too many districts, administrative positions in the central office are filled by teachers and administrators who are ineffective in schools or are tired of teaching. Maintenance and craft jobs are sometimes given to relatives or friends of school board members. Civil service rules and patronage do not attract the most qualified and competent people to these positions. Furthermore, once in the positions, there are few incentives for these nonschool personnel to be efficient.

The solution to these problems is not obvious. School districts that have tried to contract out maintenance and custodial services have not always been happy with the results. Nevertheless, whether hiring your own people or contracting out, it is highly likely that conditions will improve if decisions about the operation and upkeep of schools are delegated to the school level. Through trial and error, each school will find the services that best meet the needs of that school. Schools that rent space from a private or not-for-profit organization may have the landlord provide maintenance and service as part of the rental agreement. Schools could hire their own service employees or contract with private service companies to do the job, or make some combined arrangement. Corporate partners and parents might provide some of these services, if, by so doing, resources could be freed up for some other educational purpose. And if many schools were in the market for operating and maintenance services, new service providers would open up and compete in terms of quality and price for the schools' business. There will always be costs involved in operating and maintaining schools. A decentralized, market approach to securing these services, however, is likely to improve the quality of services and possibly reduce their costs.

The same logic applies to the provision of staff development and the purchasing of supplies and services. Once, central purchasing was much more efficient. Today, however, with computers and fax machines there are few economies of scale in purchasing. Some contract schools may decide to band together for large-order discounts on supplies and services.

They may choose to have the school district provide those services. The choice should be left to the providers so that schools can decide how best to use their total resources to improve student learning.

Teacher Retirement

Employee fringe benefits are an increasing burden for most school districts, accounting for up to 30 percent of all personnel costs and 25 percent of total school costs. These expenditures continue to grow as a percentage of total costs and are the topic of the most bitter negotiations and lobbying by school employee groups. Any reduction in these benefits is perceived as an attack on the well-being of teachers.

Retirement, along with medical costs, constitutes the majority of fringe benefits. Most public school teachers belong to teacher or state employee retirement systems. These systems generally guarantee employees a fixed benefit at the time of retirement, based upon the employee's highest career salary level and years of service. Teacher lobbies have also been successful in a number of states in obtaining legislation that permits early retirement, say after twenty years of service, without reduced benefits or penalties for subsequent employment. Most state or teacher retirement systems reward employees who remain in the same system for many years. This creates a strong incentive for teachers and other school employees to serve until they are eligible for retirement, and for teacher unions to oppose almost all efforts to establish teacher evaluation and termination procedures.

Civil service retirement systems are expensive, unpredictable, and an obstacle to the provision of effective education. The best way to provide school employees with an adequate and dependable retirement program is to change to an employee contribution system such as TIAA/CREF or any number of other tax-deferred annuity retirement plans. In the contribution system, as opposed to a fixed-benefit approach, dollars set aside for a teacher or employee's retirement belong to the employee and can be carried with them to any public- or private-sector job they have in the future. Such plans are safe because they are always fully funded, unlike many state retirement systems that have unfunded liabilities that will have to be covered by future legislative appropriations. And because these contribution systems are managed by large private-sector organizations, the long-term return on investment tends to be higher than in state-managed retirement accounts.

Under the employer contribution approach, each contract school would be responsible for contributing to its employees' retirement program. The school would agree to contribute, say, 50 percent or some fixed percentage of the cost of retirement, and the employee would contribute the balance. The funds would be deposited in a retirement plan selected by the employee from a list of state-approved retirement plans. If an employee changed jobs within the state or found employment in another state, her retirement would travel with her. Similarly, if an employee dropped out of teaching or changed to a private-sector job, she would still have all of the money contributed by the school and herself in a tax-deferred account. These funds could only be withdrawn without penalty when the employee reached a predetermined age, which under current law is fifty-nine and a half. This is in contrast to most state fixed-benefit plans in which employees must be vested, in some cases only after ten years of service, in order to be eligible for retirement benefits when they retire.

During the transition from a state fixed-benefit system to an employee contribution system, provisions would have to be made for those teachers and employees who are currently in a state fixed-benefit plan. Existing employees should be given a choice of staying with their fixed-benefit plan or shifting to a private plan. All new employees would join an employee contribution plan. The employer's contributions to the two systems would be the same. It would the option of existing employees whether to stay with the state plan or move to the more flexible employee contribution plan. The decision would depend on the circumstances of each employee.

Conclusion

This chapter describes a new approach for raising and distributing money for schools that supports a system of contract schools. The goal is a system of school finance that is more equitable, more efficient, more democratic, more flexible, and more understandable than the current complex systems found in the fifty states.

A state's school finance system should place responsibility for funding schools on the state and establish a simple formula that allocates a fixed dollar amount per student directly to schools providing the service. The amount a school receives should depend primarily on the number of students enrolled in the school. Since parents would be free to choose any school in the state and to transfer to another school if they were dissatisfied or wanted a change, schools would have a strong incentive to use resources effectively and efficiently. A school district's role in school finance should be minimal. Its primary role should be to select, facilitate, and monitor the performance of school providers.

Most decisions about the use of educational dollars should be made at the school level by people who best understand the school's program and the needs of its students. In general, budgetary decisions should be broadly shared, so the interests of parents and students are included along with teachers and administrators in choices that are made. Parents rights to choose the school for their children or to transfer to another school should provide a strong incentive for school personnel to pay attention to parent and student interests and concerns.

Other features of school budgeting that fall more closely in the area of administration should also be school-based. Decisions about school facilities, transportation, operations and maintenance, and personnel benefits need to be part of a larger plan for operating the school. Alternatives in each of these areas should at least be considered. Through trial and error, new approaches for handling all areas of school administration will be found that better serve the interests of school clients. This, of course, is the goal of contract schools: to reinvent a public school system that results in improved educational opportunities for all children.

SEVEN

Politics, Leadership, and Transition Strategies

merica's public education system is vast, and it was not designed to change quickly. It can, however, be moved by determined forces, especially ones inspired by a simple but practical idea and empowered by the natural authority of parents and advocates for children. A contract school movement is likely to start small, as it is tried out in a few urban school systems desperate for success, and as it builds on the growing number of state charter schools programs. But once its potential becomes evident, contract public schools could become widespread. Within a few years, determined national leadership, buttressed by a broad coalition of state and local leaders, parent groups, and minority spokesmen, could make contracting the dominant mode of education governance in many school systems, especially those in the biggest cities.

Though in theory contracting can provide important new benefits for virtually everyone concerned with public education, the system will be hard to change. Skeptics will rightly demand to be shown how contracting will work in detail. Stakeholders will need to be shown, in concrete terms, how it will affect them personally. This chapter considers the problems of transition from the current system to contracting in two ways: first, by identifying the changes it would imply for the roles and missions of key institutions in public education, including school boards, teacher unions, schools of education, and state education agencies; and second, by identifying possible strategies for demonstrating the value of contracting and overcoming political hurdles to its implementation.

How Laws and Agency Missions Must Change

If it is to affect the lives and opportunities of large numbers of students, the contract-based system must completely replace the existing institutions of public school governance. The basic laws now governing public education must be changed to:

- Authorize local education agencies to contract out for instructional services and the management of whole schools.

- Permit publicly supported schools to become independent legal entities capable of receiving cash from state and local sources, maintaining their own budgets, and deciding what goods and services they will buy, and from whom, and what instructional strategies they will emphasize, whom they will hire, train, and fire, what ancillary services they will provide, and what work students must do to remain enrolled.

- Define the missions of new state and local education agencies to focus on developing and maintaining healthy portfolios of contract schools rather than directly operating schools as local branches of a centralized public bureaucracy;

- Create smaller local education agencies, especially in urban areas, so that school boards and superintendents can oversee manageable numbers of school contracts.

- Ensure that virtually all the public funds available for elementary and secondary education are allocated directly to schools in the form of cash, not centrally purchased goods, services, or employees.

- Equalize real per pupil expenditures within localities, and adjusting for costs, statewide.

- Eliminate state laws and regulations that govern the days and hours schools may be open, limit the kinds of buildings that may be used to house schools, set mandatory teacher and administrator pay schedules, require schools to maintain specific mixtures of administrative and teaching staff, and require specific education courses for people who would be teachers or principals.

- Amend state labor laws that now restrict access to the teaching profession, make teachers the employees of school systems rather than of schools, and make teacher unions the monopoly providers of teachers.

- Eliminate provisions of state and federal grant programs that require schools to single out individual students for particular educational services.

Laws Permitting Contracting

Local education agencies (LEAs) are regarded as instruments of the state, and their powers and structure are defined in state law and regulation. In most states, statutory changes are necessary to enable local education authorities to contract out for the management of schools and to distribute cash, rather than predetermined assets, to the schools. Many states are, however, limited by the Dillon Rule, which forbids local public bodies to redelegate functions assigned them by state law. This apparently applies to operation of whole schools, not parts of them. School systems in many Dillon Rule states have authority to contract for trash removal and major construction, school maintenance, staff development sessions, and for specific services to handicapped children. Some bring in evaluators and testing firms, and others can hire contractors to run whole schools for the handicapped or for truant and dropout students who need "alternative" forms of schooling. But school boards cannot contract out for operation of whole schools for "regular" students who do not fit into some special category.

Affirmative state laws are necessary to make it clear that contracting is a normal and legitimate method of providing public schools. State legislation is also necessary if schools are to become, as proposed above, legal entities able to control their own budgets, hiring, and purchasing, and to defend their contractual rights in court. Unless schools become legal persons, school boards can change the terms and conditions of school operations at whim, as they do now with magnet schools. If schools had real legal status they would have definite legal rights, and school board actions toward them would be constrained by contracts law.

States with very large school districts, like New York, California, and Florida, may also need to redefine local education agencies so they serve smaller numbers of students and more compact geographic areas. Districts in large cities should be broken into smaller units. It may be possible for a local board to supervise contracts for schools numbering in the tens, but the complexity of doing so for hundreds, or a thousand in the case of New York City, is too great. New school systems, organized to supervise schools in small contiguous areas, are needed to manage contract schools. In the big cities, establishing several new local education agencies in the place of one large district has the added advantage of eliminating large bureaucracies and enabling new contracting-oriented boards and superintendents to build their central offices from scratch.

Local Agency Missions

Contracting preserves local school boards as key actors in providing public education. Local boards would remain key policy makers in education, but they would operate by letting contracts, distributing funds to contractors, and assessing whether schools were operating and performing in ways consistent with their contracts.

These missions are fundamentally different from those now performed by local school boards, and it is hard to imagine how a board established to run schools directly could adapt to such a profound change. State governments probably need to disestablish existing local education agencies and commission new ones with the new mission. One transition strategy might be to have both old and new boards working at the same time for a while. In a particular locality, a new school board entitled to start schools could coexist with a conventional local education agency for a fixed period while the new board, on a scheduled annual basis, took over a growing share of state and local funds and used the funds to contract for schools. After a fixed period the old school board's operating authority would expire and the new contract-oriented school board would control all the funds. Alternatively, new local boards could be established immediately, to run existing schools and move toward contracting as soon as possible.

To avoid regeneration of the old central-office structure, the new boards must be required to send an extremely high proportion of the total funds they receive directly to schools in the form of cash payments; be forbidden to establish any form of civil service system or to employ more than a small number of full-time persons; be forbidden to tax schools; be permitted to contract for services such as evaluation, transportation, teacher training, payroll, and so on, and offer them to schools at cost, as long as schools were free to buy services elsewhere; and use some of their set-aside funds to publish school descriptions and school performance profiles. Contract-oriented local boards might also seek grants from businesses or foundations, both for their own operations and for schools; but schools' support from public funds must not be reduced due to their receipt of private grant funds.

Contract-oriented school boards should be free to hire superintendents at market wages, not under civil service rules. School boards could also contract with private firms for all central-office functions, including the superintendency.

State Agency Mission

Once new local agencies authorized to run all-contract school systems were established, the state education agency would have three roles, as described in chapter 5: stimulating the creation and growth of organizations capable of serving as high-quality providers of contract schools; setting statewide minimum standards for school performance and arranging for objective measurement and publication of school outcomes indicators; and building a capability to intervene in school systems whose boards fail to contract for an adequate supply of good schools or tolerate the continued failure of particular schools.

These functions require a state education agency of some size, and flexible funding encourages start-ups of potential providers and permits intervention in failing schools and districts. The state would not, however, need to maintain a large monitoring staff or pay directly for the extensive testing, staff development, and school improvement efforts required by the standards/alignment system. The state education agency's job would be to ensure that local education agencies have good options in contracting for schools, and that they use them.

These state functions should be performed with as few civil servants as possible. Most states will still need a chief state school officer, whether elected or appointed, and she might be permitted to hire a small number of people to serve at her pleasure. Most other functions should be performed by independent accrediting and evaluation organizations, including consortia of local school teachers and administrators formed by the state and paid extra for their services.

State Prescriptions about School Staffing, Space, and Schedules

State laws governing school size, teacher-pupil ratios, and staff composition and workload sustain a rigid system and guarantee an artificial demand for particular skills. Such requirements needlessly inhibit contract schools' creativity.

There is no reason for the state to mandate that every school have a principal or require a specific mix of junior/senior or certified/uncertified staff. State laws might require that every contract school have at least one certified teacher. The state might even create a new master teacher status that designated teachers capable of serving as instructional leaders for schools. The state could also require that schools have boards representing parents and community members as well as education professionals. In general, there is no reason for the state to impose requirements much more specific than now attach to private schools. Schools can be expected to develop staffing patterns consistent with their instructional strategies, and to be constrained from false economies or extravagances by the need to compete for students.

Schools might also be expected to compete on how long they stay open each day, how available they are to adults in the community, whether they can package day care with other services, and the like. They might also choose to remain open all year, or to coordinate school vacations with the scheduled shut-down periods for employers. There is no need for state law or regulation to constrain innovation and competition in these areas.

Similarly, schools should be free to locate themselves wherever it suits their instructional approach and marketing strategy. School boards should be authorized to lease space in existing school buildings to contractors, but contractors should also be free to accept donations of commercial space or to lease it at market rates.

State laws should neither require contract schools to use the existing inventory of school buildings nor forbid local education agencies from leasing or selling unclaimed school space for noneducational purposes. Though many contract schools would undoubtedly use existing buildings and locate themselves in neighborhoods where many parents might choose the most convenient school, not all schools should be constrained to do so. Because schoolchildren are unlikely to complain effectively about dangerous facilities, health and safety regulations are still necessary. But contract schools should have the same range of choices about facilities as private schools.

Teacher Collective Bargaining Law

Teacher collective bargaining law differs sharply from one state to another, and the differences have important implications for any effort to authorize and promote contract schooling. As Dean Millot of RAND reports, there are essentially four different state legal environments for teacher collective bargaining:

- School systems must bargain collectively with teachers, and bargaining can affect a broad range of educational policy issues.
- Collective bargaining is mandatory but strictly limited to teacher wages, hours, and working conditions.
- Teacher collective bargaining is permitted but not required.
- Teacher collective bargaining is prohibited by state law or policy.

In states that permit collective bargaining but do not require it, school boards enjoy great discretion. Local boards may be able to establish school contracts without having to weather union legal challenges or strikes.

States that do not permit collective bargaining may, ironically, be difficult environments for the introduction of contract schools. In such states, according to Millot, school boards are often bound by the Dillon Rule, discussed above. Though unions in such states are normally weak, they would be able to sue against contract schools on the grounds that the school board lacked authority to contract with school operators just as it lacks authority to contract with teacher unions. The American Federation of Teachers sued the city of Baltimore and the Baltimore public schools on these grounds, in an ultimately unsuccessful effort to block implementation of the city's contracts with Education Alternatives, Incorporated (EAI).

To facilitate contracting, collective bargaining laws in most states would need amendment in two ways: first, to allow school boards to hire teachers through more than one agent, i.e., to release school boards from the obligation to bargain collectively with a single teacher union, and to allow individual schools to enter into contracts with individual teachers or professional associations; second, state laws should make it clear that school boards may fulfill their responsibilities by contracting out for instructional services, rather than by operating schools directly.

State and Federal Grants Programs

Though localities can contract for schools without the permission of Congress or the federal government, the structure of existing federal grant programs in education can make contracting difficult. Except in very limited circumstances, the major federal grant programs—Title I and the Education for All Handicapped Children Act—require recipient schools to single out particular students for special services. These requirements have a profound effect on school programs. As Kimbrough and Hill (1981) show, all of the instructional programs in a school are affected by the need to pull particular students out of their classes to receive federally funded services. These requirements strongly constrain school programs, and would severely restrict contractors' flexibility on choosing instructional methods and schedules.

If contract schools are to be fully in charge of their own programs and fully accountable for the results they obtain, they cannot be required to work around fixed requirements for the use of particular funds for the instruction of particular students. To make federal programs compatible with contract schools, federal funds should travel with students so that students with special needs bring extra money to the schools they attend. A disadvantaged student would therefore bring several hundred (or in the case of some handicapped students, several thousand) extra dollars to a school that admits him or her. In addition, federal funds must be available for enhancement of the entire school instructional program, not just the parts of it expressly designed for particular students. Taken together, these two changes will encourage contract schools to admit disadvantaged students. They will also enable schools to serve disadvantaged students by strengthening the basic instructional program, rather than by pulling them out of the regular instructional program to receive special services.

In order to give members of Congress some confidence that federal grant funds are used as intended, district RFPs could require contract school providers to show how the school's regular program will help disadvantaged students, and what enrichment opportunities would be available. Contract schools could also be required to prove in their regular evaluations that such promises had been kept. In place of current federal program monitoring mechanisms, the U.S. Department of Education could also hire contractors to perform an inspection function, verifying that school boards were holding schools to the terms of their contracts.

Leadership and Coalition Building

Adoption of contracting requires change in the coalition of interests that influence public policy toward education. A number of groups now act alone and in coalition to stabilize the current governance system. Teacher unions contribute more to state legislative campaigns than any other group, and many teachers have won election to legislatures. The state school boards association, organizations representing school district superintendents, school principals, school bus drivers, school maintenance workers, and many others contribute campaign funds and lobby for the benefit of their members. Organizations representing the content areas of public education, such as mathematics, music, performing arts, and English, all press for mandates that protect their areas of interest.

The influence of educational groups is also institutionalized in the regulatory structure of public education. In almost every state, education groups have been successful in building a wall of rules and regulations that makes them almost immune to change. In California the education code has grown to over 11,000 pages, many of which were written as a result of group advocacy.

For the system to change two things must happen. First, the groups favoring a new way of doing business must come to know one another, unite around a specific agenda, develop leadership that will reach out to others who might become supporters, and form coalitions that can press for change even against strong opposition. Second, the framework of laws, regulations, labor contracts, and customs that undergirds the current system must be overturned and replaced by a new and far more flexible set of legal requirements and administrative arrangements.

How can such changes come about? Who among the groups concerned with schools are natural supporters for a movement toward contracting? How can other groups be won over and opponents neutralized? By what political and legal strategies can states and localities be led to enact laws and regulations that permit public school contracting of the kind described above?

Leadership

After years of ferment on school improvement, it is clear that the school system cannot reform itself. Constituency politics limit school board members and make it virtually impossible for them to unite on a line of action that dramatically changes the ways schools do their business. Though some school superintendents are reform-minded, most are limited by their training and early career experiences: they are prepared to administer the existing system, not to dismantle or rebuild it. Most other forces in the system, including teacher unions, exist to shield their members from exactly the kinds of wrenching changes that are needed if public education is to be reformed.

Several recent studies (e.g., Hill et al. 1989; Shipps 1995) conclude that initiative from outside the school system is necessary for fundamental reform. Local civic, foundation, business, and political leaders can make school reform a major local priority and put options on the table that the regular actors in school politics would rather not consider. At the state level, governors and legislators might provide leadership, particularly in alliance with local government and community leaders. Senior civic, business, and government leaders can broaden the field of forces at play in educational policy-making, so that teacher unions and other veto groups cannot unilaterally block reform. At the local level, senior civic and business leaders can strengthen the hand of superintendents or teacher-union heads who know that their school systems need reform but cannot accomplish it alone.

Who can step up to play the necessary leadership roles? Because K–12 education is essentially a local and state enterprise, there is no obvious source of national leadership. The president and the secretary of education are logical candidates, but they are not likely to lead a movement for school contracting in the near future. Democratic administrations depend heavily on teacher union support and are unlikely to confront the education establishment. Republican administrations have no such constraints, but they have recently been preoccupied with using education voucher proposals, rather than more moderate and fully developed reform plans, as tactics in a campaign to detach Catholic voters from their traditional Democratic base. Governors, particularly those looking for an issue on which to run for higher office, might capitalize on the contracting idea. Alternately, a coalition of governors seeking to lead dramatic reform movements within their own states might provide national leadership.

However, sustained and effective national leadership for a contracting movement will almost surely have to come from private individuals. As mentioned above, national business groups could feature contract schools as parts of their reform agendas or even make it their own single issue. So might child advocacy organizations like the Children's Defense Fund and the PTA.

One potentially critical source of potential leadership is the minority community, especially among African-American elected officials, business leaders, and lawyers. These individuals have natural authority, as members of groups whose children are the most likely to suffer from inadequate schooling. They also stand to gain the support of minority parents, most of whom, according to recent Gallup polls, think the public schools fail their children. (More than two-thirds of African-American adults responding to a 1994 Gallup poll favored vouchers or other methods that would let parents choose schools other than their neighborhood public schools.)

Minority leaders can lend credibility to governance reform initiatives. They can also help to protect minority teachers and other school personnel from any disproportionate impacts of change. Most importantly, they can help to mobilize the minority community, the strongest untapped source of support for fundamental education reform.

Natural Supporters

Leaders with an agenda are likely to attract support from many directions. Groups most likely to actively support a local or statewide movement in favor of public school contracting include minority parents, as discussed above, parents who have abandoned public schools but would like to return, public school educators now attempting to run magnet and charter schools, leaders of child advocacy organizations, city mayors and business and religious leaders, and state legislators and governors, many of whom now favor deregulation of public education.

The core of a contract schools coalition must be parents. Because of the opaque and bureaucratic character of most public school systems, all but the most aggressive parents are excluded from having any voice in the policies and operations of schools. School size, school assignment procedures, and busing have limited opportunities for parent participation. A grass-roots effort to organize parents for school reform should be a key part of building a new education coalition.

Closely allied to parents are groups that advance the interests of children. In the past, children's advocates have focused on issues such as child welfare, single mothers, child care, immunization and medical services for children. Now they realize that schools must be a part of any solution to the problems of children.

A third group that must be a part of any pro-contracting coalition is teachers who want to be empowered to help children. The vast majority of teachers probably fall into this category. Local teacher unions will initially oppose the new coalition, but they might eventually be brought around because their members will demand it, realizing that the coalition will improve their own status and working conditions.

If a coalition is to become effective in localities throughout the country, it must involve senior local and state leaders, including CEOs and elected leaders of local government, and the all-important minority professionals and officeholders. These groups' entry into the coalition could be organized by national organizations such as the National Conference of Mayors, the Urban Coalition, and the Business Roundtable or the National Chamber of Commerce. If encouraged by their national organizations to do so, local business and political leaders can make common cause with parents, teachers, and others inside the educational system who favor reform but cannot bring it about alone.

Groups That Might Be Won Over

Many people are deeply concerned about the quality of the nation's public schools but cannot readily accept radical changes. Many understandably want to be sure that any reforms are at least as good as the existing system at preserving minority rights, creating opportunities for social mobility, and inculcating democratic values and respect for others. As chapter 2 has shown, the existing system is not very good at these things. But many potential supporters of change are also afraid of radical measures that would leave decisions about school supply, access, and quality entirely to a new and untried contracting process. These groups include school board members and superintendents, who are now blamed for the failures of a system that is so gridlocked that they cannot change it. Contracting can offer them enormous new leverage, especially to change the schools that fail students and disgrace the system. It lets superintendents intervene directly to change the mission and staffing of failing schools, rather than working by indirection, through policies that affect all schools alike.

Rank-and-file teachers might also become contracting supporters if they learn that contracting offers good teachers the opportunity to work in organizations that are free to succeed. Teachers in contract schools need not be saddled with unproductive coworkers relying on civil service protection. Many good teachers would earn more, as schools sought to attract and keep teachers who have rare skills or become the heart and soul of their instructional programs.

Many leaders of the local, state, and national PTAs now see that a strategy of uncritical support for public education bureaucracies has not paid off for parents and children. A new strategy of advocacy for parents who want responsive and flexible schools could give new life to PTA organizations. It would also strengthen PTA links with a huge potential constituency of minority parents who want choices, not just pleasant relationships with incumbent teachers and principals.

Local religious leaders who see the need for schools that are focused specifically on the needs of minority and disadvantaged youth might support contracting. Even church leaders who run their own private schools might support reforms that promise to expand the number of public schools that offer the climate and mission focus typical of private schools. So might state superintendents of public instruction, many of whom now acknowledge that their departments are not structured or able to help improve schools, and state legislators and members of Congress who are tired of passing mandates and categorical programs that they know have symbolic effects at best.

Though national and state teacher-union leaders face potential opposition from elements of their rank and file, many want to develop a new mission for their organizations, one that improves teacher working conditions and career opportunities and eliminates the traditional split between labor and management in schools. Similarly, universities and colleges of education are reluctant to offend leaders of conventional public school systems, but they might also value the opportunity to become school contractors and create a new mission for themselves, preparing teachers to work in schools with special curricula and approaches to instruction.

Contracting can provide many of the assurances these people require—that schools will remain public, open to all, and dedicated to equal opportunity and social mobility, while offering the prospect of far more effective and efficient public schooling. Without the kinds of leadership described above, however, they are not likely to spontaneously recognize the promise of contracting.

Likely Opponents

The goal of improving public education is not controversial; only the methods are. Adults who choose to get involved in schools, as paid teachers and administrators or as volunteers, all like to work with children and hope to make a positive difference for the children they encounter. It is, therefore, impossible to say exactly how a given reform proposal will be received. Some adults will support actions that cause them extra work, or even threaten their incomes, if they believe children will benefit. However, as in all areas of human endeavor, it is especially difficult to see the flaws in an arrangement that meets one's own interest. This section identifies those groups that are, because of their particular interests, likely to be the hardest to persuade in favor of contracting.

Leaders of traditional teacher-union locals. Contracting reduces the importance of the single district-wide teacher collective bargaining agreement, which is the union's chief mechanism of influence over education policy. By creating a more open labor market for teachers, contracting is also a threat to the job security of some members whom union leaders have pledged to protect.

State legislators who depend on union votes and funding. For many legislators, the teacher unions are the most consistent and credible interpreter of the interests of public education. As recent struggles over charter school legislation have demonstrated, unions are often able to add debilitating amendments to bills they cannot block entirely. State-capital union lobbies, in fact, often oppose reforms that some local union leaders are willing to accept.

Other professional education groups. The state school boards association, organizations representing school district superintendents, school principals, school bus drivers, school maintenance workers, and many others contribute campaign funds and lobby for the benefit of their members. Organizations representing the content areas of public education, such as mathematics, music, performing arts, and English, all propose and support legislation that protects or enhances their area of practice.

Career administrators in state and local education agencies, especially people who specialize in interpreting and keeping schools in compliance with federal regulations. These employees, whose careers depend on federal categorical programs, would have few clear functions and no job security in a system based on contracting and lump-sum funding of schools. Though many central-office staffers could go into business as private providers themselves, some could not hope to survive in a market where schools are free to make their own purchasing decisions.

Local and state school board members, some of whom relish their current opportunities to select administrative staff and to award special programs to particular schools, or who might not want to take on complex new contract oversight responsibilities. Some members, as noted above, will welcome the opportunity to play a more delimited but more powerful role. But, judging from the response of some school boards that have rejected contract and charter proposals, change will continue to be resisted.

These groups are likely to oppose contracting in the short run, and might be hard to win over in any event. Over time, however, their opposition might break down if incremental steps toward contracting, as described below, demonstrate that it can lead to school improvement.

Strategy

As the foregoing sections make clear, full implementation of school contracting requires major changes in state laws and state and local-agency authorities and capabilities. Such profound changes are unlikely to occur overnight. Some might come incrementally, through increasingly ambitious reform legislation. The continual evolution of state charter school laws, from timid statutes that defined limited autonomy for small numbers of schools to bolder statutes that provide greater school independence and that raise or eliminate caps on the numbers of schools that can participate, is a promising model. Some existing state charter schools laws might evolve into full-blown contract school laws.[1]

The first move toward a system of contract public schools is not likely to come from state legislatures. It is much more likely to come from localities that seek to encourage innovation, rescue children in intractably failing schools, or cope with stagnant per pupil funding. State legislation and

1. A new hybrid charter-contract school statute proposed for Washington State would create true contractual relationships between school boards and independent nonprofit organizations operating schools. School boards could limit the number of contracts initially, but after five years boards would have to grant a charter to every qualified applicant that could attract enough students to fund its operations.

other authoritative actions (e.g., court orders establishing systems of contract schools) are likely to follow developments at the local level.

Building Community "Comfort" and Consensus

Public officials responsible for primary and secondary education, superintendents, school administrators, union leaders, parents, need to explore the concrete implications of adopting educational contracting. To begin a productive community dialogue, representatives need opportunities to engage in a neutral forum. They need tools to help them examine various approaches to contracting in a way that is informative yet does not commit them to real-world actions.

Policy exercises involving plausible but hypothetical scenarios can serve this purpose. In a policy exercise on school contracting, local community and education leaders will face issues like those they would have to resolve in the real world, e.g., how to make a transition from a program-budget system in which schools are not cost centers and have dramatically unequal resources, to a cash budget system in which schools will all have real-dollar budgets based on enrollment. Participants might also be asked to decide how to respond when some contract schools become oversubscribed and others are in danger of closing due to falling enrollment.

Such exercises could present participants with hypothetical situations concerning the adoption of educational contracting and give them structured opportunities to develop appropriate policy responses. Because the scenario presented is hypothetical, the participants' discussion of contracting is "low stakes." Because the scenario is plausible and concrete, their discussion is focused and specific. By engaging a large number and broad range of stakeholders in a discussion of a contracting scenario, those running the exercise can develop a rich understanding of the key problems and schools of thought surrounding the issue. Participants can improve their own appreciation of the subject by playing the exercise and then hearing the approaches taken by others presented with the same facts.

Starting Small in a Few Localities

Though a few public school systems have contracted for a few schools, the ideas outlined here have never been used as the basis of a whole school system. Though good potential contract school providers exist, they could not suddenly gear up to run hundreds of schools next year. Even if the existing potential contractors decided to collaborate in providing all the schools for a whole school system, they could not hope to take over any major city's schools.

The existing providers could, however, make a very big dent in any city's supply of failed schools. As we have suggested elsewhere (Hill 1992) contracting could have a quick impact on even as large a city as Los Angeles if it were used as the way to redevelop the lowest-performing 5 percent of the city's schools. While even finding contractors to take responsibility for 30 schools (5 percent of the city's 600) would be difficult, it could be done. The key is to begin with organizations that are already running successful schools, such as churches and ethnic organizations (including African-American Christian schools). Another source of potential contractors is the staffs of existing public magnet schools. Many religious organizations are closing down schools every year and could readily supply teaching and administrative staffs to run nonsectarian schools under public contract. Others, including the public magnet schools, could "hive off" staff and students to reproduce new variants of their existing models.

Innovators and reformers from outside a community could also be enticed in. Profit-makers like the Edison Project, Alternative Schools Inc., and Sabis International are ready to go. Principals and teachers who have developed models for new schools under foundation grants—from, e.g., RJR Nabisco, General Electric, and Panasonic, and under state model-school programs, like Washington State's Schools for the 21st Century—could be placed under contract to recruit and train teachers and open a school on the site of a failed existing school.

Not all the contractors' ideas will work, and some will surely take more than one year to reach their full potential. But the decision of even one major city school system to turn around its worst schools through contracting would elicit an immense new supply of people with school ideas, ready to do the work and take the risks that contracting entails. A decision to promote contracting, made by one or more big-city mayors or the governors of a few urban states, would produce great interest among educators and unprecedented amounts of development funding from foundations and the federal government. But this strategy requires an official commitment to try contracting for several years in a large number of schools.

Building on Charter School Laws

Charter school laws in force in approximately half the states represent a significant move toward educational contracting. Although, as discussed in chapter 4, most state statutes authorize only small numbers of charter schools and fall short of providing school operators full control of necessary resources and enforceable contractual rights, they do establish the practice of relying on private persons to provide whole public schools.

Charter schools also encourage formation of organizations that can operate public schools and create a demand for independently provided support services for privately operated public schools. As an ongoing study by Dean Millot of RAND and Robin Lake of the University of Washington has found, a tiny school-support industry composed of lawyers, insurance underwriters, accountants, and property management specialists is arising in Massachusetts and other charter school states (Millot and Lake 1996).

Under existing charter school laws the charter "industry" will remain small and marginal. However, as school reformers and legislators gain experience, more recent legislative proposals (e.g., in Washington State) have no caps on the numbers of charters and provide schools true organizational independence and contractual rights. These developments, if they continue, could result in an incremental transition to an all-contract public school system.

Enactment and Funding of Contract School Laws

This section considers alternative strategies for enacting those pro-contracting laws and policies.

- Legislative enactment strategies, employing conventional information and lobbying techniques to push new laws through state legislatures.

- Statewide initiatives, bypassing legislative processes in favor of direct public appeals for new laws that would permit school contracting and dismantle contrary laws and administrative structures.

- Litigation strategies, in which plaintiffs complaining about school finance inequities and other failures to meet state constitutional guarantees of "high quality" or "thorough and efficient" education seek contracting as a remedy.

- Local school board elections, in which contracting supporters assist candidates who would use all existing authorities to create contract-like freedoms for individual schools.

Legislative enactment. A strategy seeking conventional legislative enactment has important costs and benefits. On the cost side, the legislative process requires sustained and expensive lobbying, takes considerable time, and works through forums, especially the state legislature education committees, where sworn opponents to contracting are highly influential. Legislatures seldom act precipitously, and "sudden" legislative victories are almost always the result of years of preparation. One or more powerful legislators must be persuaded to sponsor and work for legislation, committee leaders need to be informed and persuaded, rank-and-file members must be convinced, and governors must be willing to sign a bill once it passes. In most legislatures, significant new legislation must go through at least one legislative session of hearings and debates and be tabled for later consideration, before it can be seriously considered for enactment in a later session. It took three years for the National Business Roundtable's education reform strategy to win enactment in just three states, and after five years' effort less than half the states had enacted all or major parts of the agenda. Because opponents have had time to get organized, future enactment might be even more difficult to obtain than it was in the past. Teacher union lobbies in Washington, Alaska, Connecticut, and other states are also well prepared to fight enactment of charter or contract school laws or anything they consider "creeping privatization."

On the other hand, potentially pro-contracting forces are also organized to influence state legislatures. Business lobbies, organized African-Americans and other minority groups, and mayors and county commissioners can command serious attention in state legislatures. Some, especially those that have worked for systemic reforms under the Business Roundtable agenda, have developed expertise and credibility in education and have formed alliances with key legislators. In addition, senior state legislators in several states have succeeded in passing charter bills and may be ready for more ambitious system-wide efforts. Many governors also see contract and charter approaches as ways they can move recalcitrant state education establishments.

Legislative campaigns are slow and costly, but they may be the only feasible approach for most states.

Popular initiative. The initiative process is a way to avoid legislative roadblocks and work in an arena where popular support can outweigh establishment opposition. However, it requires expensive public information campaigns and risks a great deal on one unpredictable event. Though defeated initiatives can be revived, incendiary issues like tax limitation or gay rights can capture public attention from an "old" issue. Further, legislatures are seldom willing to enact ideas that have recently been rejected by the public.

Initiative might, nonetheless, be a plausible approach in a state where unions have locked up the key legislative committees, and where business groups or political figures who support contracting can lead strong media and grass-roots campaigns. (Such appeals to popular support might also assist in the passage of legislation.)

A contracting initiative might also succeed when there is an even more sweeping and controversial initiative, like vouchers, on the same ballot. When coupled with widespread discontent with the schools, a voucher initiative can be a major asset for a contracting movement. To judge from the experience of charter proposals in California and a few other states, voucher initiatives are also good stimuli for state legislative action.

Litigation. Virtually every state education system is susceptible to court actions alleging unequal treatment of students or general failure to deliver high-quality education. Though most such suits focus on school funding, some plaintiffs also cite student achievement data showing generally low school performance or highly variable student outcomes linked to race or income. Traditionally, equity lawsuits have sought financial remedies, in the form of statewide spending equalization. However, in the 1990s courts are willing to order more substantive remedies, including sweeping reforms of state education systems, as in Alabama and Kentucky.

David Hornbeck has promoted substantive reform through equity litigation since the mid-70s and has helped fashion court orders requiring alignment-based "systemic reforms." Allan Odden (1994) has recently suggested a variant on Hornbeck's strategy under which plaintiffs would request real-dollar expenditure equalization down to the school level. As Odden suggests, such remedies could be matched with statewide goals and other accountability measures. Remedies could also include many of the preconditions for contracting, including school-level control of funds, school-level teacher hiring, and a more open teacher-labor market.

Reformers have every reason to propose school contracting as part of the remedy in statewide equity lawsuits. It is, however, questionable whether equity litigation is a reliable way to produce a mandate for contracting. Plaintiffs' lawyers often have well-established agendas promoting racially based student assignment and hiring schemes and standardization of instructional practice. Promoters of alignment, vouchers, and limited charter school schemes will also compete for the courts' attention, with unpredictable results. Still, filing *amicus curiae* briefs on behalf of contracting could be a useful activity for a national school contracting coalition.

Local board elections. Many local school boards already have the authority to purchase some instructional services via contracts. In addition to the few well-known districts that have contracted with Education Alternatives Incorporated and the Edison Project to manage schools, there is a larger number that contract for special education services and for "alternative" high schools for potential dropouts. Unions and other opponents of contracting may sue school boards that consider contracting, arguing that boards cannot redelegate the power to run schools. (That was the argument in the American Federation of Teachers' 1994 lawsuit against Baltimore's contracting effort.) But many districts may be able to assert the authority to contract, and defeat legal challenges.

Under such circumstances only local politics and labor relations would stand in the way of contracting. Contracting could be introduced to those districts through the local ballot box, if school board candidates pledging to pursue contracting could be elected. A national coalition for school contracting could work with local education reform groups to recruit and train candidates and test campaign themes.

Local electoral campaigns may be necessary even in those states that pass laws permitting contracting (or, equivalently, amending charter schools laws to eliminate numerical limits and torturous approval and start-up processes). Because state laws are likely to be permissive rather than mandatory, contracting supporters must still prevail in local politics. A national coalition for contracting could help train candidates, provide campaign materials explaining the advantages of contracting, and broker information about likely opposition tactics.

All of the foregoing alternatives are plausible under certain circumstances. None can be pursued quickly or easily. Even the litigation strategy, which dangles the possibility of avoiding political processes, will ultimately require extensive interest organization and public information campaigns. As supporters of systemic reform have found, unless there is strong pressure for a reform, its implementation can be derailed by establishment resistance. Given the complexity of the legal and administrative changes required for contracting to work on a widespread basis, contracting advocates might need to pursue all alternatives at once. Though they might hope for lower-cost victories, most will have to work through the conventional state legislative process.

Conclusion

The system of contracting we have proposed for the operation of public schools is radical in some ways and conservative in others. Compared to proposals for incremental adjustment of the existing system of public education, contracting is a radical proposal. It is intended to transform the roles of local school boards and superintendent and of state departments of education. It could also transform the roles of teacher associations, from conventional industrial unions preoccupied with collective bargaining into professional organizations dedicated to helping members find placements that match their skills and to maintaining the quality of teaching in schools.

Contracting could also lead to dramatic changes for teachers and families. Individual teachers could gain greatly expanded choices of places and conditions for work: they could choose schools on the basis of instructional philosophy, work environment, pay, personal influence, or personal advancement opportunities. Teachers would not all have the same choices: those with excellent reputations would have greater choices on all dimensions than those who had not distinguished themselves. Families, like teachers, could choose schools on the basis of instructional philosophy, emotional tone and climate, reputation, availability of ancillary services, and responsiveness to parents. Parents would also have the advantage of knowing that schools depend on family patronage and are controlled by the adults who work in them, not by remote and inaccessible regulators.

Compared to proposals for a completely market-based system of education, or for de-institutionalization of education in favor of a system in which parents assemble their children's educational experiences by choosing different vendors for different instructional programs, contracting is a conservative proposal. It is intended to maintain public oversight and community control over public schools, relying on boards of education to maintain a portfolio of schools that meet the needs of the students and families in a locality. Though contracting has many market-like features, it also recognizes a community-wide interest in school quality, and thus maintains public capabilities for assistance to troubled schools and investment in providers of new school to replace failed ones.

Contracting is also intended to strengthen, not weaken, schools. Under contracting, each school could invest in its own future by hiring, training, and developing teachers to work effectively within its specific context. Schools would run on adult personal responsibility, rewarding teachers and administrators for contributions to school performance as measured by students' instructional success, and saying frankly what they require of students and their families. Under contracting, schools could also be stronger communities, acting on behalf of the families that choose them, and on behalf of the broader society, ensuring that children learn enough to become informed voters, decent citizens, productive taxpayers, and full participants in a future economy.

We think a system of school contracting has great promise because it creates the right incentives for earnest adult collaboration on behalf of children. Under contracting, public officials have strong incentives to create portfolios of effective, accountable schools, and they have weak incentives to divert funds from use in schools to less productive enterprises like central administration. School operators, similarly, have strong incentives to make their schools effective, welcoming to parents, and economically efficient. They also have incentives to tell families frankly what kinds of effort the school expects of children and families. Teachers have strong incentives to sort themselves into schools where their skills are most appreciated and best used, and to work together to produce student outcomes that build their schools' reputations and secure their own jobs. Finally, parents have both incentive and opportunity to find schools with which they and their children are comfortable, and to commit themselves to the levels of student attendance and effort that the school requires.

Incentives, or course, are not guarantees. Contracting is a way of organizing human affairs, and human frailties can and will come into play. As we have already seen in EAI's experience in Baltimore and Hartford, arrangements that go under the name of contracting but that do not create real freedom and accountability at the school level, do not have good results. Half-baked contracting systems, in which public officials control spending and staffing decisions, or unions can staff a school with teachers who are hostile to the contractor, or contractors can take public money without clear advance agreement on performance standards and measures, do not improve on the current arrangements for delivery of public education. Contracting is meant to be a system of transparent adult relationships, in which freedom and responsibility are clearly defined in advance. Obfuscation and ambiguity, even when they are introduced to salve feelings or deflect conflicts, destroy the positive incentives that contracting is intended to create.

Contracting does not require false precision. No one can know in advance exactly how much children will know before they enter a school, or how quickly a good school can help a particular group of children overcome the harm done them by a failed school or a hurtful neighborhood environment. Public officials and school contractors can work together to establish performance baselines and realistic expectations for individual schools. But they cannot duck the issue of performance expectations. A contracting system in which performance expectations are vague can quickly revert to a system of entitlements based on compliance.

We have done our best in this book to help public officials, community leaders, and educators understand how contracting might lead to a more effective system of public education and how it can be done. We cannot, however, anticipate all the issues that will arise or all the lessons that will be learned by communities that sincerely try contracting. There is much to be learned. If, as we hope, this book generates widespread discussion and experimentation, future analysts will be astounded at how little we understood.

As this chapter has made clear, contracting will upset many comfortable adult arrangements in public education, and it will have fervent detractors and critics. Critics will demand to know whether contracting guarantees that adults will not misallocate money, neglect children, handpick students to make themselves look good, or fudge data. Those who think contracting is a promising approach toward more just and effective public education should respond that there are no guarantees. No system, whether governed by rules or by markets, is proof against abuse and neglect. Even systems based on so-called legal guarantees (i.e., opportunities to sue in court for vindication of rights) fully expect failures and routinely deliver remedies that the claimants consider disappointing. In an imperfect world where there are no guarantees, those who would serve children must talk candidly about incentives, opportunities, and probabilities. We have tried to make our case in those terms, and hope our critics will respond in the same spirit.

Two Hypothetical Contract Schools

Selden Middle School

Selden Middle School was different from most of the contract schools in the district. The others had been organized by experienced individuals and forceful entrepreneurs who recruited teachers to be part of their planning teams and eventually part of the operating faculty of the school. However, the schools more often reflected the ideas and personality of a strong leader than a group of professional colleagues. Selden was different—it started as a part of the district's teacher union, and had evolved into a nonprofit teacher-controlled cooperative. The lead teacher, who served as the school's chief executive officer, was more highly paid than her peers, in recognition of the added responsibility of the position. The other teachers in the school were paid simply on the basis of their seniority in the school and the level of their professional preparation. In effect, they had adopted the district's teacher salary schedule. It worked fine from their viewpoint, and they adopted the district's salary scheme for teacher aides as well.

The initial decision to bid to operate a middle school was exceedingly controversial within the local union. Many senior members opposed the entire idea of contracting for instructional services. They had worked diligently since the mid-1970s to gain the perquisites and benefits of unionization, and they were reluctant to risk those hard-fought gains for an idea that had yet to be tried on a wide scale. Moreover, many had the security of a tenured position in the school district. Why, some argued, should they give up union gains for what seemed like more risk and more work?

The local's executive director took the position that teachers should have options, and she strongly supported establishment of the Selden school contract. In order to reassure teachers who were interested in working at Selden, the citywide union promised it would, in exchange for a teacher's foregoing tenure with the school district, ensure that individual teachers had lifetime employment as a teacher, though not necessarily in a particular school or even school district. Of course part of this trade-off was that individual teachers agreed to continually be effective as instructors, willing to upgrade their own teaching skills on a regular basis and participate in the in-service preparation and career evaluations of their peers.

Selden School's own internal labor relations were highly positive, though one teacher who said, "I just can't deal with having to discuss my teaching methods with others," left, with the school's encouragement. As the school's reputation grew, the staff occasionally had to turn down an applicant who claimed seniority rights but who did not appear to have the right mixture of skills and attitudes. These incidents were painful, and sometimes put strain on the teacher community, but the staff had learned to get through them.

The school's lead teacher had experienced many of the stresses associated with leadership. Though she tried to preserve the spirit of partnership that characterized the start-up phase of the school, she found that some teachers thrust her into the role of boss. Teachers outside the school often criticized her for turning down applications from senior teachers, and for requiring that the funds for in-service training be controlled by the school as a whole, rather than by individuals. The lead teacher's lowest moment had come when she expelled a boy—the son of a teacher in another local public school—for twice pulling fire alarm levers in the main hallway. She relied on the local union's executive director for counsel, but they had both come to be regarded as "the enemy" by a minority faction in the citywide local, who said that the union's business was collective bargaining, not school management.

Selden was evaluated in the same way as the other schools in the district. Enrollment was voluntary, the choice of parents who could place their children at other middle schools in the district if they desired. Selden was also the subject of the comprehensive outside evaluation processes to which all schools were subjected on a three-year cycle. If the school failed in the eyes of the independent evaluators, or failed to attract students, then its contract would be subject to revision or nonrenewal. As in other local contract schools, concerns for the school's performance and survival ultimately dominated decisions about staffing, time off, and spending. Under the school's contract with the school board, Selden evaluated teachers and decided what forms of in-service training were required for teacher-salary step increases.

Selden Middle School enrolled 600 students, generally between the ages of 10 and 14. If the school had been heavily dependent upon conventional grade groupings, these youngsters would have been in the sixth through eighth grades. However, Selden did not depend exclusively upon either egg-crate classrooms or Carnegie-unit grade levels. Rather, the school was highly oriented around three yearlong projects. The three projects were the "Eighteenth Century," "Chocolate," and "Gender."

All of this had initially seemed whimsical at best. The awarding of the contract by the school board to a teacher cooperative had itself been controversial. When the media got hold of the proposed curriculum, a number of politically conservative and devoutly religious groups were quite alarmed. However, the depth of the project curriculum, and the seriousness with which the topics were pursued, eventually overcame resistance. It became clear the students were interested, learning projects were sensible, and student evaluation and grading were rigorous. High scores on statewide examinations went a long way to convince initial skeptics, and the attendance rate and civil behavior of students were impressive, both for parents and for the surrounding neighborhood.

Selden School was formulated around several learning principles. First, the teacher cooperative believed that whatever students were studying should have meaning in their everyday lives. In some manner the students had to be engaged in activities which meant something to them—something they could connect to their lives outside of school. Thus, Mr. Rhoads, a skilled social science and history teacher, began to discuss with students at the school the Federalist Papers in the context of neighborhood teenage gangs or cliques. Notions of representative government and the preservation of minority rights took on a liveliness and intensity in class discussions that few adults would ever have anticipated.

Similarly, the chocolate curriculum was a big surprise. Students learned about commodity futures and hedging; using recipes, they learned math and measurement; they learned geography by studying about cocoa plantations and transoceanic shipping, sugar production, butter contracts, and retail trade routes. Psychology was taught through a unit on marketing. Science was easy—the chemistry and biochemistry of chocolate became fascinating, and the technology of mass production and packaging offered numerous opportunities to teach general science and introductory applied physics.

The gender unit, or as waggish students renamed it, the "sex" unit, had been extraordinarily controversial initially. However, parents had, in time, become enormously impressed with the subject matter involved and the maturity of their children in handling the topics. The initial focus of the unit concentrated on interactions between males and females in society, both past and present. However, the underlying theme explored through a variety of subjects the manner in which gender roles have been continually shaped and reshaped by economic and technological forces. The roles of men and women in agricultural, industrial, and postindustrial societies were the backbone of the unit. The interaction between technological innovation, economic change, and alterations in roles for males and females was thus placed in a historical context. This context served as an excellent backdrop for discussion and learning about contemporary careers, laws, literature, fashion, the media, and dozens of other facets of contemporary society. Science for the gender project dwelled initially upon human biology and reproduction, and it was far more intense than the superficial treatment of sex education required by the state education code. Early in the semester, however, Ms. Holland, the biology teacher, had an opportunity to teach science fundamentals about all kinds of flora and fauna, as well as human evolution. A Selden School eighth grader could pronounce and explain "ontogeny recapitulates phylogeny" in a manner which stunned all but the most scientifically sophisticated parents.

The project and problem-solving basis of the Selden curriculum was an exceedingly time-consuming activity for the teachers. It was much easier to compartmentalize instruction in fifty isolated minutes of history, followed by fifty minutes of foreign language, followed by fifty minutes of general science. To integrate all of these plus three or four other subject areas into a project aimed at planning the first meeting of Congress and the first State of the Union Address under the newly adopted Constitution was far more difficult.

A second learning principle which undergirded instruction at Selden was the notion of cooperative learning. Not only were students actively engaged in projects which brought their textbook reading, library research, and homework assignments together into a vivid experience; they also engaged in many of these projects as a team. Teams had shifting student membership, depending upon the task at hand. Johnny or Susie might well be part of the Hamiltonian faction at the Constitutional Convention, while on different teams when it came to bargaining on the price of butter for the chocolate candy production project. Similarly, Johnny and Susie might be part of yet other different teams when it came to writing a play adapted from a Michael Crichton novel about sexual harassment in the workplace.

Project teams conducted research, constructed sets for dramatic productions, engaged in science experiments, arranged field trips, scheduled outside experts, wrote reports, visited production facilities, interviewed civic officials and dignitaries, identified CD-ROMs that could be used for research, and produced daily news programs reporting on events at the Constitutional Convention, the Chicago Board of Trade, and the UN Conference on Human Rights.

Generally, the sixth grade concentrated on the "Eighteenth Century," the seventh grade on "Chocolate," and the eighth grade on "Gender." However, numerous projects in all three areas depended upon cross-age project teams. Eighth graders were expected to help with sixth- and seventh-grade projects, and this cross-age tutoring was an essential part of the curriculum. Eighth-grade tutors were taken, as a reward for their service, on an end-of-year field trip to Williamsburg. Here much of their three years of study and preparation came together when they debated, in the restored colonial capital building, the role of the colonies in boycotting English goods, including imported chocolate.

Despite the project and problem-solving orientation of the Selden curriculum, teachers took pains to ensure that the state core curriculum in science, mathematics, history, civics, geography, literature, and language was covered. Selden also maintained an extensive after-school program of electives in areas such as athletics, music, and foreign language and in practical fields such as cooking and carpentry.

King Comprehensive High School

It was an unusually humid spring day at King High School. Principal Fox, devoid of his school-crested blue blazer, was taking his usual noon walk around the campus. He stopped at the broad plaza where all the campus walkways merged. Each day, from 12 to 12:30 P.M. he made a point of touring the school. This was one of the several techniques he used to stay abreast of developments in every part of King High School.

From his central vantage he observed the flow of students, faculty, volunteer tutors, and others moving from one part of the campus to another. Some students were headed for lunch in the cafeteria or on the grassy commons area. An almost equal number were headed for the parking lot or for the nearby rapid transit stop. For those leaving the campus, the academic portion of their school day was complete, and they were carrying their belongings and backpacks with them. For most of these students the afternoon would be spent at a nearby hospital and outpatient clinic, where they would work as laboratory assistants, orderlies, nurses' aides, physical therapy aides, physicians' assistants, and in other health-training capacities. What they did at their afternoon job was linked to their morning classroom subjects. Their hospital and clinic duties were the applied side of the mathematics, chemistry, and technical writing classes in which they had been enrolled for two years. Some of these students would reappear at the school later in the afternoon to participate in intramural sports and other activities.

For the other portion of the student body—ninth graders in the common-school core and upper-school students engaged in the college preparatory curriculum—the afternoon would consist of elective courses and then either a performing-arts, athletic, community service, or intramural activity.

Fox enjoyed the hurly-burly of the King campus. He worked hard to ensure that students were engaged in activities of which they were proud and from which they could derive subsequent benefit, both personally and as citizens. He was proud of other features of his school as well. Many of the parents and community volunteers waved or stopped for a few seconds to chat as they headed for their cars. He knew most of them; indeed, through his many years of involvement in community activities, he had personally recruited many of them to volunteer in the school. Fox wanted many adults, in addition to teachers, on the campus. He liked the intellectual and practical stimulus these successful individuals brought to classes. He also liked the notion of having many adult role models readily available for students to see, and with whom they could identify. Fox also liked the easy manner in which King students, regardless of their academic program, race, or economic status, interacted with each other.

The school board was on Fox's mind. A prominent member had phoned that morning to request that a math teacher be transferred from one of King's major academic programs to another. This was perplexing. Never before had he received such a call. The operating contract, which King's professional cooperative had signed with the board three years before, was loaded with evaluation criteria by which the overall success of the school and its programs could be judged. However, the contract expressly prohibited school board interference in the school's day-to-day operation.

Fox had listened attentively on the phone to the school board member's complaints, and said he would talk to her again later. He did not agree with her criticisms of the teacher. He intended to discuss the issue next Monday evening with the cooperative's board of directors and gain the advice of the attorney he used who specialized in school matters. He did not want any embarrassment to come to the board member, but when he would phone her back on Tuesday to explain that he was not acting positively on her request, he wanted to know his legal grounds firmly. He also wanted advice about how, diplomatically but emphatically, to inform her that she was out of line and should not engage in such an activity in the future.

Parents and students could easily speak with the principal if there was a problem with a teacher—and many had. When they had a good point, Fox took an appropriate action. If parents and students were dissatisfied with his solution, they were also within their rights to file a grievance with King High School's own governing board. In theory, parents could also complain to the local school board, but only on grounds that the school was violating its contract. If a complaint could not be resolved, as had happened four times in the three years he had been the principal and contract director, a student could always transfer to another public high school. Several, including two contract schools regarded by Fox as amiable competitors, were located nearby.

Fox hated disputes with parents and sometimes longed for the old days when disciplinary matters and complaints could be referred to the central office. He believed, however, that the school defined itself and evidenced seriousness of intent in its dealings with fractious students and their families. He also admitted that his spine was stiffened by the experience of some other contract middle schools that had lost parental support after failing to maintain the studious atmosphere promised in their recruiting brochures.

Fox did not have long to reflect favorably upon his school and to muse about the school board member's call. He had a busy afternoon. He was meeting at 12:30 P.M. with the senior segment of the student council to hear plans for the spring semester graduation ceremonies. He had a 1 P.M. meeting with the school's biology and health science teachers. They had been redoing the laboratory science curriculum in keeping with recently released national standards. He wanted to hear the results of their deliberations and decide whether or not to alter the science offerings in the forthcoming school year. At 2 P.M. he would meet with the school's business manager, Mr. Hayward, to review the month's financial accounts. King had approximately 1,000 students and a total annual budget approaching $7 million. Finances were a big part of Fox's overall responsibilities as contract director, and he was proud that he and the school staff had saved sufficient funds each of the past two years to purchase added equipment for the school, and to award the staff and faculty salary bonuses with the other half of the savings.

Fox typically allocated from 3 to 4 P.M. as a time when students, faculty, parents, or virtually anyone could drop by and speak with him without an appointment. He looked forward to these informal conversations. This was another mechanism that enabled him to stay in touch with the wide range of individuals who attended or worked in the school. He was planning on leaving a little before 4 P.M. today. The school's tennis team was playing in the conference finals, and he was eager to watch several of the matches.

At the tennis matches, Fox knew he would have a chance to speak with an influential parent, Dr. Robinson, about the possibility of financing for several creative evaluation ideas the health academy faculty had conceived. Robinson headed a philanthropic foundation, one of the few that actually invested in experiments and innovations in testing and the measurement of student and school program performance. Fox was unhappy with King's continued reliance upon standardized test scores and conventional performance measures such as student dropout rates. He and his faculty were eager to find additional means of appraising the effects of their school, and Robinson was always a constructive critic and generous donor. His son was also a good tennis player.

Robinson, as well as other foundation officials, civic activists, university faculty, and prominent local business executives, had helped Fox and his teacher colleagues during their year of volunteer work designing the contract proposal for what became King High School. Fox had called together a design group of teachers, almost all of whom he had worked with in one school setting or another during his ten years as an assistant principal and then principal, and they had agreed to create a completely new secondary school program. They formed a nonprofit organization and adopted the label "Teaching Cooperative." They knew approximately how much money per pupil they would have to spend. The new state school-finance laws specified how much a school district would receive in per pupil revenues, and the teachers knew that at least 95 percent of that had to be spent at schools.

In the beginning, uncertainty had prevailed for contractors. For example, they would not be able initially to judge how many students would want to come to their new school. Since students no longer had to attend a school in an assigned neighborhood, proposal designers always carried with them the notion that they had better render schooling attractive and useful or there would be few takers. They also had to find a way to "market" their school—to let prospective enrollees know what King stood for, and what services it would provide.

Early in their planning meetings, Fox and the teachers decided that they would operate a comprehensive high school, but not one in the conventional mold. There would be two major curriculum options. One would emphasize college preparatory academics. However, the teachers intended that the last year of study at King High School would be like the freshman curriculum at most good colleges. King would have high standards, and students would know that their studies would be rigorous. They would also know that successful completion of those studies would virtually guarantee them admission to a good college and the high probability of being able to skip most or all of their freshman year at that college. In effect, King could lead to success and save their families money in the process.

Fox and his planning companions were not satisfied in catering only to a student body immediately interested in college. They also were challenged by the notion of making secondary school useful and interesting to youths who might not want to go to college or who did not want to go to college immediately. For this group of students, they initially designed a "Partnership Health Academy." This was a school within a school, a component of King High School which, while drawing heavily upon the King faculty and facilities, had a stand-alone image and practical identity.

King's partnership was with nearby Oakmont Hospital and Outpatient Clinic. Students had to apply to the hospital to be admitted into the partnership program. Fox liked this part of the plan. With this approach, students knew from the beginning that the activity was a serious one. Applicants had to assemble a portfolio of materials, write an essay, provide evidence of interests, and arrange for a personal interview. Finalists were interviewed jointly by school and hospital staff.

Approximately 100 applicants were accepted annually into the Partnership Academy. They had a three-year health services curriculum. Classes were scheduled from 8 in the morning until 12 noon. Students worked in the hospital or clinic, or participated in a related activity, from 1 until 4 p.m. For their service in this setting, students were paid the legal minimum wage their initial year. Higher amounts were paid in each succeeding year, consistent with the students' academic success in school, assumption of added job responsibilities, and progression through the ranks of their practical training assignments.

In their morning classes, Health Academy students took a language arts, history, and social science core which emphasized literature, communication skills, social science, history, and philosophy concepts related to health science. They also took mathematics, biology, and chemistry. For their senior year, should they elect, courses were also available in physiology, advanced algebra, biochemistry, and advanced laboratory techniques. They also met three hours a week for a class on health and hospital protocol and practical operations. This class met once a week in large groups and then twice each week in small sections specializing in whatever component of the medical or health field that the student was performing in the hospital or clinic.

One morning hour per week was reserved for a period during which a group of twenty students met as a group with their "academic advisor." This teacher counseled them personally and academically, and served as their school liaison with their hospital "clinical advisor." At least twice a month their King academic advisor visited with students in the hospital setting and discussed their work performance and the relationship of school and work.

Students' afternoons were actively spent in practical hospital and clinic activities. In their initial year, they did a great deal of observing and menial activity. By the end of year one they were expected to be intimately familiar with the institution and its procedures, have qualified in several technical areas necessary to begin their specialized tasks in the fall of the second year, and have gained familiarity with whatever equipment they would be expected to operate beginning in their second year.

Health Academy students, in addition to their academic advisor at King, had a clinical advisor at the hospital. Each clinical advisor oversaw twenty student trainees. This involved at least once-a-week observations and conversations. It also meant providing advice and ensuring that extra assistance was provided for any student who was falling behind or in danger of dropping out. Day-to-day training and supervision in students' hospital tasks were handled by one or more of the hospital employees to whom trainees were assigned.

Hospital testing tended to be quite practical. There was a series of developmental activities that trainees were expected to master. Many of these had immediate feedback connected with them, and student trainees could themselves assess their performance. There were, however, formal examinations at the end of each semester, and students received report cards summarizing both their King School academic learning and their hospital and clinic performance

It was too early to predict, but it appeared as if many of the first cohort of students would be offered jobs upon their completion of the program. Fox was particularly pleased with the four students who had become excited about health matters and had decided to alter their graduation goal. They had transferred to the academic program at the high school in order to prepare to go to college. They would have to take an additional year at King, but they were prepared and motivated to do just that. Despite these successes, Fox knew that many parents hoped King would help their children get work directly after high school, and he feared some loss of enrollment if the promised jobs did not materialize.

Heartened by the health-training experiences, Fox and his staff had begun the planning for an additional Partnership Academy program. This was a link with the city's major hotel and tourist industry.

The Health Academy enrolled 300 students, evenly divided over the three years of its curriculum. The Hotel and Recreation Program in its initial year would enroll only 100, but it presumably would grow by a similar amount for each of the subsequent two years. When both academies were in full operation, King enrollment would stabilize at 1,200. This seemed a good size for a secondary school, and Fox was not eager for King to grow beyond that. If the demand for the school remained high, then Fox and his colleagues would think of bidding to operate a second school.

The Academic Academy at King was a rigorous school. Students applied midway through the ninth grade, based on their interests in going to college. The Academic Academy also had a stream for science and one for humanities. Students enrolled in one stream took courses in the other field, but not as intensely as in their major. For example, science majors took a full program in mathematics and then specialized in either chemistry, physics, or life science. They also took a course in literature and history or a humanities course each semester. However, whereas they took only ten hours a week in these two subjects, they took twenty hours a week in their science courses. This included laboratory time.

Humanities students were almost the mirror image of the science students in their course load. They took ten hours of science and mathematics a week and twenty hours of integrated literature, history, and humanities. All students, humanities and science majors, took at least one foreign language. Humanities students could opt for a second foreign language in their junior and senior year. All senior year courses, and many junior year offerings as well, were rated as advanced placement courses. Students obtaining a B or better in these classes were highly assured of receiving college credit for them.

There were 300 Academic Academy students, 100 in each of three classes. Their courses did not meet every day—they were scheduled more like college classes. with some meeting on Monday, Wednesday, and Friday; others, particularly the science laboratory classes, clustered on Tuesdays and Thursdays. The Health Academy laboratory classes tended to be clustered on Mondays and Wednesdays. Thus, the school could derive maximum benefit from its specialized physical facilities.

King had a 300-student ninth grade class. The ninth grade was the final grade in which all students attended a common school with a state-prescribed core curriculum. Thereafter, students had to select—actively had to make a choice and had to apply for—whatever kind of schooling they wanted. Thus, the ninth-grade curriculum was heavily oriented toward state and national history, civics, and electives. Another ninth-grade component was filled with information about the secondary school choices available to students beginning in the tenth grade. Ninth-grade homeroom teachers, themselves familiar with King's Academic and Partnership Academies as well as secondary programs in other schools throughout the geographic area, spent virtually an entire year providing students and their families with information, assisting them in making choices, and, eventually, helping to complete admission applications.

The Academic Academy shared faculty, particularly in afternoon elective courses, with the ninth-grade common school and the two Partnership Academies at King School. However, Fox continued to search for means for more fully integrating the three curricula at the school. He wanted to maintain the intellectual integrity of all the programs, but simultaneously he wanted the students to interact with each other more often. His biggest success so far on this dimension was with the athletic teams. Even here, however, it was a strain on the Partnership Academy students because they often had to shorten their working time. He had altered schedules, and both the hospital and hotels were flexible, but he knew he had more planning to do to accomplish this aim.

Fox would meet with the health-science faculty in the morning and convey the new ideas for a proposal to formulate a "value added" means for assessing pupil performance. If he and his teachers could develop a means, even experimental, for determining the entry-level skills of health-science students and their incremental levels of additional skill and knowledge each year thereafter, Robinson would give serious consideration to providing the school with development funding.

Testing was on Fox's mind in yet another manner. Later that week the school schedule would have to be altered substantially for a day. This was to accommodate the end-of-year state testing program. These examinations, proctored by outside monitors, were high stakes, both for the school and for the students. Individual student scores would be reported to colleges to which they applied and to prospective employers. Also, the school's contract renewal and overall community reputation would in large measure be linked to these scores. Fox felt confident that he and his staff had emphasized the correct concepts and skills, and, thus, students and the school would do well. But he had been surprised by test scores, both high and low, in the past. Nevertheless, it was difficult to dismiss the state-administered examinations as a useless activity. The consequences were high.

As Fox entered his car to drive home, he reflected on the day. What he liked about his current job was the freedom and responsibility. A lot rode on his ability to organize and motivate both faculty and students. Sometimes he longed for a quiet day free of crises and threats to the school's reputation. As a dedicated supporter of public education, he was not happy to hear his brother-in-law say, "what you are running is a medium-sized business, and you have to worry about survival every day." But he knew his brother-in-law was essentially right. In the past year, Fox had started meeting monthly with the heads of local independent high schools, and had found that they had much in common.

On the other hand, the rewards were tremendous. As he drove he thought about the number of times, under the old arrangements—before taking charge of a contract school, he had attended endless central-office meetings in which he had been told by assistant superintendents how to use his time and to run a school. Now, he almost never went to the central office. He had advice aplenty from his teachers, the parent council, and others. Whether he took or ignored the advice, the payoff or penalty was felt by the school: staff members and parents would decide whether to stay with the school or transfer, and the school would either flourish and retain its contract or not. However, now he and his staff were virtually unfettered bureaucratically in their ability to pursue what they knew was good education. He also was feeling good about the tennis team victory and took a mental note to phone the coach that evening and congratulate him on the results.

A Primer on School
Finance Systems

Anew system for financing contract schools must build on the
strengths of the current system and correct its weaknesses.
Describing the current system will not be easy, however.
Most state school-finance systems have become so complex
as the result of years of legislative deal-making, that only a few people in
each state truly understand how schools are financed. Just to clear out the
underbrush choking the current system may be reason enough to consider
our proposed changes.

State Finance Systems

Almost every state constitution requires the state to provide free public
education, or provide for a system of free public schooling from elementary through high school. Attendance through some age, usually sixteen,
is compulsory, and it is the state's responsibility to assure equity or fairness in the way schools are financed.

There are fewer similarities among state school-finance systems once
you go beyond state constitutional guidelines. Although states on average
pay about 50 percent of the cost of schools, the actual percentage varies
from a high of over 90 percent in Hawaii to a low of 5 percent in New
Hampshire. Average state expenditures per child vary from over $9,000 in
New Jersey to about $4,000 in Mississippi. States also use different rev-
enue sources to pay for schools, although the property tax still provides
most of the local support, and income and sales taxes make up the bulk of
state school dollars.

Variations within are as great as the variations among states. In states
like Hawaii, California, Oregon, and Washington that rely heavily on state

revenues to support schools, the variation in expenditure per pupil at the local level is less. States that rely more heavily on local support have a harder time equalizing school expenditures.

The current "system" of school finance in the United States is anything but systematic. It is instead a hodgepodge of political compromises that often seem to contradict the very purposes of public education. Many states ignore the importance of adequate facilities for high-quality education, leaving the construction and maintenance of schools to local authorities. And almost all state financial systems allocate resources for school inputs without much attention to what those inputs are producing.

School Finance Formulas

While education is a state responsibility, most states delegate responsibility for managing schools, and part of the responsibility for financing them, to local school districts. States generally establish some level of basic funding, called a foundation level, which is expected to provide a minimum basic education. It agrees to pay a percentage of the basic amount per student or classroom (or some other instructional unit), with the local school district picking up the rest. Because local districts vary in their ability to raise funds from property or sales taxes, states generally provide additional funds for what is called equalization. Equalization means that extra state money is given to low-wealth districts that, despite making an average- or above-tax effort, cannot raise sufficient local revenue to reach the state's foundation level of support. This is a nice concept, but states seldom allocate enough money for equalization to substantially reduce the expenditure differences between rich and poor districts. Rich districts lobby to have the basic allocation available for all districts made as big as possible and resist efforts to redistribute local money from high-wealth to low-wealth districts. The result is that spending disparities persist between high-wealth and low-wealth districts in most states. These disparities generally will be greater the larger the number of districts in a state, and the larger the local share of total school revenues.

The state's basic school-finance formula usually only covers the operating costs of the regular education programs. Federal and other state funds are passed through the states to districts that have students with special needs. These "categorical" programs provide some equalization in that they are often targeted to disadvantaged children, who tend to be more concentrated in low-income areas. Categorical programs are expensive to administer, however, and a high proportion of the funds support professionals and administrators before trickling down to help students in classrooms. The funds are often provided to districts, not schools, and not on a per pupil basis. Other funds are provided to local districts by states for transportation services, and occasionally to offset the high cost of small schools.

How State Education Dollars Are Spent

Pockets of school poverty persist, especially in many of our declining rural areas. In some places, the entire school district is poor. In many urban districts, however, poor schools exist within more prosperous districts because of the way resources are assigned to the schools. In fact, as we pointed out in an earlier chapter, it is not uncommon for a poor inner-city school to have as little as half of the resources of a suburban school in the same district, solely because of personnel policies that permit vacancies to be filled on the basis of teacher seniority. The inequity of such a teacher-assignment system is even greater because many new teachers leave after the first year or two of teaching. The consequence is that urban schools not only have less experienced teachers, but also have constant teacher turnover, both of which are detrimental to successful student learning.

These inequalities are a blight on the nation and threaten our economic and social welfare. But despite these problems and their widely recognized importance, national, state, and local governments have struggled to find solutions. We believe that the educational system has become so large and politically entrenched that it cannot be changed without a major reform of governance and finance.

This point can be made more clearly by looking at the way educational dollars are spent in the United States. One observation is that too little of public tax dollars are actually spent on the instruction of children, and too much is spent to support a bureaucracy filled with a wide variety of non-classroom professionals and service employees. These noninstructional personnel are aggregated principally in school district central offices. They are too seldom assigned to school sites. The only way this unbalanced condition will change is to require that dollars go directly to schools for instruction. The pressures at individual schools, particularly if a contract school is subject to the four kinds of evaluation we have discussed elsewhere in this book, are to deploy every conceivable person for instruction. Individual schools have far less tolerance than central offices for personnel who are not engaged in instruction. Principals and teachers at a school are eager to ensure that everyone around them is engaged in the activity for which the school was established.

Placing resources at school sites was the approach used in Great Britain. Under Margaret Thatcher's Educational Reform Act of 1988, local education authorities were ordered to pass most of the money directly to schools on a per student basis. The result was a substantial increase in the allocation of education dollars in England and Wales to the schools (Guthrie and Pierce 1990). But we're getting ahead of the argument.

According to the 1994 edition of the Digest of Education Statistics, total current expenditures for public schools in the United States in 1991–92 were $211.2 billion. Of this amount $128.4 billion, or 60 percent, was spent for instruction. $82.8 billion, or 40 percent, was spent for noninstructional costs. Eleven percent was spent on operations and maintenance; 4 percent on transportation; and the remaining 25 percent for other student support services, including general and school administration, academic support, and health programs. Of the $128.4 billion available for instruction, $118 billion, or 92.4 percent, was spent on teacher salaries and benefits; only $4.7 billion, or 3.7 percent of total instructional expenses, was spent for supplies. The striking finding from this analysis is how much goes to support personnel and how little is spent for research, training and development, or instructional materials and supplies. Many of the nation's schools are without science laboratories and equipment, current textbooks, or computers. No other kind of organization could hope to survive spending so little for these items, especially an organization that is supposed to prepare students for contemporary employment and citizenship.

There never seems to be money available for equipment, materials, and research because new dollars raised for schools are needed for teacher salaries or existing programs. Even when districts pass a new operating levy, the moneys are already allocated for deferred maintenance, additional teachers to reduce class size, salary increases, or some other purpose selected by the central administration.

The Politics of the Budgetary Process

Why do school systems find themselves in this over-constrained condition where there is never enough money for necessary equipment and materials, staff training and development, or new ideas to improve instruction? Some argue that it is because we just spend too little for education. We believe it has more to do with the structure and politics of the budgetary process in public education.

This is also a complex topic, and we probably do it an injustice by this short discussion. We are reminded of the adage that for every complex problem there is a simple answer that is wrong. In this case, however, the facts are strongly on the side of a political impasse.

Most states require school districts to prepare an annual budget for the fiscal year that begins on July 1. The primary focus of the school board and administration is in balancing expected revenues with expected expenditures. Little attention is paid to how the allocation of the budget affects student learning.

A school board, like most units of local governments, first attempts to estimate the resources it is likely to receive based upon the current law and a projection of students. If the estimate of revenues from the federal government, the state, and local property tax levies or sales tax receipts falls short of the current budget or expected minimum needs, the board considers asking local voters for additional support. Only when alternative revenue sources have been denied them, will the board consider budget cuts or other strategies for using funds more efficiently. Faced with a budget deficit, districts usually cut those activities whose elimination will create the least opposition. Deferred maintenance and custodial services go before busing and athletic programs. Personnel are let go on a last-hired, first-fired basis, usually regardless of the need for their services or the quality of their work.

School districts, like most public-sector institutions, engage in incremental budgeting. Incremental refers to the tendency to make resource allocation changes only at the margins. The vast majority of expenditures in a school system continues year after year, and from one budget cycle to the next. In other words, the budget base changes very little. The budget for each unit in the system is seldom changed regardless of changes in demand for the services of the unit or changes in state policy. One reason school districts get so angry at new federal or state mandates, especially when unaccompanied by a new appropriation, is that any change would require a reallocation of funds, and that is difficult to do. Generally budgets change only when there are new dollars, or increments, to pay for the proposed change.

The reason why incremental budgeting is so pervasive is the political influence of individuals and groups who benefit from the way things currently are. The groups with the most influence over school budgets are the administration and teacher unions or teacher representatives. Their first impulse is to protect the jobs and privileges of those already in the schools. If there is a prospect for new resources, the central administration and the teachers lobby to have those resources used for their own benefit. The central office asks for more supervisors and program coordinators. Teachers lobby or bargain intensely for higher salaries and smaller classes. Many parents of children in school side with the teachers on these issues, because their primary contact with the schools is with the teachers, who provide them with nearly all the information they receive about schools. Consequently, a school board and administration are likely to be under tremendous political pressure to spend the new money on those who are already employed, who believe they are entitled to receive what they got last year plus a "fair share" of any additions.

The best that policy makers can hope for under the current school organization is to gain control over a portion of an anticipated increase and direct those resources toward new goals. When resources are declining, entrenched interests are even more adamant in protecting the base. For these reasons, it is difficult for policy makers to make decisions about the total school budget, or to even consider systemic change. Typically, only a portion of new money can be redirected to a new program or goals. Reform is almost impossible when resources are declining.

One important reason school budgeting is incremental is that power to make budgetary decisions is concentrated in the central office and teacher unions. With this power they can generally determine the organization's direction. Budget control, in other words, is power. This is conventionally referred to as the "power of the purse." With budgetary control concentrated, there is little incentive for the power holders to reallocate the budget in ways that diminish their financial situation or their power.

Conclusion

There are two major problems with the way we finance schools in the United States. The first is that, in dividing responsibility for supporting public schools among units of government with widely varying abilities to support education, it is almost impossible to provide every child with an equal opportunity for a quality education. The second is that bureaucrats have too much control over the way dollars are spent and little incentive to allocate budgets efficiently, if by efficiently we mean where the dollars will produce the most education. A solution to the current inequities is to shift the responsibility for financing basic education to the state and then distribute those dollars to schools on a per student basis. The solution to the inefficiency of school budgets is to give more control over the budget to those people who are most concerned about educational quality: school principals, classroom teachers, and the parents of children in school.

Questions and Answers about Contract Schools

I n this appendix, we attempt to answer a number of questions that people ask about contracting for instruction and other education services. The following answers are intended for policy makers who might be considering the adoption of such a system, for parents and others who may wish to explore such a system with policy makers, and for education professionals who might want to bid to operate a "Contract School."

The questions cover the following topics: (1) parent choice and parent participation, (2) school board operation, (3) provider or contractor operations, (4) citizen concerns, (5) accountability and efficiency, and (6) miscellaneous items.

Parent Choice and Parent Participation

How would a parent choose a school for a child?

This is a crucial question because the answer to the "Where to go to school" decision might be substantially different under contract schools than what usually happens now.

Presently, in most public school systems, parents simply send their child to the nearest neighborhood school. If the district has a court-ordered or voluntary racial desegregation plan, then a child may not attend a neighborhood school but, nevertheless, will attend whatever school the district decides. In effect, presently, the school district is the deciding agent in these transactions. Children are compelled to go to school wherever the district determines.

There are two possible exceptions to this traditional pattern of school-attendance assignment. If parents can afford a private school, then they can exercise a larger element of choice. Or, if the district has a magnet school plan or some other kind of public choice program, then there may be an element of household discretion in the matter.

Under a contract school system, each school's provider would be encouraged to operate a school with an individual style, theme, or unique mode of operation. This style would be a component of the contract, and the character of the school would become part of the manner by which the school advertised itself to its potential parent and student clients.

Parents, under a contract plan, would have a choice of public schools either throughout the entire school district or, in large districts, in a region or sector of the district. Also, under cooperative arrangements among school districts, parents might even have a choice of public schools across district or even county lines.

How would parents be guaranteed they were not denied entry to a school because of unfair discrimination?

School districts would distribute information about the nature of each school within a district. They also would establish clear procedures for applying to attend a particular school. Priority might easily be given to children who resided within a geographically bounded attendance area. Enrollment priority might also be given to students whose siblings already attended a specific school. Similarly, a school district could establish racial balance guidelines: in effect, specifying that a school had to have room to admit students of particular races in order to achieve whatever balance was deemed by the school board to be appropriate. Also, under certain circumstances, a school for which the number of applicants outstripped the number of available student spaces might rely upon a random lottery to determine admission. In this manner, no child would be unfairly favored over another.

Districts would also be expected to establish attendance appeal procedures, similar to those which often exist presently. Under such arrangements, an applicant believing himself or herself to be wronged, could file a grievance and have the attendance decision reviewed by a district-overseen neutral process.

How would parents obtain information regarding schools or sets of schools?

School districts would be responsible for overseeing an information distribution process and for providing households with responses to inquiries. Such services should be able to provide objective and accurate data regarding each school for which a prospective applicant was eligible.

How accurate would be the information provided by schools to parents?
One of the functions served by outside evaluators, called upon periodically to appraise the performance of a school and the school contractor operating the school, would be to review the information distributed by the district about the school. In effect, information available to potential clients would also be subject to an external "audit" to ensure its accuracy.

What if a parent were unhappy about a school, and could a parent choose to switch schools for a child?
Parents have multiple avenues through which to express their displeasure with a school and attempt to arrive at a more satisfying situation for their child. First, conventional channels of personal communication with teachers and other school officials will continue to be available and should be exhausted. In that the contractor's overall level of revenue, not to mention eventual contract renewal, would be subject to favorable client opinion and student enrollments, one would think that contractors and their employees would be unusually sensitive to claims of displeased clients. However, if a parent were still unsatisfied, he or she could ask the school district ombudsperson to intervene or rely upon a district-wide grievance resolution process. Failing to gain satisfaction through such avenues, and as a last resort, parents could also move their child to another school in the district or possibly to a school in a nearby district.

How can parents influence the spectrum of available schools from which to choose?
School boards will be the agency responsible for deciding what kinds of schooling to offer. School boards will construct the dimensions of Requests for Proposals (RFPs). Thus, an appropriate initial leverage point at which parents who desire a particular kind of school can make their desires known is the board proceeding at which RFP dimensions are the subject of deliberations.

Through what mechanisms can parents express their views regarding the performance of schools and their satisfaction levels?
One of the several components by which a contract school should be appraised is the satisfaction of clients. A principal measure of parent satis-

faction is enrollment. If a school is repeatedly undersubscribed, then the message is "something is wrong here."

In addition, the third-party independent evaluations, to which contract schools should be subjected in order to determine the extension or renewal of a contract, should explicitly call for systematic polling of parent opinion.

Parents, as well as other citizens, will vote in school board elections and interact with school board members. Here again are opportunities to convey personal impressions of school performance.

Could a parent choose a school which was located in another school district from the one in which he or she resided?

The controlling authority in such instances is state law. Increasingly, states have enacted statutes which facilitate interdistrict transfers of students. In the absence of such an overarching authority, districts can enter into agreements among themselves regarding interdistrict transfers. However, all such complexities aside, there is nothing inherent within contracting which either mandates or prevents interdistrict opportunities for students.

How would a parent express a complaint or file a grievance against a teacher or another school employee?

Effectively, parent grievances or complaints against teachers or other school employees would be handled in a contract situation as they are now, with one crucial addition. Presently, parents have conventional means for filing complaints: first through informal conversations, and, if matters escalate, through formal channels. These generally begin at the school site and proceed through district-level officials, ending with the local school board itself. Of course, failure to achieve eventual satisfaction in this manner can lead to legal action. All of these steps remain available under contract schooling.

In addition, and crucially important, under the contract education plan described in this book, households would also have an opportunity to place their child in another school, if they were dissatisfied.

School Board Operation

Why have a school board?

Education in a democracy is too important to leave completely to the control and operation of professional educators, or to private entrepreneurs. There is a vital public interest to be served by education, and this interest justifies maintaining a publicly responsive governance system. Thus, contract education retains school boards as representatives of the public's long-run interests. However, maintaining the public's interests does not necessarily mean maintaining public operation. A system of contract schools balances public accountability, private-sector efficiency, and parent freedom to choose.

Who could run for school board elections?
There is nothing inherent within the idea of contracting that dictates a change in school board selection procedures. If citizens are currently satisfied with the manner in which school boards are selected and operate, then they can be maintained as now, but with a different set of regulatory authorities. If citizens are dissatisfied, then the arrangements pertaining to school board selection also should be altered.

How many school board members would each district have, and how long would school board terms be?
The response here is, effectively, the same as above. Whatever now prevails on dimensions such as school board membership, selection processes, single-member voting areas versus at-large district election, and length of members' terms can all be maintained or changed. What must change, however, is the operating authority of the school board. State statutes must be altered to make it clear that the principal role of the school board is representing the public's will in designing schools and evaluating their performance. What school boards no longer should be authorized to do is employ school-site administrators and teachers. These personnel should be under the authority of the successfully bidding contractor.

What powers would a school board have?
School boards will have an opportunity to assume true policy-making status. Specifically, schools boards should be authorized to: (1) employ a chief executive officer for the district and a restricted number of central-office subordinates, (2) hold public hearings regarding the qualifications of contractors and the nature of the school characteristics to embed in RFPs, (3) select among competitively submitted contract bids, (4) arrange for evaluations of schools by objective, third-party, qualified evaluators, (5) compile and effectively distribute information regarding individual local schools, and (6) establish a grievance or complaint review process and sit as a panel of near last resort in this local undertaking.

What kind of budgetary discretion would school boards have under the contract system?

School financing would continue to be a principal undertaking of state government. However, if a state decided to maintain local revenue generation as a discretionary item, then the locally elected school board might additionally have revenue discretion. However, the revenue for any particular school within a district would be a function of state per pupil specification for the grade levels involved, whatever categorical aid was available (e.g., funding for handicapped pupils), and the numbers of pupils enrolled at a school. School boards would have little discretion over spending or resource allocation within an individual school. That would be subject to the authority of the successfully bidding contractor.

Why would anyone want to run for election as a school board member?

Candidates' motives, presumably, would be as pure or as distorted as at present. The only factor that might change is that under a contracting strategy, school board members would have many fewer hassles to deal with. They would not have to engage in collective bargaining or have to manage large numbers of employees. They also would not have to engage in detailed budget considerations. Individual school budgets would be a function of contractor decisions, and the district would have no employees, except a few central-office staff. A school board member's job might be far more enjoyable. Under a contract school system, they could actually concentrate on generating educational specifications for schools, deliberating upon the qualifications of contract bidders, and reviewing school evaluation results. In other words, they would again become boards of *education.*

What is the relationship between a school board and state government?

School boards would continue as the local representative of the state in the operation of schools. Lines of state authority involving agencies such as state education departments, the legislature, governor, and state board of education would remain the same as now. The dramatic difference is that the authority of local school boards would be altered.

How could school board members make informed judgments regarding proposals submitted by contractors?

Principally by relying upon the recommendations of the chief executive they employed for just such purposes. Since superintendents of schools would no longer be employed for their consummate skill in managing large organizations, or motivating communities and citizens to support schools, or engaging in local politics, they should be expected to be unusually knowledgeable about educational matters such as the curriculum, instructional strategies, and school climates. Superintendents should be expert in sorting through proposals and deciding what to recommend to a school board.

In addition, school board members themselves should take the time to become informed about educational matters and, thus, be in a better position to make sophisticated judgments.

What kinds of employment contracts would central-office educational administrators have with school boards?

The board's chief executive officer should be on a three-to-five-year rolling contract, which would be renewable. All other employees should be under the supervision of the chief executive, and their contracts should be whatever he or she recommends, subject to board approval. In no event should central-office employee contracts extend in time beyond that of the chief executive.

What would be the relationship between contractors and school boards?

It should be an arm's-length relationship. Contractors should be selected for their qualifications, the forcefulness of the ideas contained in their proposals, and their eventual ability to deliver services as proposed. School board members should have an objective capacity to review evaluation results and determine if contracts should be renewed or extended. There should be no personal or illegal relationships which would impede the ability of a school board member to exercise objective judgment in behalf of the public's interest.

What would be the relationship between school boards and third-party evaluators?

Virtually the same as between school boards and contractors. Evaluators should be regarded simply as a different class of contractor. Their obligation is to supply objective, third-party, independent, technically competent appraisals of school operation and performance. Their views must not be compromised by inappropriate relationships either with school board members or contractors. Evaluators should be selected because of their qualifications, their capacity for providing comprehensive appraisals, their objectivity, and their ability to communicate with a wide range of audiences.

Would all schools in a district have to be contract schools?

During a phase-in period, in which school boards are establishing bidding procedures, contract monitoring routines, and determining evaluation strategies, there may be room for both the conventional system and contract schools. However, a contracting strategy envisions that, eventually, all schools in a district would be operated by contractors. One of the reasons for having complete contracting is that school boards are not intended to be employers under this system. Contracting makes an important distinction between policy makers and providers, and a school board should not be in the providing business, only in the policy business.

Provider or Contractor Operations

Who could bid on school contracts?

Any individual, association, institution, nonprofit organization, partnership, company, college or university, or government group capable of meeting at least three minimal tests: (1) obtaining liability insurance, (2) not having a criminal record, and (3) pledging not to violate applicable laws and judicial rules. In fact, bidders are likely to possess qualifications far in excess of these. Groups such as teacher unions, private entrepreneurs, professional education administrators, and private-sector firms are likely to possess high levels of professional qualifications and to boast proudly of them. It is to be hoped that one of the dimensions on which competition will take place is the qualifications of bidders.

Practically speaking, groups such as the following can be anticipated to bid: teacher associations, administrator-led groups, private companies, religious groups, not-for-profit groups such as the Girl Scouts or YMCA, and professional associations.

Why would anyone or any group want to bid to operate a school?

The ability to earn a livelihood would undoubtedly be a large part of the reasoning of many individuals and groups. Additionally, motives may include professional fulfillment, civic responsibility, zeal, personal aggrandizement, fame, media visibility, and opportunity for self-expression.

Could profit-making companies bid to operate schools?

This will depend upon the decision of state officials in establishing the contracting authority. The plan will operate best if both public and private, and profit and nonprofit, groups are permitted to bid. That is, contracting will work most effectively when a wide range of prospective contractors are empowered to bid. However, the probability is also great that there exists sufficient enthusiasm among not-for-profit groups that plenty of bidders would stem from their ranks alone.

Could religiously affiliated contractors bid to operate a school?

Yes, but not for purposes of promulgating religious doctrine. Moreover, any successful bidder will have to guarantee access regardless of a student's religion. Bidders will have to agree to abide by existing statutes and court decisions regarding religion in public schools. No matter if operated by private contractors or churches, these will still be public schools.

Would contractors bidding on an RFP know the award criteria in advance?

Absolutely. One of a school board's major responsibilities is to construct and distribute the education criteria sought in the bidding and to specify the bases on which contracts will be awarded. A principal point of the entire contracting endeavor is to persuade public bodies to specify the qualities desired in public education.

How much discretion would a provider have, once awarded a contract?

A great deal. However, the basis of discretion is within the boundaries of the agreed-upon contract. Successful bidders will be expected to abide by the terms they set forth in their proposals. However, assuming that a contractor's actions are consistent with the winning bid, then he or she should be able to select personnel, determine levels of employee remuneration and working conditions, select instructional strategies, facility arrangements, communication means, and instructional materials.

What protection would a contractor have against school board micromanagement or unfair parent grievances?

The contract would serve as both the public's and provider's best protection. A contract would specify the contractor as having the authority to decide on management matters such as personnel, budget, instructional strategies, materials, and so on. School board members might attempt, after contract signing, to influence these activities, but a contractor would have the document as protection, if he or she desired to resist such intrusions. Also, if the school were popular among parents, the threat "to go public" about the school board member's inappropriate behavior might well serve to persuade a school board member to desist. Finally, the terms of the contract would be legally enforceable. A contractor would have the right to sue a district for contract violations.

Under what circumstances could a school board terminate or refuse to re-new a contract?

When a school board has good reason to believe that (1) students are at risk, either physically, psychologically, or academically, or (2) if a contract were being violated on other significant dimensions and after suitable warnings had been issued. This assumes that there is sufficient evidence to ensure that the school board can prove its case, if there is resistance on the part of the contractor.

What would a contractor have to pay teachers and other school employees?

Whatever the market demanded or whatever the contractor thought correct. There would be no specific minimum or maximum salary schedule. However, contractors would be responsible for adhering to appropriate state and federal statutes regarding employment. Also, contractors would be responsible for providing fringe benefits, including medical insurance, to their employees.

Who could be teachers in a contract school?

Contractors need more discretion to employ teachers of their choosing than under the current system. Teachers should not be required to be a part of a district bargaining unit, and not all teachers need to be state certified. There should be room for a variety of adults in schools, including other professionals, teacher aides, student teachers, and social service providers. On the other hand, schools would want to have a high proportion of professionally trained and licensed teachers to give parents confidence in the program being offered. A contractor employing low-quality teachers would jeopardize the competitiveness of its contract bid, risk the confidence of its clients (parents), and contribute to its own long-run demise by failing to produce high achievement in students. In fact schools are likely to compete for students on the basis of teacher qualifications.

What would be the relationship of subcontractors to an overall school contractor?

Principally, subcontractors, such as food service providers and maintenance workers, would be accountable to the school contractor, not the school board. Subcontractors would have to fulfill their contractual obligations and do so in a manner consistent with the general contractor's overall master contract with the school district. There might be exceptions to such an arrangement wherein a school board had a separate contract for a service such as after-school child care, and the provider reported both to the general contractor and, perhaps, to the school board. However, such bifurcated arrangements are generally to be avoided.

Could contractors determine what courses or subjects to teach in a school?

Yes, they could, as long as the courses met the terms of their contract. Contractors should agree to meet the expectations of the school board, but how those expectations are met should be decided at the school level. How the courses are taught, what instructional materials are used, who teaches the courses, and an assortment of other operational matters fall within the purview of the contractor.

Could a contractor determine what textbooks and other instructional materials to use in a school?

Yes. These are the kinds of operational matters which rightfully should be left to the discretion of contractors. However, contractors might well make such decisions in collaboration with parents.

How would contractors handle federal funding for special-needs students?

These matters should also be incorporated into the school-board-issued RFP. Presumably, if a contractor is expected to handle one or more special populations in a school, then the applicable state and federal categorical financial aid should follow the students involved who enroll in the school. The contractor would be responsible for meeting whatever state and federal categorical funding regulations apply.

Who, contractors or parents, would provide school supplies (paper and pencils) to students?

This should be specified as a component of the contract. If the RFP makes clear that instructional supplies are to be provided by the contractor, then the answer is clear. If the RFP or the bid specifies to the contrary, then that is clear. What should not happen is for the contract to omit specifications on the matter. Presumably, if a contractor is intending to provide such materials, then the contract amount will include such items in the budget.

Who would determine the range and quality of peripheral services at a school, e.g., child care, food service, recreation, counseling services, and elective courses?

The school board has the responsibility of specifying in an RFP the scope of desired services. Contractors, in responding, will specify the manner in which they intend to meet these obligations, either directly or through subcontractors.

Citizen Concerns

Who would set the local property tax rate?

The same parties as do now. There is nothing in this arrangement that need alter the taxation system. However, the state's interest in providing equal educational opportunity would be enhanced by a fully state-funded system of school finance as described in chapter 6.

Who would determine how much money would be spent for schools, for the state and locality?

Same answer as above. Whatever political system decisions are now made about school financing would be made under a contract education strategy.

Could citizens vote for school board members?

If they do now, then they could continue to do so under a contract strategy.

Could citizens vote in tuition add-on elections?

No. If state officials see fit to permit a contract school strategy to contain a parental discretionary fee add-on arrangement, then such additions are to be borne completely by parents, and only parents vote to approve or disapprove. Citizens do not participate in such elections because they bear none of the potential tax burden.

What if nonparent citizens should have a complaint against a school or a contractor?

They would initially engage in conversations with the individual contractor. Assuming this did not solve the problem, then they would file a complaint with the school board which should have formal procedures for handling such matters.

How would citizens know about the quality of their locality's or state's education system?
Citizens would have multiple avenues to information about their community's schools. One would be annually published results of state-wide testing programs. Such programs would be school-by-school and would be published for each community. Second, citizens would have the results of district or school annual testing, which should be publicly distributed. Third, school evaluation reports, undertaken by third-party independent evaluation contractors, should be distributed publicly by the school board. Last, citizens could attend school board meetings at times when contracts are up for renewal and listen to and participate in discussions.

Accountability and Efficiency

How would state officials know about the quality of schooling?
A principal means for evaluating education performance would be results of statewide examinations. Additionally, a state agency should be responsible for obtaining third-party local school evaluation reports and annually providing the legislature and governor with a synthesis of such results.

How can state officials and the general public ensure that schools are operating efficiently?
The state can contract annually, or over longer periods, for outside experts to conduct appraisals of the state's schools. They would rely upon the statewide examination outcomes and other data, on comparative information from other states and nations, and they would mix into their analyses a consideration for resources. In this way a judgment can be made regarding the efficiency and effectiveness of the system statewide.

What might a state testing system be like?
Many states already have testing schemes. The important components a system should possess in order to be useful are as follows: (1) State subject-matter curriculum frameworks which specify what ideas are of sufficient importance that they should be transmitted to students. These serve as the backbone of the examination system. Test questions should be constructed to appraise pupil knowledge of these dimensions. (2) Test questions which have been piloted to ensure that they possess the technical components of validity and reliability. (3) Sampling procedures which enable generalization at least to entire schools and possibly inclusion of

each student, so as to be able to provide not only sample results but results for the entire universe of students. A last component for consideration is "consequence." Should the state test results make a difference for a student? Should, for example, awarding of a high school diploma be contingent upon successful test passage?

Could some schools kick back some state money to parents?

No. Schools would be required to spend all the money they received from public sources on school operations, less any fees or profits allowed by the contract. A school could not make refund payments to parents, though it could use some of its retained income to pay for extracurricular activities or supplemental instruction.

Would some schools attract students with glossy sports or extracurricular programs?

Some contractors might choose to offer special extracurricular activities, and some might invest in competitive sports teams. Others might avoid interscholastic sports but offer intramurals or outdoor adventures. Still others might minimize extracurricular programs in favor of enhanced academic offerings. Any of these approaches would be possible under contracting, as long as contractors delivered the instructional programs promised and met their student performance goals.

What would happen if parents strongly supported a low-performing school?

The school contract would require that the school achieve specific performance levels. If a school consistently failed to meet those performance standards, the local district would be required to terminate the contract and seek another provider. A public hearing process that develops a district-wide consensus on performance standards would help board members make the hard decision to close a popular, low-performing school.

Miscellaneous Questions About Contract Schools

How do contract schools differ from charter schools?

Charter schools have been initiated in approximately twenty states. Their operation, like contract schools, necessitates a change in state laws. Their existence depends upon the local board of education, or other designated public agency, approving a charter, a compact of sorts which specifies the school's mission and certain important operating modes. Presumably, if dissatisfied with its operation, a school board could foreclose on the charter.

The principal difference, however, is that many charter schools are run by school district employees, administrators, teachers, and classified staff. These employees may have volunteered to work at the school in question. They, as teachers, may also have agreed to operate in a manner different from most schools in the same district. However, they are district employees and maintain all the rights, privileges, and, possibly, rigidities of a conventional public school district. Many charter schools also lack independent legal status.

How do contract schools differ from voucher schools?

The principal difference is that contract schools maintain public control over the school. The school board, through its contract, evaluation, and contract renewal procedures, maintains control over the school. The contract operator cannot unilaterally change its curriculum or services. The nature of the school and the range of offerings is specified in advance and subject to review in a contractual sense. A contract school permits the flexibility of a voucher or charter school plan, but, importantly, maintains public control over the institution.

What precedent exists for contracting in public education?

"Contracting" for educational services is not a completely original idea. The earliest and most successful examples of the contracting idea in public education are university laboratory schools, some of which were established in the early part of the nineteenth century. Most of these schools operate under a contract of sorts with either the state or a local school district. Laboratory schools use a variety of criteria for admitting children and offer a wide range of educational programs. Most still are involved in initial teacher preparation and often serve as laboratories for experimentation with new pedagogy. Most laboratory schools are highly regarded, but because of their independent status are more often compared to private independent schools than to public schools.

Another successful example of "contract" schools are the Department of Defense Section 6 schools that operate in the United States. They are free-standing public schools operated for defense department employees. It is interesting that the Section 6 schools are highly regarded in comparison to the Defense Department Schools overseas that are highly bureaucratic and generally of poor quality.

A variant of contracting was the subject of a small-scale project in the

1960s. As a part of the Johnson administration's War on Poverty, a special agency was formed within the office of the president to experiment with innovative means for dampening sustained poverty. Part of the experimental agenda was improving educational opportunity. This highly specialized federal agency, the Office of Economic Opportunity (OEO) undertook a number of education experiments.

One such project was known as "Performance Contracting." Local school districts, with students from low-income households, were provided with federal funds to contract with private-sector instructional providers. These contractors were paid in exchange for teaching specialized subjects such as reading and mathematics. The amount contractors were paid was on a per pupil basis and the remuneration was contingent upon gains in achievement test scores. The experiment was a scandalous failure. It was discovered in Texarkansas, Texas, that the contractor's instructors were systematically providing students with copies of the test questions in advance of the "objective" examination on which the contractor's overall performance would be judged and payments determined. This scandal marked the end of the experiment.

Even more modern attempts, though still on a small scale, have run into difficulties. For example, in a much-reported effort, Boston University contracted with the school board of Chelsea, Massachusetts, to operate that city's elementary and secondary schools. This experience was widely publicized initially, but Boston University officials were not able to deliver on their promises of vastly improved education. Similar contracting efforts by private entrepreneurs in Minneapolis and Baltimore have had a rocky start. Some of these experiments have promised substantial external support which either did not materialize or ran out. Without that support the schools were unable to produce the promised results.

What would make matters different, or better? What are the fundamental components of contract schools which will render them more effective than existing public schools?

Public schools currently operate without fear of failure. Regardless of performance, pupils show up in classrooms, teachers are paid, administrators generally hold their jobs. To fail has few, if any, serious consequences under the current system.

Under a contracting strategy, the guarantee of "success" is lifted. If parents do not choose to attend a contractor's school, or if the contractor fails to abide by specified terms of reference in the contract, then the contract can be withdrawn. In short, there is no guarantee of success, and contractors will have to expend substantial efforts ensuring that their clients and their sponsors are satisfied.

Why not rely upon a full-blown voucher plan instead?
Contracting has many features in common with voucher plans, but it also has crucial differences. Among the common features is the empowerment of clients. If they do not like a school, they can attend another. One of the important differences, however, is that contract schools remain public schools. They remain under the aegis and legal control of a body of publicly elected officials. They are, thus, in a position to ensure the well-being of schools not only for immediate clients but also for the general public. In a voucher plan, the general public is a more remote constituency, having to exert influence at the state or federal level but having little influence at the local school level. In sum, contracting provides for a greater degree of public control than does a voucher plan, while still relying upon competition to ensure higher quality and responsiveness to clients.

What would happen to teacher unions under contract schooling?
Their role would change, but they would be unlikely to disappear. The bargaining unit would no longer be school districts because the latter would no longer be hiring teachers. Teachers would be employees of contractors, and unions, if they were to represent teachers at all, would represent them in their relationships with contractors.

Teacher unions might still play a vital role for teachers. For example, unions might operate "hiring halls" from which contractors could recruit able and experienced classroom instructors. Unions might play a vital role in providing various kinds of fringe benefits, e.g., medical insurance, to teachers. Finally, unions might decide to operate schools, to bid on RFPs. If they were awarded a contract, then teacher unions would no longer simply be "labor," they would also become entrepreneurs or providers.

What happens to school superintendents under a contracting strategy?
Superintendents continue to play a vital role, as the chief executive officer of school districts. However, that role changes dramatically. Under contracting, the superintendent is the principal education advisor to the school board, providing counsel about the contents of RFPs, assisting in the evaluation of bids, overseeing contractor performance, arranging for third-party evaluations, administering parent and student grievance procedures, and making recommendations to the school board regarding the renewal or termination of contracts. However, as busy as a superintendent

would be under such arrangements, he or she would not be the supervisor of vast numbers of employees. In that manner the role would change.

What would happen to so-called "alternative" schools and "community" schools under a contract strategy?

If their teachers and administrators are district employees, they would have to decide on whether or not they desired to bid for the operation of their school. If they bid and won the competition, then they might continue to operate the school in the past manner. However, if the school board altered the specifications for the school, through the RFP process, or the old "operators" chose not to bid to become the new providers, then the school as it was might disappear, only to be replaced by whatever the school board specified and bidders thought useful.

Will not contractors simply employ white teachers and neglect minority employees?

They might, but doing so would probably imperil their success. For example, if minority parents were impressed by the spectrum of teachers put forward by a contractor-operator, they might gravitate toward that school and drain away the attendance of an all-white contractor. Similarly, school boards might judge proposals with multiethnic instructional workforces more favorably than any slate of all-white or all-anything teachers. In short, there are plenty of mechanisms through contracting by which minority entrance can be protected as well or better than today. State and federal laws about fair hiring practices would still apply.

If contracting is successful, won't more private school students be drawn into the public system, costing the taxpayers more money?

Yes! If contract schools are successful, they may well draw students from existing private schools, and the cost burden to taxpayers would increase. However, one should remember that such parents and students are due public schooling, if they want it. Moreover, their presence, or return to, the public system will increase the political influence of public schools and, thereby, enable such schools to draw more resources from federal, state, and local governments.

Can contract schools be part of a network?

Absolutely, yes. If a contractor chooses to bid on multiple RFPs, and successfully negotiates multiple contracts, then that contractor might have a network of schools. However, this would be a system of schools, not

243

a school system. Indeed, teachers, parents, students, and others might well benefit from such networks, if it meant better teacher training, lower prices for supplies through bulk purchasing, and curriculum innovation.

Won't contract schools become as custom encrusted and inflexible as existing public schools?

That is possible but unlikely. Remember there is no longer a guarantee of "success." Dissatisfied parents can seek schooling elsewhere. No one is compelled to attend a particular contract school, except perhaps in a sparsely settled rural area where there simply are insufficient numbers of students to justify a competitive arrangement. (This is a problem of the current system, not an added problem imposed by contracting.) Without a sufficient number of students, a school would fail. Also, school boards believing that a school should be different than what has existed can always alter the RFP in the next round of bidding and seek a different kind of school.

Do contract schools have to issue an annual report to their various constituents, parents, citizens, school boards, and so on?

The answer here depends upon what the school board specifies in the RFP. If annual reports of a certain type and distribution are specified, then, no doubt, contractors will comply. If not required to, some contractors may offer annual reports anyway.

What happens to a contract school which does not attract a sufficient number of students?

The amount of money paid to a contractor should be contingent upon enrollment. If the contractor is incapable of attracting clients, then the school budget will be decreased. This can have a downward-spiraling effect. Fewer students, less money, poorer-quality services, less ability to live up to contract specifications, and the school becomes less attractive to parents. Under such arrangements, a contract school should go out of business.

Under current arrangements with public schools, if parents are unhappy, they seldom can migrate to another school. Moreover, if a public school draws too few students it may still survive if a reluctant school board is unwilling to counter political pressures to close it.

What does a school board do if a contractor forfeits on school operation in midyear? Who protects the interests of students in such an arrangement?

This is one reason for using contracting instead of vouchers. If a school defaults on its contract, the school board would step in with an interim or emergency provider. Per pupil funding that would have gone to the defunct contract school would go instead to the new provider or to existing schools in which the students enroll.

Will school boards have sufficient intestinal fortitude to close down an operator who is not complying with contract provisions?

This could be a problem. School boards currently have difficulty recognizing failure in a public school and almost never make dramatic changes, even when students are failing and dropping out. What would be different under a contract scheme? There would be at least four differences.

First, parents do not have to use the school. They can simply opt to attend another contract-operated school. A sustained loss of revenue would eventually force the school board to close the ineptly operated school.

Second, the contract provisions would also empower parents to sue or seek other redress if the contractor was not providing services as agreed.

Third, the required, objective, third-party evaluations would be made public. Their independent nature might require that school boards take them more seriously than the timid evaluations that now take place.

Fourth, teachers would no longer be employees of a school district. Their substantial political influence, under current arrangements, would be diluted. Perhaps, with a different political dynamic in operation, a political dynamic which empowers parents, school boards might be emboldened to act when a contractor does not perform.

Where else does government oversee services but not directly provide services? Are there any precedents for school contracting?

One good example is in the area of public utilities and transportation. Public utilities commissions and transportation commissions are free to specify performance levels and, thereafter, contract with providers through a bidding process.

Is there any limit to the number of contract schools that a school board can reasonably oversee?

Probably yes. Many of today's school districts, certainly in cities such a New York, Chicago, and Los Angeles, are simply too large. They are of a scale which virtually defies rational public-sector management. If their school boards were only the policy makers, not additionally the providers, they might perform more effectively. Nevertheless, we believe that a school board could only effectively manage the contracts of approximately two, perhaps three, senior high schools, and the feeder schools they serve. Thus, a successful contract school arrangement would almost assuredly necessitate the downsizing of very large school districts.

Can a contracting strategy be compatible with other school reforms?

Yes. For example, the Clinton administration has promulgated a strategy known as Goals 2000. A principal component here is that schools should establish goals for their districts, specify these goals in terms of expected performance for students, utilize objective means for assessing performance, rely heavily upon in-service teacher and administrator preparation, and utilize textbooks and other instructional materials which stress higher-order thinking skills and downplay drill and skill rote practice.

Contracting can fit with such ideas easily. In fact, contracting can provide the mechanism which permits the Goals 2000 top-down strategy to become effective by supplying a means by which schools actually would want to undertake reform.

Similarly, contracting is compatible with ideas such as the Essential School movement founded by Theodore Sizer, the Accelerated School Plan of Henry Levin, the reform ideas of James Comer and Robert Slavin, the New American Schools, and so on, for all reform movements directed at making individual schools more effective.

What about schools of education under a contracting strategy?

They too must become more market-oriented. Their graduates would still undertake practice teaching or apprentice teaching but would do so under the aegis of contractors. Also, contractors, not school boards, would be the employers of new teachers. Thus, schools of education would have to persuade contractors that their graduates were appropriately prepared to perform well. If they could not, then their graduates would risk not gaining employment. In effect, schools of education would become more like other professional schools, e.g., business, engineering, law, or architecture. They would have to prepare candidates who were attractive to other professionals in the field. They would not have to comply with state-imposed, often irrelevant, credentialing statutes.

What about state teaching credentials? Would they still exist under contract schools?

Probably, but they wouldn't be as important or be required for all instructional employees. The test of whether or not a teacher was fit to teach would be the judgment of a contractor. Contractors would be motivated to employ good teachers because, otherwise, they would not be able to satisfy their clients and meet their contract specifications. They could not risk hiring bad teachers. However, most credential requirements, now imposed by state government, do not assure good teaching. They guarantee only that the candidate successfully sat through a prescribed number of required classes and had a minimal experience as a practice teacher. Contractors would probably want more than this before agreeing to hire a teacher.

What about the notion of "career ladders" for teachers?

Contract schools would encourage this idea greatly. Most contractors would be able to afford, and would eagerly seek, a few master teachers. However, they would quickly want these master teachers to distribute their influence by supervising and teaching larger numbers of journeyman or apprentice teachers. Here is the hierarchy or professional ladder that is beginning to dominate other professions.

What about the National Board of Professional Teaching Standards?

This is a voluntary national certification that teachers with at least three years of successful teaching experience can now seek. If this idea catches on widely, then contractors will be eager to employ nationally certified teachers as a means for ensuring their clients that they had good teachers.

Anderson, Beverley. 1994. "Permissive Social and Educational Inequality 40 Years after Brown." *Journal of Negro Education*, 63, no.3, p. 443.

Areen, Judith, and Christopher Jencks. 1971. "Education Vouchers: A Proposal for Diversity and Choice." *Teachers College Record*, 72, p. 327.

Berliner, David C., and Bruce J. Biddle. 1995. *The Manufactured Crisis: Myths, Fraud, and the Attack on America's Public Schools*. Redding: Addison-Wesley.

Bierlein, Louann, and Lori Mulholland. 1993. *Charter School Update: Expansion of a Viable Reform Initiative*. Tempe: Morrison Institute for Public Policy.

Bimber, Bruce. 1991. *The Decentralization Mirage: Comparing Decision-making Arrangements in Four High Schools*. Santa Monica: RAND.

Bimber, Bruce. 1993. *School Decentralization: Lessons from the Study of Bureaucracy*. Santa Monica: RAND.

Booz-Allen and Hamilton. 1992. *Cost Allocations in the Chicago Public Schools Chicago*. 1995 Chicago School Finance Authority.

Bracey, Gerald W. 1992. "The 5th Bracey Report on the Condition of Public Education." *Phi Deltan Kappan*, 77, no. 2, p.149.

Brandon, Richard N. 1993. "Sustaining Political Support for Systemic Education Reform." Human Services Policy Center, University of Washington. Prepared for the Pew Forum on Education Reform. Working Draft.

Carver, John. 1990. *Boards That Make A Difference: A New Design for Leadership in Nonprofit and Public Organizations*. San Francisco: Jossey-Bass Nonprofit Sector Series.

Celio, Mary Beth. 1994. "Building and Maintaining Systems of Schools: Lessons from Religious Order School Network." Working papers of the University of Washington Graduate School of Public Affairs.

Chow, Stanley H. L., et al. 1991. "Administration and Instruction Costs." *School Business Affairs*, 57, no. 4, pp. 37–41.

Chubb, John E., and Terry E. Moe. 1990. *Politics, Markets and America's Schools*. Washington, D.C.: The Brookings Institution.

Cohen, D. K., and Farrar, E. 1977. "Power to the Parents? The Story of Education Vouchers." *The Public Interest*, 48:72–97.

Coleman, James S. 1967. "Toward Open Schools." *The Public Interest*, 9, no. 20 (Fall).

Commission on Chapter I. 1992. "Making Schools Work for Children in Poverty: A New Framework." Prepared by the Commission on Chapter 1, U.S. Department of Education.

Coons, John E., and Stephen Sugarman. 1978. *Education by Choice: The Case for Family Control*. Berkeley: University of California Press.

Cooper, Bruce S. "School-Site Cost Allocations." 1993. Paper presented at the general meeting of the American Educational Finance Association.

Cooper, Bruce S. 1994. *The Finance Analysis Model: Linking Resources for Education*. Chicago: Center for Workforce Preparation, Coopers and Lybrand L. L. C.

Crain, Robert, et al. 1992. *The Effectiveness of New York City's Career Magnets*. Berkeley: The National Center for Research on Vocational Education.

Dansberger, Jacqueline, Michael Kirst, and Michael Usdan. 1992. *Governing Public Schools: New Times, New Requirements*. Washington, The Institute for Educational Leadership.

Davies, Howard. 1993. *Fighting Leviathan: Building Social Markets That Work*. London: The Social Market Foundation.

Davis, Evan. 1993. *Schools and the State*. London: The Social Market Foundation.

Dianda, Marcella R., and Ronald G. Corwin. 1993. *What a Voucher Could Buy: A Survey of California's Private Schools*. Los Alamitos: Southwest Regional Laboratory.

Doyle, Dennis. 1977. "The Politics of Choice: A View from the Bridge." *In Parents, Teachers and Children*. San Francisco: Institute for Contemporary Studies, p. 227.

Drucker, Peter. 1994. "The Age of Social Transformation." *Atlantic Monthly*, November.

Educational Economic Policy Center. 1993a. *Between Goals and Improvement: Sanctions and Rewards for Educational Results*. Austin: University of Texas.

Educational Economic Policy Center. 1993b. *A New Accountability System For Texas Public Schools,* vol. 1. Austin: University of Texas.

Elmore, R., and MacLaughlin, M. 1988. *Steady Work: Policy, Practice and the Reform of American Education.* Santa Monica: RAND.

Elmore, Richard F. 1986. *Choice in Public Education.* Center for Policy Research in Education. Santa Monica: RAND.

Elmore, Richard F., and associates. 1991. *Restructuring Schools: The Next Generation of Educational Reform.* San Francisco: Jossey-Bass.

Encarnation, Dennis J. 1983. "Public Finance and Regulation of Nonpublic Education: Retrospect and Prospect." In *Public Dollars for Private Schools: The Case of Tuition Tax Credits,* Thomas James and Henry M. Levin, eds. Philadelphia: Temple University Press, 3:175–95.

Farcas, Steve. 1993. *Divided Within, Besieged Without.* New York: The Public Agenda Foundation.

Finn, Chester E., Jr. 1991. "Reinventing Local Control." *Education Week,* January 23, pp. 32 and 40.

Finn, Chester E., Jr. 1993. "What If Those Math Standards Are Wrong?" *Education Week,* January 30, p. 36.

Fisher, Roger, William Urey, and Bruce Patton. 1991. *Getting to Yes: Negotiating Agreement Without Giving In.* Boston: Houghton Mifflin.

Friedman, Milton. 1962. *Capitalism and Freedom.* Chicago: University of Chicago Press.

Fuhrman, Susan H., and Richard Elmore. 1990. "Understanding Local Control in the Wake of State Education Reform." *Educational Evaluation and Policy Analysis,* 12 (Spring): 82–86.

Garfinkel, Irwin, and Edward Gramlich. 1972. *A Statistical Analysis of the OEO Experiment in Educational Performance Contracting.* Washington, D.C.: Brookings Institution, Technical Service Reprint T-002.

Gemello, John M., and Jack W. Osman. 1933. "The Choice for Public and Private Education: An Economist's View." In *Public Dollars for Private Schools: The Case of Tuition Tax Credits,* Thomas James and Henry M. Levin, eds. Philadelphia: Temple University Press, 3:196–209.

Glazer, Nathan. 1983. "The Future Under Tuition Tax Credits." In *Public Dollars for Private Schools: The Case of Tuition Tax Credits,* Thomas James and Henry M. Levin, eds. Philadelphia: Temple University Press, 2:87–100.

Governor's Council on Education Reform and Funding. 1993. *Putting Children First: Improving Student Performance in Washington State.* Olympia, Washington.

Grissmer, David, and Sheila Kirby. 1991. *Patterns of Attrition Among Indiana Teachers, 1965–1987.* Santa Monica: RAND.

Guiton, Gretchen. 1995. "Matchmaking: The Dynamics of High School Tracking and Within-School Segregation." *American Education Research Journal,* 32, no. 1.

Guthrie, James W., Walter I. Garms, and Lawrence C. Pierce. 1988. *School Finance and Education Policy: Enhancing Educational Efficiency, Equality, and Choice.* Engelwood Cliffs: Prentice-Hall.

Guthrie, James W., and Lawrence C. Pierce. 1990. "The International Economy and National Education Reform: A Comparison of Educational Reforms in the United States and Great Britain." *Oxford Review of Education,* v. 16, no. 2, pp. 179–205.

Hannaway, Jane, and Martin Carnoy, eds. 1993. *Decentralization and School Improvement: Can We Fulfill the Promise?* San Francisco: Jossey-Bass.

Hannaway, J. 1993. "Political Pressure and Decentralization in Institutional Organizations: The Case of School Districts." *Sociology of Education.*

Hannaway, J. 1992. "School Districts: The Missing Link in Education Reform." Paper prepared for the Association of Public Policy and Management Association annual meeting, Denver.

Hannaway, J., and L. Sproull. 1977. "Who's in Charge Here?: Coordination and Control in Educational Organizations." *Administrators Notebook.*

Hanushek, Eric Alan, et al. 1994. *Making Schools Work: Improving Performance and Controlling Costs.* Washington, D.C.: Brookings Institution.

Hardcastle, A. J. 1994. "The Voices of Organizational Culture: An Ethnographic Study of Total Quality Management Implementation at the Douglas Aircraft Company." Ph.D. dissertation, UCLA Graduate School of Education.

Harvey, James. 1994. "The Lake Union Statement: Reconciling Systemic Reform, Charters, and Contracting." Working paper. Seattle: University of Washington Graduate School of Public Affairs.

Hill, Paul, T. 1992. "Urban Education." In *Urban America: Policy Choices for Los Angeles and the Nation,* James Steinberg, David Lyon, and Mary E. Vaiana, eds. Santa Monica: RAND, pp. 127–51.

Hill, Paul T. 1996. "The Educational Advantages of Choice." *Phi Delta Kappan,* June.

Hill, Paul T., and Josephine Bonan. 1991. *Decentralization and Accountability in Public Education.* Santa Monica: RAND.

Hill, Paul T., Gail E. Foster, and Tamar Gendler. 1990. *High Schools with Character.* Santa Monica: RAND.

Hill, Paul T., and Doren Madey. 1982. *Education Policymaking Through the Civil Justice System.* Santa Monica: RAND.

Hill, Paul T., Leslie Shapiro, and Arthur Wise. 1989. *Educational Progress: Cities Mobilize To Improve Their Schools.* Santa Monica: RAND.

Hirschman, Albert. 1969. *Exit, Voice and Loyalty: Responses to Decline in Firms and Organizations.* Cambridge: Harvard University Press.

James, Thomas. 1983. "Questions About Educational Choice: An Argument from History." In *Public Dollars for Private Schools: The Case of Tuition Tax Credits,* Thomas James and Henry M. Levin, eds. Philadelphia: Temple University Press. 1:55–70.

Jencks, Christopher. 1966. "Is the Public School Obsolete?" *The Public Interest,* 2, no. 18 (Winter).

Jencks, Christopher, and Judith Areen. 1970. *Education Vouchers, A Report on Financing Elementary Education by Grants to Parents.* Cambridge: Center for the Study of Public Policy.

Jensen, Donald N. 1983. "Constitutional and Legal Implications of Tuition Tax Credits." In *Public Dollars for Private Schools: The Case of Tuition Tax Credits.* Thomas James and Henry M. Levin, eds. Philadelphia: Temple University Press, 2: 51–174.

Johnson, S. M. 1984. *Teacher Unions in Schools.* Philadelphia: Temple University Press.

Johnson, S. M. 1987. "Can Schools Be Reformed at the Bargaining Table?" *Teacher College Record,* 89(2), 269–80.

Kearns, D. T., and Doyle, D. P. 1988. *Winning the Brain Race.* San Francisco: Institute for Contemporary Studies Press.

Kerchner, C. T. 1986. "Union-Made Teaching: The Effects of Labor Relations on Teaching Work." In E. Z. Rothkopf, ed., *Review of Research in Education,* 12. Washington, D.C.: American Education Research Association.

Kimbrough, Jackie, and Paul T. Hill. 1981. *The Aggregate Effects of Federal Education Programs.* Santa Monica: RAND.

Kirp, D., and Jensen, D. 1986. *School Days, Rule Days.* London: Falmer Press.

Kolderie, T. 1988. *School-Site Management: Rhetoric and Reality.* Minneapolis: Humphrey Institute, University of Minnesota (pamphlet).

Koretz, Daniel 1992. *Evaluating and Validating Indicators of Mathematics and Science Education.* Santa Monica, RAND.

Kozol, Jonathan. 1992. *Savage Inequalities: Children in America's Schools.* New York: Harper Perennial.

Lankford, Hamilton, and James Wyckoff. 1995. "Where Has the Money Gone? An Analysis of School District Spending in New York." Educational Evaluation and Policy Analysis,. 17, no. 2 (Summer): 195–218.

Levin, Henry M. 1983. "Educational Choice and the Pains of Democracy." In *Public Dollars for Private Schools: The Case of Tuition Tax Credits,* Thomas James and Henry M. Levin, eds. Philadelphia: Temple University Press, 1:17–38.

Levin, Henry M. 1991. "The Economics of Educational Choice." *Economics of Education Review,* 10, no. 2, pp. 137–58.

Lipsitz, J. 1983. *Successful Schools for Young Adolescents.* New Brunswick: Transaction Publishers.

Lipsky, M. 1980. *Street-Level Bureaucracy.* New York: Russell Sage Foundation.

Longanecker, David A. 1983. "The Public Cost of Tuition Tax Credits". In *Public Dollars for Private Schools: The Case of Tuition Tax Credits,* Thomas James and Henry M. Levin, eds. Philadelphia: Temple University Press, 2:115–29.

Malen, Betty, et al. 1990. "Unfulfilled Promises." *School Administrator,* 47, no. 2, pp. 30, 32, 53–56.

Malen, B., and A. W. Hart. 1987. "Career Ladder Reform: A Multi-Level Analysis of Initial Efforts." *Educational Evaluation and Policy Analysis.* 9(1), 9–23.

Malen, Betty, and Rodney T. Ogawa. 1988. "Professional Patron Influence on Site-Based Governance Councils: A Confounding Case Study." *Educational Evaluation and Policy Analysis,* 10, no. 4, p.251

March, James G., and Johan P. Olsen. 1989. *Rediscovering Institutions.* New York: The Free Press.

McDonnell, Lorraine, and Anthony Pascal. 1988. *Teacher Unions and Education Policy.* Santa Monica: RAND.

McDonnell, Lorraine, and Paul T. Hill. 1993. *Newcomers in American Schools: Meeting the Educational Needs of Immigrant Youth.* Santa Monica: RAND.

Meyer, J. W., and B. Rowan. 1978. "The Structure of Education Organizations." In M. W. Meyer and Associates, *Environments and Organizations.* San Francisco: Jossey-Bass.

Miller, L. Scott. 1995. *An American Imperative: Accelerating Minority Educational Advancement.* New Haven: Yale University Press.

Millot, Marc Dean. 1994. "Autonomy, Accountability, and the Values of Public Education." Seattle: University of Washington Institute for Public Policy and Management.

Millot, Marc Dean. 1995a. *What Are Charter Schools?* Seattle: University of Washington Institute for Public Policy and Management.

Millot, Marc Dean. 1995b. *How Does the Washington State Education Code Compare with the Charter Schools Statute of Other States?* Seattle: University of Washington Institute for Public Policy and Management.

Millot, Marc Dean, and Robin Lake. 1996. *So You Want to Start a Charter School?* Seattle: University of Washington Institute for Public Policy Management.

Moe, Terry M. 1996. "Private Vouchers." In *Private Vouchers,* ed. Terry M. Moe. Stanford: Hoover Institution Press.

Mohrman, Alan, Susan Albers Mohrman, and Allan Odden. 1993. *The Linkage Between Systemic Reform and Teacher Compensation.* Los Angeles: University of Southern California School of Education, Consortium for Policy Research in Education.

Mohrman, Susan Albers, and Priscilla Wohlstetter. 1994. *School-Based Management: Organizing for High Performance.* San Francisco: Jossey-Bass.

Muller, Carol Blue. 1983. "The Social and Political Consequences of Increased Public Support for Private Schools." In *Public Dollars for Private Schools: The Case of Tuition Tax Credits,* Thomas James and Henry M. Levin, eds. Philadelphia: Temple University Press, 1:39–54.

Muncey, Donna E. and Bruce MacQuillan. 1996. *Reform and Resistance in Schools and Classrooms: An Ethnographic View of the Coalition of Essential Schools.* New Haven: Yale University Press.

Murnane, Richard J. 1983. "The Uncertain Consequences of Tuition Tax Credits: An Analysis of Student Achievement and Economic Incentives." In *Public Dollars for Private Schools: The Case of Tuition Tax Credits,* Thomas James and Henry M. Levin, eds. Philadelphia: Temple University Press, 3:210–22.

Murnane, Richard J. 1986. "Family Choice in Public Education: The Roles of Students, Teachers, and System Designers." *Harvard Education Review,* 88, no. 2 (Winter).

Murphy, Joseph, and Lynn G. Beck. 1995. *School-based Management as School Reform: Taking Stock.* Thousand Oaks: Corwin Press.

Nathan, Joe. 1989. *Public Schools by Choice: Expanding Opportunities for Parents, Students, and Teachers.* Bloomington: Meyer Share Books.

Oakes, Jeannie. 1985. *Keeping Track: How Schools Structure Inequality.* New Haven: Yale University Press.

Oakes, Jeannie. 1995. "Two Cities' Tracking and Within-School Segregation." *Teachers College Record,* 96, no. 4, p. 681.

O'Day, Jennifer, and Marshall S. Smith. 1991. "Systemic School Reform." In *The Politics of Curriculum and Testing: The 1990 Yearbook of the Political Education Association,* Susan H. Fuhrman and Betty Malen, eds. London: Falmer.

O'Day, Jennifer, and Marshall S. Smith. 1992. "Systemic School Reform and Educational Opportunity." Stanford University School of Education (paper).

Odden, Allen J. 1994a. "Including School Finance in Systemic Reform Strategies: A Commentary." *CPRE Finance Brief.* New Brunswick: Consortium for Policy Research in Education.

Odden, Allan J. 1994b. "Decentralized Management and School Finance." *Theory into Practice,* 33 no. 2 (Spring): 104–11.

Odden, Allan J., et al. 1995. "The Story of the Education Dollar: No Academy Awards and No Fiscal Smoking Guns." *Phi Delta Kappan.* 77 no. 2 (October): 161–68.

Odden, Allan J., 1996. "The Finance Side of Implementing New American Schools." Arlington: The New American Schools Development Corporation.

Ogbu, John U. 1994. "Racial Stratification and Education in the United States: Why Inequality Persists." *Teachers College Record,* 96, no. 2, p. 264.

Orfield, Gary. 1994. "Asking the Right Questions." *Education Policy,* 8, no. 4, p. 404.

Osborne, David, and Ted Gaebler. 1992. *Reinventing Government.* Menlo Park: Addison-Wesley.

Powell, Arthur, Eleanor Farrar, and David Cohen. 1985. *The Shopping Mall High School: Winners and Losers in the Educational Marketplace.* Boston: Houghton-Mifflin.

Purkey, Stewart, and Marshall Smith. 1983. "Effective Schools: A Review." *Elementary School Journal,* 83:427–51.

Raywid, M. A. 1985. "Family Choice Arrangements In Public Schools: A Review of the Literature." *Review of Educational Research,* 55 no. 4, 435–67.

Raywid, Mary Anne, and Thomas A. Shaheen. 1994. "In Search of Cost-Effective Schools." *Theory into Practice,* 33, no. 2 (Spring): 67–74.

Robinson, Glen. 1988. "Too Much Administration: Myth or Reality?" *School Business Affairs.* 54 no. 12 (December): 10–14.

Rosenholtz, S. J. 1984. "Effective Schools: Interpreting the Evidence." *American Journal of Education,* 93, no. 3: 352–88.

Senge, Peter. 1990. *The Fifth Discipline.* New York: Doubleday.

Shanker, Albert. 1990. "A Proposal for Using Incentives to Restructure Our Public Schools." *Phi Delta Kappan,* 71, no. 5 (January): 344–57.

Sherman, Joel D. 1993. "Public Finance of Private Schools: Observations from

Abroad." In *Public Dollars for Private Schools: The Case of Tuition Tax Credits*, Thomas James and Henry M. Levin, eds. Philadelphia: Temple University Press, 1:71–86.

Shipps, Dorothy. 1995. "Big Business and School Reform: The Case of Chicago, 1989." Ph.D. dissertation, Stanford University School of Education.

Shires, Michael A., Cathy S. Krop, C. Peter Rydell, and Stephen J. Carroll. 1994. *The Effects of the California Voucher Initiative on Public Expenditures for Education.* Santa Monica: RAND.

Sizer, Theodore. 1984. *Horace's Compromise: The Dilemma of the American High School.* Boston: Houghton-Mifflin.

Smith, James P., and Finis R. Welch. 1986. *Closing the Gap: Forty Years of Economic Progress for Blacks.* Santa Monica: RAND.

Smith, Marshall S. 1991. "A National Curriculum in the United States?" *Education Leadership*, 49(1), 74–81.

Tyack, David, and Thomas James. 1986. "State Government and American Public Education: Exploring the Primeval Forest." *History of Education Quarterly*, 26(1) (Spring).

Tyack, David. 1974. *The One Best System: A History of American Urban Education.* Cambridge: Harvard University Press.

Tyack, David. 1990. "Restructuring in Historical Perspective: Tinkering Toward Utopia." *Teachers College Record*, 92, no. 2, (Winter): 170–91.

Walberg, Herbert J. 1994. "Educational Productivity: Urgent Needs and New Remedies." *Theory into Practice*, 33 no. 2 (Spring): 75–82.

Willms, J. Douglas. 1983. "Do Private Schools Produce Higher Levels of Academic Achievement? New Evidence for the Tuition Tax Credit Debate." In *Public Dollars for Private Schools: The Case of Tuition Tax Credits*, Thomas James and Henry M. Levin, eds. Philadelphia: Temple University Press. 3:223–34.

Wilson, James Q. 1989. *Bureaucracy: What Government Agencies Do and Why They Do It.* New York: Basic Books.

Wise, Arthur E. 1970. *Rich Schools Poor Schools.* Chicago: University of Chicago Press.

Wise, Arthur E. 1979. *Legislated Learning.* Berkeley: University of California Press.

Wohlstetter, Priscilla. 1995. "Getting School-Based Management Right: What Works and What Doesn't." *Phi Delta Kappan*, 77, no. 1, p. 22.

Wohlstetter, Priscilla, and Allan J. Odden. 1992. "Rethinking School-Based Management Policy and Research." *Educational Administration Quarterly*, 28, no. 4, p. 529.